Communications for Legal Professionals

Helen Wilkie

John Roberts

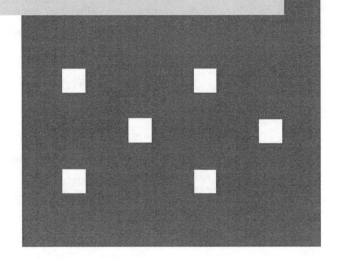

emp
2006
Emond Montgomery Publications
Toronto, Canada

Emond Montgomery Publications Limited
60 Shaftesbury Avenue
Toronto ON M4T 1A3
http://www.emp.ca/highered

Printed in Canada.
Reprinted July 2013.

We acknowledge the financial support of the Government of Canada through the Canada Book Fund for our publishing activities.

The events and characters depicted in this book are fictitious. Any similarity to actual persons, living or dead, is purely coincidental.

Acquisitions editor: Jennifer McPhee

Marketing manager: Christine Davidson

Director, sales and marketing, higher education: Kevin Smulan

Copy editor: Jamie Bush

Production editor: Jim Lyons

Proofreader: David Handelsman

Text designer and typesetter: Tara Wells

Indexer: Paula Pike

Cover designer: Susan Darrach, Darrach Design

Library and Archives Canada Cataloguing in Publication

Wilkie, Helen, 1943-
    Communications for legal professionals / Helen Wilkie, John Roberts.

Includes index.
ISBN 978-1-55239-139-6

    1. Legal composition.   2. Forms (Law)—Canada.   3. Communication in law.   4. Legal assistants—Canada.   I. Roberts, John A., 1944-   II. Title.

PE1479.L3W45 2006   808′.06634   C2005-907478-7

Contents

Preface ix

INTRODUCTION

The Importance of Communication in the Legal Field 1
Learning Objectives 1
What Is a Law Clerk? 1
What Is a Legal Assistant? 1
Working Environments 1
Importance of Communication 2
Communicating in a Multicultural Society 3
Communicating with People with Disabilities 4
Working Together 4
Summary 5

CHAPTER 1

Effective Listening 7
Learning Objectives 7
Introduction 7
Your Listening Profile 8
    Quiz 1 Analysis 8
    Quiz 2 Analysis 8
    Quiz 3 Analysis 10
Nine Rules for Lively Listening 10
    Rule 1: Decide To Listen 10
        Listening Keeps Us Informed 10
        Listening Keeps Us Out of Trouble 11
        Listening Makes Us Appreciated 11
    Rule 2: Avoid Selective Listening 11
    Rule 3: Give Acknowledgement and Feedback 12
        Reflective Listening 13
    Rule 4: Ask Appropriate Questions 13
        Broadening Questions 14
        Clarifying or Confirming Questions 14
        Questions That Change the Direction 14
    Rule 5: Look for Non-Verbal Cues 14
        Body Language 15
        Tone of Voice 15
    Rule 6: Listen with Your Whole Body 15
    Rule 7: Separate Fact from Opinion and Propaganda 16
    Rule 8: Control Your Emotional Response 16
    Rule 9: Make Notes 17

Some Additional Principles 17

Barriers to Effective Listening 18

Drawing It All Together 19

Spelling and Definitions 24

Summary 25

CHAPTER 2

Spelling 27

Learning Objectives 27

Introduction 27

Improving Your Spelling 28

Useful Spelling Rules 32

Rule 1 32

Rule 2 33

Rule 3 33

Rule 4 33

Plurals 34

Word Problems 37

Summary 49

Spelling and Definitions 50

CHAPTER 3

Grammar Skills 51

Learning Objectives 51

Introduction 51

Grammar Pre-Test 52

Grammar Essentials: Sentences 56

Subject 56

Verb 57

Subject–Verb Agreement 60

Sentence Fragments 63

Run-on Sentences 65

Modifiers 66

Misplaced Modifiers 66

Dangling Modifiers 67

Pronoun References 68

Pronouns and Case 69

Ambiguous and Indefinite Pronoun References 70

Parallel Structure 71

Correlatives 71

Grammar Essentials: Punctuation and Capitalization 72

Commas 72

Apostrophes 74

Possessives 74

Contractions 75

Periods 76

Question Marks 77

Exclamation Points 77

Quotation Marks 77

Semicolons 77

Colons 78
Capital Letters 78
Voice 80
Summary 82
Spelling and Definitions 82

CHAPTER 4

Writing: Letters, Memos, Reports, and E-mail 83
Learning Objectives 83
Introduction 83
Writing Strategies 84
Direct Order 84
Indirect Order 85
Letters 86
Formats 86
Figure 4.1   Basic Business Letter Format 86
Figure 4.2   Modified Block Style with Modified Open Punctuation 87
Figure 4.3   Traditional Style with Closed Punctuation 88
Figure 4.4   Full Block Style with Open Punctuation 89
Style 90
Date 90
"Without Prejudice" 90
Inside Address, Attention Line, and Salutation 90
Subject Line 92
Complimentary Close 94
Copies 94
Enclosures and Attachments 95
Content 95
Figure 4.5   Sample Letter 96
Tone 97
Readability 97
Paragraphs 97
Writing Strong Paragraphs 98
Memos 99
Figure 4.6   Memo Format 99
Addresses 100
Subject Line 100
Closing 100
Content 100
Tone 100
Readability 100
The "You" Approach 100
Formats and Writing Strategy 101
Information or Instruction Memo 101
Figure 4.7   Sample Information/Instruction Memo 102
Problem-Solving Memo 102
Figure 4.8   Sample Problem-Solving Memo 103
Opinion or Proposal Memo 103
Figure 4.9   Sample Opinion or Proposal Memo 104
Planning Your Memo 105
Language and Grammar 105
Memorandum of Law 106

Legal Citation 107
   Case Citations 107
   Parallel Citations 108
Writing a Memorandum of Law 109
   Figure 4.10   Sample Memorandum of Law 110
Reports 117
   Organizing the Report 117
   Figure 4.11   Sample Report 118
E-mail 119
Spelling and Definitions 122

CHAPTER 5

Summary and Paraphrase 123
Learning Objectives 123
Introduction 123
Writing a Summary 123
   Changing Direct Speech to Indirect Speech 125
   Counting Words 125
   Sample Summaries 126
Writing a Paraphrase 130
   Methods of Paraphrasing 131
   Bias in Reporting 131
Writing a Summary and Bias Essay 133
Summary 134
Spelling and Definitions 135

CHAPTER 6

Speaking Effectively 137
Learning Objectives 137
Introduction 137
Effective Oral Presentations 138
   Purpose 138
   Selecting a Topic 138
   Narrowing the Topic 139
   Research 140
   Preparation 142
   Organization 144
   Mechanics 144
   Answering Questions 145
   Nervousness 146
   Visual Aids 147
Non-Verbal Communication 148
   Visual Elements 148
      Eye Contact 148
      Facial Expression 149
      Gestures and Posture 149
      Body Orientation 149
      Manner of Dress 149
   Vocal Elements 149

   Loudness 149

   Rate 150

   Emphasis 150

  Spatial Elements 150

Impromptu Speaking: Say What You Mean, S.I.R. 151

A Last Word about Oral Presentations: Don't Read 152

Workplace Communication 152

  Dealing with a Difficult Client 152

  Conferencing with Peers 154

Summary 155

Spelling and Definitions 155

CHAPTER 7

Legal Forms 157

Real Estate 158

  Forms 158

   Figure 7.1 Transfer/Deed of Land 159

   Figure 7.2 Charge/Mortgage of Land 160

   Figure 7.3 Discharge of Charge/Mortgage 161

   Figure 7.4 Land Transfer Tax Affidavit 162

Wills and Estates 163

  Forms 163

   Figure 7.5 Notice of an Application for a Certificate of Appointment
of Estate Trustee with a Will 164

   Figure 7.6 Application for Certificate of Appointment of Estate Trustee
with a Will 167

   Figure 7.7 Affidavit of Service of Notice 170

   Figure 7.8 Certificate of Appointment of Estate Trustee with a Will 172

   Figure 7.9 Affidavit in Support of Request for an Order that the
Requirement of Posting a Bond Be Dispensed With 173

   Figure 7.10 Order to Dispense with Bond 174

Litigation 175

  Forms 175

   Figure 7.11 Statement of Claim 176

   Figure 7.12 Jury Notice 184

   Figure 7.13 Notice of Examination 187

   Figure 7.14 Affidavit of Service 190

   Figure 7.15 Offer to Settle 192

   Figure 7.16 Notice of Discontinuance 195

Corporate Procedures and Transactions 198

  Forms 198

   Figure 7.17 Articles of Incorporation 199

   Figure 7.18 Articles of Amalgamation 202

   Figure 7.19 Articles of Continuance 205

   Figure 7.20 Articles of Dissolution 208

   Figure 7.21 Articles of Amendment 209

   Figure 7.22 Annual Return 211

APPENDIX A

Proofreading 213

Proofreading Techniques 213

APPENDIX B

Readings 231
Clients Without Lawyers Disturb Chief Justice 231
Some Day, Victims Won't Fear Us 232
Pleading Case for Reform of Legal Aid System 233
The Formula from Hell 236
The Secret Document 238
Judgement Day 240
Top Court Lets Dads Appeal Payments 241

INDEX 243

Preface

Communications for Legal Professionals is a complete communications program that enables students both to improve their writing skills and to become familiar with the various forms of communication required of law clerks and legal assistants. The format of the book allows instructors to work with an entire class at the same pace or at different levels, and allows students to work on their own or in groups, using extensive exercises, examples, readings, and other student-friendly materials.

The book focuses on improving students' verbal and writing skills, using examples drawn from the legal field. It emphasizes spelling, grammar, listening, and speaking skills, and provides extensive guidance on writing and formatting memos and letters.

The book includes the following features:

1. *Learning objectives, exercises testing new skills, summaries, and spelling and definitions tests.* Each chapter begins with learning objectives that clearly define the skills that students will acquire. The relevance of particular communication skills to the legal field is demonstrated through discussion and examples, and numerous exercises test students' mastery of the skills presented in the chapter. Following a summary, each chapter concludes with a brief spelling and definitions test that involves words of a general nature, rather than those specific to law clerks and legal assistants, allowing students to practise and retain spelling skills throughout the semester.

2. *An emphasis on listening skills.* Effective listening—to colleagues, clients, and others—is a skill that needs to be developed. Chapter 1 shows students how to identify and overcome barriers to effective listening, and demonstrates the importance of listening skills for law clerks and legal assistants.

3. *An emphasis on defining words and terms, and building a vocabulary of legal terminology.* Along with spelling new and troublesome words, students are required to define these words and thereby expand their vocabulary. There is little advantage to spelling words if students do not know the meanings. Students are also introduced to legal terminology throughout the book, through spelling tests and law-related examples and exercises.

4. *An analysis of spelling and grammar rules, and an emphasis on the use of words and grammatical constructions in legal documents.* Chapters 2 and 3 contain exercises drawn from the legal field and emphasize the

importance of spelling and grammar in legal correspondence, reports, and everyday legal office situations.

5. *An emphasis on the writing process.* Chapter 4 addresses the composition of letters, memos, reports, and e-mail. It explores various strategies for writing and formatting these documents in a legal setting, using law-related examples, and emphasizes the importance of spelling and grammar skills as they apply to various legal documents. The chapter includes a discussion of the memorandum of law.

6. *Separate consideration of summary and paraphrase.* Mastery of summarizing and paraphrasing skills is invaluable in the analysis of legal documents. Chapter 5 is devoted to summary and paraphrase, and also considers bias in reporting.

7. *An emphasis on the importance of speaking skills.* Law clerks and legal assistants must interact with clients, colleagues, lawyers, and others outside the firm. Chapter 6 discusses the speaking skills that students need to master to be effective professionals in the legal field. The chapter also discusses the importance of non-verbal communication when dealing with clients, and the importance of effective speaking skills when dealing with difficult clients or when making a workplace presentation.

8. *Inclusion of a variety of legal forms.* Law clerks and legal assistants deal with real estate forms, wills and estates forms, litigation forms, and corporate forms on a regular basis. Chapter 7 presents scenarios in a variety of legal areas, followed by forms filled in with scenario details. Students can therefore see the reason and purpose of the forms, along with their formats and contents.

9. *An extensive appendix on proofreading skills.* Besides being able to spell correctly and use proper grammar, law clerks and legal assistants must also be able to proofread legal documents effectively. This appendix discusses proofreading techniques and offers numerous exercises to improve students' proofreading skills.

10. *An extensive appendix of readings.* An understanding of relevant legal issues in Canada today helps prepare students for their careers as law clerks and legal assistants. The readings in this appendix also complement various exercises on summary and paraphrase in chapter 5.

We gratefully acknowledge the generous advice and support of Giselle Piper, Michele Mendes, and Sylvia Morris, experienced law clerks who willingly gave their time and expertise and kept us on track by providing the sort of knowledge that comes only from daily immersion in a legal environment. Jane Clarke of Mohawk College and Marguerite Moore of Fanshawe College provided invaluable advice at many stages in the writing process. Finally, we owe a debt of gratitude to Jennifer McPhee, our editor, whose hard work, skills, and dedication have earned our utmost respect.

Toronto and Hamilton, Ontario
November 2005

The Importance of Communication in the Legal Field

Learning Objectives

After reading this introduction, you should be able to

- See the need for effective communication in the legal field.
- Understand the communication process and the barriers to it.
- Realize the importance of communicating with people of diverse cultures.
- Realize the importance of communicating with people with disabilities.
- Understand the importance of communicating as a member of a group.

What Is a Law Clerk?

In Ontario, a law clerk is a person qualified through education, training, or work experience to do the following kinds of work for lawyers, law offices, government agencies, and other entities: to perform, under the direction of a lawyer, administrative or managerial duties; and to undertake, when delegated to do so, substantive legal work that, in the absence of a law clerk, the lawyer him- or herself would perform.

What Is a Legal Assistant?

Legal administrative assistants gather information and assemble legal documents and correspondence using their knowledge, initiative, and creativity. They communicate directly with clients, lawyers, law office personnel, judicial and government offices, and other professionals in the community as part of their daily activities.

Working Environments

Law clerks and legal assistants usually work in law firms, but they can also work in

- corporate legal departments,
- accounting firms,
- government departments,
- banks, and
- associations.

■ Importance of Communication

Everyone communicates. You speak, write, read, and make gestures, all of which can be considered methods of communication. Even when you aren't speaking, writing, reading, or gesturing to someone, communication takes place.

Statistically, 70 percent of our conscious day is spent in communicating. Of the time we spend communicating, 9 percent is devoted to writing, 45 percent to listening, 30 percent to speaking, and 16 percent to reading. Communication involves more than one person. Even as this material is being read, for instance, it becomes a form of communication between the authors who wrote the material and the student who is reading it.

Even when your attempt to communicate feels quite unsuccessful, the person you're addressing does *receive* your communication. But perhaps he or she is not listening, or is not responding in a manner that you feel is appropriate, or is not responding at all. This means that your message isn't getting through to the listener for some reason. No response, or an inappropriate response, is still a form of feedback to your message. A traditional diagram used to illustrate this theory is set out in the figure below.

Communication Theory

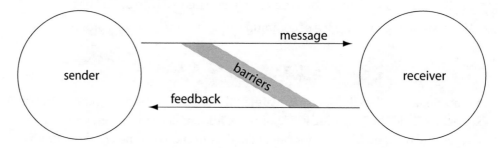

The person communicating (the sender) sends a message to another person (the receiver). The receiver gives feedback to show that the message has been received and how it has been received.

When someone doesn't appear to respond to your communication or responds inappropriately, there are reasons for this breakdown; they are called *barriers to communication*. Possibly the receiver can't hear your message clearly; possibly the receiver doesn't agree with what you said and doesn't want to tell you so; possibly the receiver is not responding for some other reason.

There are a number of possible barriers to communication:

1. **Difficult environment**: The room is hot, stuffy, too large or too small.

2. **Technical problems**: Static on telephone lines or computer crashes can hinder communication.

3. **Resistant attitude**: The listener may lack interest in what is being said, or may disagree with the speaker.

4. **Cultural differences**: The speaker's age, gender, or ethnicity may be remote from the listener's.

5. **Stereotyping**: The receiver may have a fixed set of ideas about the speaker or the speaker's message; these ideas are often based on rumour or assumption and may be incorrect.

6. **Inappropriate body language**: The speaker's body language may not match the message.

7. **Wrong time of day**: The speaker or listener may not be alert during part of the day. For example, a night person may have trouble listening during an early class.

8. **Noise**: Aural distractions may impede listening.

9. **Inappropriate audience**: The audience may not be the right one for the particular message.

10. **Weak language**: The speaker's language may be vague or confusing.

EXERCISE 1

IDENTIFYING BARRIERS TO COMMUNICATION

Take a moment to look around your classroom and at your timetable. What are some of the possible barriers to communication that you see? Do the following barriers, for example, apply to you?

1. Books for the course are expensive. You resent having to pay that much money for one book that you feel you probably won't use entirely.

2. You've had three classes in a row; this is the third. You're tired and just want to get finished and get home.

Whether or not these examples apply to you, try to identify other barriers to communication in the classroom.

These barriers can seriously affect the communication process. For instance, think of how difficult it might be, in the case of a bitter divorce suit, to communicate with a client reacting to what is perceived as a paltry settlement offer from a spouse. Emotions are running high, and a desire for vengeance is in the air. In these circumstances, you might find it difficult to communicate with someone who is too emotional to listen. These factors, and many others that will be discussed in this book, make the communication process difficult; it can be difficult to obtain the information you need or to convey the information the other person needs.

Communicating in a Multicultural Society

Law clerks and legal assistants must sometimes communicate with people whose first language is not English. This occurs in the corporate world, and is even more likely to occur in the areas of law that involve individuals, such as family law, real estate law, employment law, and insurance law. You must be able to obtain the information you need to assist these clients, and to convey the appropriate information to them, without making them feel awkward or uncomfortable. Make every attempt to pronounce names properly, be a good listener, be compassionate, and be aware of cultural differences. For example, in some cultures, direct eye contact is a sign of respect, while in other cultures, it is a sign of disrespect.

Be aware of problems that may arise from differences in vocabulary and intonation. Similar words can have different meanings in different cultures and languages, and the way something is said is often more important than the words used. In addition, lawyers, law clerks, and legal personnel are viewed differently from culture to culture, and in some cases may be seen as threatening.

Some general guidelines for communicating in a multicultural society are as follows:

1. Use words that are commonly known.

2. Avoid slang or colloquial expressions.

3. Use simple sentences that contain a subject, a verb, and an object.

4. Don't use acronyms, contractions, or abbreviations.

5. Be aware of signs of confusion on the part of the listener.

6. Be an active listener yourself. Active listening skills are discussed later in this book.

7. Be aware that an imperfect understanding of what you are saying doesn't indicate a lack of intelligence.

8. Use gestures and facial expressions whenever possible to clarify your meaning.

Communicating with People with Disabilities

Here are a few broad guidelines for communicating with people with disabilities:

1. Acknowledge the existence of a disability. People with disabilities sometimes use gestures to draw the speaker's attention to their condition; they would prefer that it not be ignored.

2. Understand the nature of the disability.

3. Be resourceful in attempting to establish communication. For example, written notes are usually the best way to communicate with a hearing-impaired or a speech-impaired person.

Working Together

Communicating is often a one-on-one situation. As seen in the figure on page 2, a sender sends a message, a receiver receives the message, and the feedback indicates how much of the message was received, understood, and accepted.

There are many situations, however, when you will be dealing with more than one person. After all, dealing with the process of law is a group effort; for example, you don't complete all of the work on a large real estate transaction by yourself. You need the assistance of land titles agents, gas or electricity department personnel, local government officials, other law firms, and more—an entire range of people to whom you must communicate vital information and from whom you must receive information in return. These people are members of your group. When mixed messages are sent between members of the group, or when various members interpret a message differently and fail to assist one another in the communication process, confusion usually ensues—another communication barrier.

EXERCISE 2

FORESEEING BARRIERS

Imagine that you are a legal assistant involved in the large real estate transaction mentioned in the paragraph above. List some of the potential barriers to communication that might be encountered with the following:

1. The buyer of the property

2. The seller of the property

3. The other law firm that you are dealing with

4. The land titles agents

5. The local government

Summary

Everyone communicates, but the effectiveness of the communication process varies. Effectiveness is reflected in the types of feedback given and depends on how well the barriers to communication between sender and receiver are overcome. Law clerks and legal assistants must be effective communicators. They must understand that certain barriers to communication, such as language difference or physical disability, present special communications challenges. Law clerks and legal assistants particularly need to communicate effectively as members of a group.

CHAPTER 1

Effective Listening

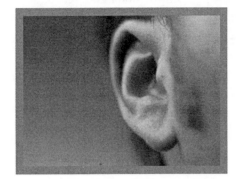

Learning Objectives

After completing this chapter, you should be able to

- Recognize personal listening tendencies.
- Identify barriers to effective listening.
- Develop better listening habits.
- Understand the importance of listening skills for law clerks and legal assistants.

> *We have been given two ears and but a single mouth in order that we may hear more and talk less.*
>
> —Zeno of Citium

Introduction

"No one listens anymore!"

This is a complaint that many students have heard from their instructors, but is it correct? You sit in class and "listen" to what is being presented—except, of course, when you're looking out the window, or talking to someone, or daydreaming, or not concentrating because the room is too hot or too cold, or when you just don't feel like listening.

So, are you really listening? Are your instructors correct? Do the words go in one ear and out the other?

Listening skills are essential for law clerks and legal assistants. You must continually listen to instructions from your superiors, and to what is being said by lawyers, clients, court officials, colleagues, and many other people who will be part of your career. The best place to learn how to listen is in the classroom.

▪ Your Listening Profile

This chapter includes three quizzes to help you rate yourself as a listener. There are no correct or incorrect answers. Your responses, however, will extend your understanding of yourself as a listener and show you where improvement is needed.

These are not particularly difficult quizzes, but your answers will reveal something about your listening skills in relation to others who have done the test.

> **LISTENING PROFILE QUIZ 1**
>
> - Circle the category that best describes you as a listener:
>   excellent / (above average) / average / below average / weak
>
> - On a scale of 0 to 100 (100 being the best),
>   how would you rate yourself as a listener?   _82_

QUIZ 1 ANALYSIS

- Eighty-five percent of all people questioned rate themselves as "average" or worse. Fewer than 5 percent rated themselves as "excellent."

- On the 0 to 100 scale, the extreme range of all respondents was 0 to 90, the general range was 35 to 85, and the average was 55.

> **LISTENING PROFILE QUIZ 2**
>
> On a scale of 0 to 100 (100 being the best), how do you think the following people would rate you as a listener?
>
> - Your best friend: _40_
> - Your instructor: _?_
> - An acquaintance: _20_
> - Someone in your class: _80_
> - Your girlfriend / boyfriend / spouse / partner: _90_
> - Your employer, if you have a part-time job: _90_

QUIZ 2 ANALYSIS

Most respondents rated themselves highest in the role of listeners to their best friends. In most categories, respondents rated themselves higher than they did in quiz 1.

What does this tell us? If people are in fact, as most of them suspect, strong listeners in relation to best friends, it is perhaps because such relationships, unlike others, necessitate good listening. It is interesting to note that most respondents felt that they were seen as poor listeners by spouses and partners. Does "familiarity breed contempt"? The results seem to indicate that respondents talk a lot to their partners but don't listen much.

The implications of all this for law clerks and legal assistants are startling. The quiz contains no categories for clients, colleagues, or other law firm associates, but if you assume that your overall listening performance would remain the same in connection with these people, you have to wonder how much information is being missed. What are you hearing? If you are an average listener, what happens to the information you missed, information that ought to appear on, say, a court document? Obviously, this information gets lost, and the implications can be serious. The outcome of a lawsuit or a criminal action can significantly affect a client's future. It's important not only to hear what is being said, but to listen to what is being said. There's a lot riding on the information you listen to.

> ### LISTENING PROFILE QUIZ 3

Choose one of the following answers for each of the questions below, and score yourself accordingly.

Answer	Score
Almost always	2
Usually	4
Sometimes	6
Seldom	8
Almost never	10

As a listener, how often do you . . .	Answer	Score
■ consider a subject uninteresting?	_____	_____
■ criticize a speaker's delivery or mannerisms?	_____	_____
■ become passionate about something said by a speaker?	_____	_____
■ listen only for facts?	_____	_____
■ try to outline everything?	_____	_____
■ fake attention?	_____	_____
■ look for distractions?	_____	_____
■ ignore difficult material?	_____	_____
■ become antagonistic?	_____	_____
■ daydream?	_____	_____
Total		_____

AT A LECTURE, ONLY 12 PERCENT LISTEN

Bright-eyed college students in lecture halls aren't necessarily listening to the professor, the American Psychological Association was told.

If you rang a bell at sporadic intervals during a lecture and asked students to record their thoughts and moods at that moment, you'd find the following:

- About 20 percent of the students, men and women, were pursuing erotic thoughts.
- Another 20 percent were reminiscing.
- Only 20 percent were paying attention to the lecture.
- Only 12 percent were understanding what was being said.
- The remainder were worrying, daydreaming, or thinking about something else.

— *Paul Cameron, Wayne State University*

QUIZ 3 ANALYSIS

The lower your score, the weaker are your listening skills. Think about it: if your listening skills are weak, what are you really hearing at your job?

Most of us engage in ineffective listening, an obvious barrier to good communication. People are generally poor listeners, usually out of habit or lack of attention or interest, or because the message is complex. Here are some suggestions about how to listen effectively.

■ Nine Rules for Lively Listening

Poor listening habits are the cause of more communication breakdowns than most of us realize; we tend not to think of listening as a communication skill. The first thing to realize about listening is what it's not. First of all, listening and hearing are not the same thing. Hearing is the physiological event of sound hitting the eardrum. Listening is complex; it involves receiving a message, interpreting the message, interpreting the speaker's feelings, eliminating personal biases, understanding what is being said, and practising other skills, which will be discussed in this section.

When someone else is speaking, usually you are not; there is silence from your side of the conversation. But if you are running over your reply in your mind and just waiting for the other person to finish so that you can jump in, that's not real listening.

Lively listening is a conscious act, and if you don't practise it actively, you simply cannot communicate effectively.

RULE 1: DECIDE TO LISTEN

Human beings deal with the noise in their environment by filtering out what doesn't interest them, so that they can concentrate on what does. For example, people who live on busy streets often claim that they don't hear the cars going by. The problem is that we often rely too heavily on this filtering mechanism and end up filtering out messages that we need to hear.

In business settings, we can't afford to let that happen, so we must actually *decide* to listen and then listen actively, with concentration and intent, using all of the skills that we'll be discussing in this section.

Why should we listen? Here are three good reasons: listening keeps us informed; listening keeps us out of trouble; listening makes us appreciated.

Listening Keeps Us Informed

A common cry in business today is, "Nobody ever tells me anything around here!" This is usually heard just after someone has found out something that he or she should have known before. This exclamation reflects an attempt to blame others for one's own lack of knowledge. How often, on the other hand, have you heard someone say, "I never listen to anything that anyone says around here"? Make a point of paying attention to what's going on around you—of listening to messages and information from your colleagues—so that you will always be well informed. Knowledge is power; the best way to acquire knowledge is to listen.

Listening Keeps Us Out of Trouble

Perhaps you remember your mother saying, when you were quite young, something like, "I've told you over and over not to do that. Don't you listen?" The answer, of course, is that we didn't listen. We didn't realize it at the time, but we had more important things on our minds than instructions from Mom, so the information went, as my own mother used to say, in one ear and out the other.

Unfortunately, that situation isn't confined to childhood. Many of us carry poor listening habits into adulthood and the business world. If someone is giving you instructions and you don't listen well, there's a good chance that you won't be able to carry out those instructions properly. Over time, this can be detrimental to your career.

Listening Makes Us Appreciated

One of my best friends in university was very popular. More than once I heard people say that when they were with her, she made them feel as if they were the most important people in the world. They felt that way because she was a great listener. She listened with her ears, her eyes, her smile, her body, her mind—her whole self. When you put that much of yourself into the listening end of a conversation, the other person can't help but admire and appreciate you.

In business, the good listeners will often find themselves respected and trusted simply because other people enjoy working with them.

RULE 2: AVOID SELECTIVE LISTENING

Selective listening occurs when we listen only to what we want to hear: we select the message. In business as in life, we can't afford to practise selective listening. The fact that we ignore bad news or uninteresting material doesn't make it go away or become irrelevant. In fact, things may well become worse if we act on just one part of a complex message.

One way we listen selectively is by not listening to all of what the other person is saying. We listen to half a sentence and then, assuming we know what the person is about to say, we don't bother listening to the rest. Has anyone ever done this to you when you were speaking? Then you know how annoying it is. "That's not what I was going to say!" is like a dash of cold water in the listener's face, and it is well deserved.

A common cause of selective listening is personal bias or stereotyping against the speaker. For example, you might attend a staff meeting of law clerks from your firm where a new office procedure is being discussed. You overhear one of your colleagues whisper to another person, "This procedure won't work. One of my friends at another firm has tried it. It's going to break down the minute we get busy." Obviously, someone with this attitude is not going to listen to the presentation with an open mind, and in fact may not listen at all. That's selective listening.

It's also tempting to discount the opinions of people you simply don't like. If you feel yourself switch off when a certain person begins to speak, you are guilty of selective listening. Remember, the information may be valid and useful even if the person delivering it isn't someone you would have over for dinner—so listen up!

RULE 3: GIVE ACKNOWLEDGEMENT AND FEEDBACK

You can encourage a speaker either through a verbal or a non-verbal response. A simple nod of the head, a smile, a raising of the eyebrows—these are all forms of non-verbal acknowledgement. They let the speaker know you are paying attention. Remaining silent at the appropriate times also indicates you're listening.

If you prefer to acknowledge the speaker verbally, you might interject encouraging words into the conversation, such as "Tell me more about it," "I didn't know that," or "I understand." Note that this indicates your understanding, not your agreement. Your chance to disagree will come later. You could also ask for clarification, with such expressions as "Are you saying that … ?" or "Do you mean that … ?" You may want to paraphrase the speaker's words, and begin your rephrasing with an expression such as "I hear you saying that … ." We'll look at the paraphrase in more detail in chapter 5. These forms of acknowledgement let the speaker know that you understand what is being said. They demonstrate your interest and establish a rapport between the two of you. In a meaningful conversation, each party acknowledges the other's *feelings* as well as the actual words that are spoken.

For example, suppose that a co-worker is complaining about a seemingly trivial matter. She frowns and says angrily, "Why don't they print these meeting announcements on coloured paper or something? How do they expect me to pay attention to another piece of white paper that just gets lost on my desk?" If you simply agree with her, or say that *you* don't have a problem with white paper, you might be missing the point. Respond instead with a statement such as "This really seems to have you upset." This response opens up the possibility for further conversation. Indeed, you may find that white paper isn't the problem so much as the fact that she is feeling overwhelmed with her workload and apt to view another piece of paper on her desk as the last straw. This is another example of how effective listening could contribute productively to the discussion.

Men and women tend to react differently to this type of acknowledgement. Of course, this is not always the case, but as a general rule, men are often reluctant to discuss their feelings, and are likely to deny them. When responding to a man in this situation, preface your remarks with phrases such as "It seems to me," or "Could it be," or "I wonder if." Women tend to be more direct about their feelings, although you still need to be careful.

It's important to watch the language you use in giving feedback. If you use preliminary phrases such as "My advice is" or "Your problem is," your feedback may not be welcome. You want to tune in fully to what is being said without offering your own judgment or ideas or feelings. If you give speakers the opportunity to talk a problem through, they will often come up with the answer themselves, which is much more effective than having you impose an answer.

Don't downplay a problem. Avoid responses such as "Don't worry" or "That's not so bad." These responses can be perceived as devaluing the speaker's concerns.

Reflective Listening

Reflective listening is a form of feedback that involves carefully rephrasing a speaker's message and returning it to him or her for confirmation, such as in the following exchange:

> *Richard*: "I'm fed up with writing draft reports for my supervisor to take to meetings and never hearing whether they went anywhere or not."

> *Jerry*: "It sounds as if you're frustrated by not receiving feedback about your reports. Is that right?"

That's reflective listening. It isn't suitable for all situations, and you have to avoid merely parroting what the speaker has said, but it can be a useful method of making sure, for example, that you have heard instructions correctly.

RULE 4: ASK APPROPRIATE QUESTIONS

Questioning is an important part of the listening process, because it helps the speaker convey his or her thoughts. By asking the right questions, you can greatly increase the scope of the conversation, which is the real art of listening. Compare the following modes of questioning:

1. *Employer 1*: "Has Jenny been to work every day this week?"

2. *Employer 2*: "How is Jenny doing now that we've taken away some of her workload?"

Here we see two different types of questions: **closed** and **open**. Employer 1 asks a closed question, which means that it can be answered with a simple "yes" or "no." Employer 2 asks an open question, which means that the other person must elaborate and give information in order to answer it.

If you want to develop and broaden a conversation, start by asking open questions. Then, as the need for confirmation arises, insert closed questions where appropriate. Let's continue with the sample dialogue from above:

> *Employer*: "How is Jenny doing now that we've taken away some of her workload?"

> *Office Manager*: "Okay."

> *Employer*: "Do you think her work habits have changed?"

> *Office Manager*: "She seems a lot happier and a lot more efficient."

> *Employer*: "How so?"

> *Office Manager*: "She used to take a lot of time off, complaining about headaches and stress. She didn't seem to be very happy. Now, she actually comes in early, is more outgoing than she used to be, and handles her files quickly and efficiently."

> *Employer*: "And you attribute this to having someone help her with her workload."

> *Office Manager*: "Definitely."

Employer: "I'm glad we were able to figure out the problem. What else do you think we need to do?"

Office Manager: "I think Jenny will be fine. We should look at the workloads of all of our law clerks and see if there are any other problems."

You can use both types of questions, closed and open, to broaden a conversation, to clarify or confirm meaning, or to move the conversation in another direction. Below are examples of questions that accomplish these three goals.

Broadening Questions

"Mary, you've told us about the new procedure they're using in the Toronto branch, and it seems to be working well. How do you think we can adapt it to suit our conditions in Montreal?"

As you can see, this question calls for an analytical response that will bring in more information and broaden the discussion.

Clarifying or Confirming Questions

"What do you mean? Are you saying you agree with Doug's assessment?"

By asking questions like these, you give the speaker an opportunity to restate a position and clarify it for others.

Questions That Change the Direction

"We've discussed your proposed program in depth and it seems to have merit. Can you tell us what impact it will have on the budget?"

The first sentence brings closure to one part of the discussion, and the ensuing question moves it on to another part.

Do you see how the open-ended questions elicit information, and the closed-ended questions serve to confirm information or opinion? Think about your own conversations. Do you use questions effectively? Questioning is a valid and helpful aspect of listening, so it's important to work on it.

RULE 5: LOOK FOR NON-VERBAL CUES

Suppose for a moment that you now live in a different place from the one where you grew up, and that you have gone home on vacation. For the first week you have spent every day and evening with your mother, and you have thoroughly enjoyed her company. Now, an old friend has invited you out for dinner. As you leave, you say, "Okay, Mom, I'm off. I'll probably be at Barbara's place for a couple of hours, so I won't be too late."

Instead of looking at you with her usual cheerful face, Mom looks down at the carpet, her head leans forward and down to one side, and her voice seems to slow down and age 20 years as she says in a world-weary tone, "Oh, don't worry. I'll be fine. Just you go ahead and enjoy yourself, and don't give a thought to me."

This is a classic case of the non-verbal cues—body language and tone of voice—being in direct conflict with the spoken words. Mom's non-verbal message is clear: "I don't want you to go, I'd prefer that you not enjoy yourself, and I have no intention of being fine!"

People send non-verbal messages in the workplace all the time, and effective listeners learn to "hear" them. How you decide to respond is not the issue here; the important thing is that you recognize the non-verbal message.

Body Language

Interpreting body language is not an exact science. There is danger in interpreting individual gestures and mannerisms according to a fixed set of rules; the meanings of gestures and mannerisms vary from one person to another. For example, we are told that folded arms indicate defensiveness or an unwillingness to be persuaded; however, many people fold their arms simply because it is a comfortable position.

It is important to look at "body language clusters" if you want to interpret body language accurately. If your boss stands in front of your desk with his arms folded and asks for information, it doesn't necessarily mean anything. But if he folds his arms while tapping his foot, frowning, and clenching his teeth, you can be sure that a problem exists.

What the good listener looks for is body language that *seems* to contradict the words of the speaker. When words and body language are in direct conflict, the body language is usually a truer indicator of meaning.

Tone of Voice

Have you ever heard a speaker stand up on a platform and begin a speech with the words, "I'm pleased to be here with you today"—spoken in a flat monotone that indicated no pleasure at all? You probably noticed that the tone of voice didn't match the words, and you probably believed the tone. Most people would. What did that do for the speaker's credibility? Likely, not much.

Tone of voice plays a larger role in our conversations than we realize. On hearing their voices on a tape recorder for the first time, most people refuse to believe that they sound "like that." People don't realize that they speak in such a flat tone.

Alertness to tone of voice is another tool for evaluating the truth and sincerity of a person's actual words in relation to the real feelings behind them. Ideally, for a message to be clear and uncomplicated, the words, body language, and tone of voice should all be in agreement; in other words, they should all send the same message.

Lively listeners always pay attention to non-verbal cues because they are a vital component of communication.

RULE 6: LISTEN WITH YOUR WHOLE BODY

Picture this: something exciting happened at work today. When you and your partner sit down to dinner, you begin to relate the incident. Your partner doesn't look at you, doesn't say a word, shows no reaction—just keeps on eating. Do you feel listened to? Is your partner using the tools of lively listening? The fact is that

that person might well be listening, might be taking in every word you say. But is it lively listening? No.

The lively listener not only takes in information, but also indicates in many ways that the speaker's message is getting through. If you want to make it clear that you are listening, use your entire body.

First, *look at* the person speaking. Give the speaker plenty of non-verbal feedback: nod your head, smile, frown, vary your expression to suit your response, lean toward the speaker; the speaker is encouraged to continue because you have made it clear that you're listening.

Using your body also helps you as the listener; if you're active, your attention is much less likely to wander. In other words, by physically indicating to the speaker that you *are* listening, you will actually improve the quality of your listening.

RULE 7: SEPARATE FACT FROM OPINION AND PROPAGANDA

The challenge of this rule is that you must learn to distinguish what is fact from what is merely opinion or what someone would like you to believe. People colour their words in many ways, which adds to the challenge of lively listening.

"These people are doing it. Why don't you join them?" This is the familiar message of what the advertising industry calls "lifestyle advertising": a group of happy, laughing adults enjoys a certain brand of beer. The implication, the suggestion, the unspoken message is that if you drink this brand of beer, you too can enjoy this lifestyle. You are encouraged to jump on the bandwagon.

We recognize this tactic in advertising, but we don't always notice it in normal conversation. Any time someone is trying to persuade you to do something or believe something, listen carefully for the facts and strip away the opinion.

Another way that facts can be distorted is with biased words and expressions. People sometimes have so much invested in their opinions being accepted that they sound like a circus pitchman in full swing. "This process will revolutionize the way our company operates!" This may well be true, but it may not be the kind of revolution you want. Or it may not be true at all. Learn to strip away the opinion and propaganda and listen for the facts before you respond.

RULE 8: CONTROL YOUR EMOTIONAL RESPONSE

We all have hot buttons. We all have attitudes and beliefs that make us respond with a quick flash of anger when people raise certain topics in particular ways.

What are your hot buttons? It's important to be aware of them so that you can decide how to react when someone pushes them in a conversation. As a lively listener, you need to take several steps to control your emotional response to what someone says to you.

First, you must recognize your response. When someone says something that makes you angry, what does it feel like? What happens in your body? Usually, one of the first things we notice is a change in our breathing pattern—breathing becomes shallower and faster. Perhaps you find that blood rushes to your face, and you feel heat there. Some people feel a headache suddenly begin; others automatically clench their hands into fists. How do you feel if one of your hot buttons is pushed? Take some time to really think about this, because it needs to be immediately recognizable to you if you want to be a lively listener.

How do you control an inappropriate emotional response? First, acknowledge it to yourself. Then, take a momentary pause and breathe deeply. This will change your physiological state while giving you time to consider what to say. In that brief interval, you can get control of yourself and choose your reaction.

Depending on various factors—the subject under discussion, the identity of the person who has upset you, the purpose of the conversation—you might take one of three paths:

1. *Ignore the comment and move on.* This will enable you to continue the conversation, but it might leave you simmering below the surface.

2. *Mention it and make an issue of the remark.* If the same person constantly pushes the same hot button, at some point you will need to do this just to clear the air. It is possible that the person is pushing your buttons unwittingly and only needs to have it mentioned in order to stop.

3. *Respond in passing and continue the conversation on the right track.* Say something like, "You may be right, but that's not what we're discussing."

An inappropriate overreaction can put an end to any conversation, so you would do well to learn how to control your emotional response.

RULE 9: MAKE NOTES

Notes can be on paper, on a computer screen, or just in your head, depending on the situation. If one of your colleagues is explaining a situation and asking for your help, begin by saying, "I'll just make a few notes as we talk," and make it obvious that you are doing so. The person now knows that you are really listening and paying attention, and the notes serve as focal points to help you formulate your response. Don't overdo the note taking. It's one thing to make occasional notes; it's quite another thing to write down every word that was said and make the speaker feel as if he or she is being interrogated.

Of course, in order to decide which points need to be noted, you need to take steps we have already discussed: provide feedback, ask questions, and listen with your whole body. All these practices help elicit information that you can use to make effective notes. Note taking is a vital step in becoming a lively listener.

SOME ADDITIONAL PRINCIPLES

1. Remember that the listener's job is to assimilate information, understand the information, and act on it.

2. Don't ignore the speaker's silence. Silence is a behaviour that has meaning, and it's often important to discover that meaning. You might try the following question: "You seem reluctant to discuss this matter. What's on your mind?"

3. Organize your perceptions: decide whether the speaker is angry, unreasonable, or open to advice. Also, recognize stereotypes and prejudices in others. Keep your perceptions tentative.

4. Interpret the speaker in the speaker's own terms, not yours.

5. Get agreement: summarize what you've heard and have the speaker agree to your version.

EXERCISE 1

KNOWING YOURSELF AS A LISTENER

1. Identify some topics of discussion to which you listen attentively. Why do these topics interest you?

2. Identify some topics that don't usually cause you to listen attentively. Why not?

3. For those topics that don't compel your full attention, develop a list of strategies that will improve your listening skills in these areas.

Barriers to Effective Listening

There are a number of reasons why people don't listen effectively. These barriers to effective listening can affect both the message being sent and the message being received. They include the following:

1. **Lack of interest**. If you're not interested in what's being said, you don't listen; or you listen only to those things that interest you—in other words, selectively—and ignore the rest.

2. **Daydreaming**. Your mind is occupied by something other than what's being said.

3. **Emotional concerns**. You may be emotionally involved in the topic and therefore interested in only one point of view; or you may have recently suffered an emotional or traumatic experience in your personal life that is occupying your thoughts.

4. **Judgmental approach**. You hear what is being said through the distortion of your own ideas, judgments, or feelings. Your biases and prejudices take over.

5. **Environmental and physical distractions**. These include background noise, uncomfortable seating, heat, cold, cramped space, colleagues who talk while you're trying to listen, and many others.

6. **Lack of understanding**. You lack the background needed to fully understand the speaker's topic.

7. **Unclear presentation**. The speaker is discussing the topics in a vague manner and not providing elaboration.

8. **Incorrect interpretation of the message.** You misunderstand the motives behind the message, being unable to interpret others in their own terms.

9. **Lack of retention.** Statistically, we forget more than half of a message immediately, and remember only about 35 percent after eight hours.

Drawing It All Together

Now that we have identified both the skills involved in lively listening, and some of the barriers to listening effectively, we can summarize the steps you need to take:

1. *Pay attention.* The speaker may be saying something you can use to your advantage. (Skill enhancer: *Efficiency*)

2. *Concentrate on the message.* The message conveyed is more important than what the speaker is saying. (Skill enhancer: *Clarity*)

3. *Hear the speaker out.* Let the speaker finish speaking before you make any judgments. (Skill enhancer: *Objectivity*)

4. *Listen for main ideas, principles, and concepts.* Be aware of the large picture. (Skill enhancer: *Perception*)

5. *Listen two or three minutes before taking notes.* Do not begin writing immediately. (Skill enhancer: *Ability to conceptualize and summarize*)

6. *Relax while listening.* Tension detracts from listening ability. (Skill enhancer: *Self-discipline*)

7. *Eliminate distractions.* Distractions are any barriers to listening, such as noise, which will detract from the message. (Skill enhancer: *Decisiveness*)

8. *Learn how to listen to difficult material.* Do not withdraw your attention when the factual or the emotional content is difficult. (Skill enhancer: *Perseverance*)

9. *Identify your own greatest word barriers.* Word barriers are words or concepts that trigger bias or negative attitudes. (Skill enhancer: *Objectivity*)

10. *Make your interpretation skills an asset.* Use the following techniques to assist you:

    a. Anticipate the next point to be made.

    b. Make comparisons and contrasts.

    c. Identify the speaker's evidence.

    d. Practise mental summarizing.

    (Skill enhancer: *Resourcefulness*)

EXERCISE 2

TRACKING YOUR LISTENING BEHAVIOUR

1. For the next five days, pay attention to your listening behaviour. Make note of the times you genuinely try to listen and understand what someone else is saying and of the times when you aren't listening.

2. Keep a record of this information. For each entry include

   a. the day and time,

   b. the people involved,

   c. the situation (the topic of conversation, the emotions involved),

   d. the outcome (how did your listening style affect the outcome?), and

   e. your level of satisfaction with the situation.

3. At the end of the five-day period, ask yourself the following:

   a. Which of the listening styles described in this chapter did you use?

   b. In what situations did you use the various styles?

   c. Are you satisfied with your listening behaviour?

   d. What improvements do you need to make to your personal listening style?

EXERCISE 3

CASE STUDY

I didn't want to go to work today. It had been raining all weekend, but now the weather was great; it figures that Monday would be warm and sunny. But I had a meeting first thing in the morning, and my supervisor had been on my case to finish a couple of files, so I dragged myself out of bed, thought about calling in sick, realized that I was late, and rushed out of my apartment without stopping for breakfast. At least, I rushed as far as my car; it wouldn't start. I called a cab. The cab came right away, but when I got to the office, I discovered that I didn't have any money with me, so I had to find an ATM to get the cash to pay the cab driver. He was a bit peeved with me, because he had another call waiting. I guess I could have given him a bigger tip, but I didn't like his attitude. It's not as if it's my fault that my credit card was maxed out. I was a few minutes late, and my supervisor, Mary Kim, was already speaking. She always starts on time. She should consider people like me, who have good reasons for being late, and give us an extra few minutes. I had wanted to get to work early, because there had been a big party on Friday night and I wanted to catch up on the gossip. Now I had to sit there for an hour or so until I could find out what went on. So Mary droned on for another 15 minutes. She usually doesn't have anything to say in any case, so I ignored most of her presentation. I was thinking about how, now that I didn't have a car, I was going to get to the bank at lunch hour to pay some bills. I made up my mind to pay attention to the rest of the meeting, but Joel King was making a presentation, and as far as I'm concerned, there wasn't much he could tell me. What a sycophant! Always running up to the boss and asking if there's anything he can help with. It makes me sick! I think he's after my job. And the topic bored me to tears. Something about legal research or new government regulations or something like that. I can't imagine who'd be interested in that stuff. I don't remember much about the rest of the meeting. The room was stuffy; you'd think they could have opened a window. So I guess you could say that, as far as my attention level was concerned, the lights were on, but no one was home. I was catching up on some missed sleep, even though my eyes were open. I should paint some eyes on my glasses so everyone will think I'm awake. But my body was there even though my mind wasn't. That's all that counts in these big law firms.

ACTIVITY

Identify the barriers to listening in this case study. For each barrier listed, describe what could be done to overcome it.

EXERCISE 4

LISTENING IN SCHOOL

Take a look at the courses you're studying this semester. It is easy enough to determine those in which you are succeeding and those in which you are struggling. Analyze the "good" courses to determine why you are successful in them. Then, decide why you aren't successful or as successful in the others. How can you apply good listening skills to improve your grades? Before analyzing your own case, however, practise on the one that follows:

When I was in university, I had to take a biology course. I couldn't get out of it; everyone in an arts program had to take one science course. My problems were as follows:

1. I didn't like biology; I was an English major.

2. I didn't like cutting up animals.

3. The course was dull, dull, dull.

4. The members of my group all wanted to be biologists.

5. The classroom smelled like a funeral home.

6. The instructor was dull, dull, dull.

7. I had no skills in math or chemistry.

Believe it or not, I didn't do well in this course. Suggest ways in which I could have improved through active listening.

EXERCISE 5

LISTENING IN GROUPS: MOTIVATION

1. Select groups, with four to six participants in each group.

2. Appoint one referee per group.

3. Ask each participant to make a list of items—thoughts, feelings, complaints, wishes, plans—that he or she would be willing to share with other group members. It could be a to-do list, a wish list, a "things-that-bug-me" list, a "what-I'd-do-if-I-won-the-lottery" list, or something similar.

4. The referee will collect the lists from each member, shuffle them, and select one. The member whose list it is will be "it" and will speak first.

5. The referee will give each participant two minutes to tell the rest of the group what is on his or her list.

6. The rest of the group, while not being visibly rude, should do their best not to listen to the speaker. Group members can make occasional eye contact, but this should be minimal. The group members might, for instance, concentrate on their own lists as a way of ignoring the speaker. Group members should not speak to each other or to other members of the class.

7. The referee will also ignore the speaker, and will discourage nervous laughter from the group, attempts to distract the speaker, and the like.

8. When two minutes have elapsed, the referee will select another speaker, and repeat the process until all members of the group have been "it."

9. The referee will then lead a group discussion based on the following questions:

    a. How did you feel when you were "it"?

    b. How did being ignored affect or influence your motivation to continue speaking?

    c. How did being ignored affect your sense of self-esteem?

    d. How do you think others feel when you either don't listen to them or don't give them your full attention?

    e. How do you think your inattention would affect children, adults, co-workers?

    f. How did you feel when you weren't "it"?

LISTENING IN GROUPS: MEANING

Take several minutes to discuss strong feelings, moral convictions, and personal beliefs. Record the findings on the blackboard, on a flip chart, or by some electronic means. Topics may include, but should not be limited to, the following:

a. Whether to legalize "soft drugs" and invest the tax profits in education and health care;

b. Whether to legalize prostitution (both male and female) and invest the profits in health care and research;

c. Whether to ban all forms of corporal punishment for children (including parental "discipline");

d. Whether to ban the use of cellphones or any other electronic devices for drivers of automobiles;

e. Whether to make licences mandatory for the operation of motorized recreational vehicles such as snowmobiles and motorboats, and whether to restrict these licences to people 16 years of age and older;

f. Whether to stop funding any system of education that is not public (e.g., religious schools, other private schools);

g. Whether anyone caught with illegal possession of firearms while committing a crime should get an automatic 10-year prison term on top of what the judge imposes;

h. Whether religious institutions (e.g., churches, mosques, temples, synagogues) should be taxed and the profits invested in municipal infrastructures such as roads, sewers, and the like.

Having compiled a list of this sort, proceed with the following steps:

1. Select groups of three participants.

2. Appoint one referee from each group.

3. Ask the two others in the group to select a topic from the list (or come up with an alternative) that will produce a disagreement between them.

4. Ask one participant to explain to the other his or her point of view on the topic. Limit the speaker to two minutes and ask him or her to focus on a small number of points. The speaker will be allowed to continue later in the exercise if more points need to be made. The listener may not speak during this discussion or express disagreement by any gestures or expressions.

5. When the speaker's time is up, ask the listener to paraphrase what the speaker has said.

6. When the person who was listening is finished with the paraphrase, ask the person who first spoke, "Is this what you said?"

7. If the person who spoke first agrees that the paraphrase was accurate, the two participants will change roles. The person who listened first becomes the speaker and gives his or her point of view on the topic. Repeat the process.

8. Go back to the person who spoke first, and ask whether he or she has any additional points to make or has a response to the second speaker. Repeat the process.

9. When both participants have finished, ask them to paraphrase what the other one has said.

10. The referee's role will be to keep the discussion on track, to limit the two-minute discussions to a few specific points, to make sure that the listener does not speak or gesture while the other participant is speaking, and generally to maintain order.

Participants can then discuss the feelings and attitudes they had while listening, how difficult it was to listen and not interfere, whether they changed their point of view on the topic after listening to the speaker, and how important it was to listen to the entirety of what the other had to say.

Summary

Listening skills are difficult to master because of the various distractions, external and internal, that exist in any listening situation. Understand your own listening habits, and learn how to improve any shortcomings in your personal listening skills. Proper questioning methods will likely result in more useful responses.

SPELLING AND DEFINITIONS

Be able to spell and define the following words:

abatement	corroborate	guardian	testify
attendance	decision	litigious	transitory
behaviour	discrepancy	prejudice	trustee
benefited	duress	promissory	urgent
citizen	exaggerate	quash	
correspond	grievance	remittance	

CHAPTER 2

Spelling

Learning Objectives

After completing this chapter, you should be able to

- Understand the importance of spelling to law clerks and legal assistants.
- Follow spelling rules.
- Spell troublesome words.
- Increase your personal vocabulary.
- Increase your professional vocabulary.
- Differentiate between words that are commonly confused.

Introduction

Spelling in English is difficult because the language contains so many words that defy the basic spelling rules. In addition, irregular verbs, double *l* words, *ou* words, irregular plurals, possessives, and contractions make spelling a chore.

However, law clerks and legal assistants must know how to spell. Poor spelling casts doubt on the quality of reports and correspondence. Law clerks and legal assistants are expected to be professionals, and poor spelling brings their professionalism into question.

In spite of the many spelling irregularities in the language, there are some basic rules. Some of these spelling rules are set out in this chapter. Also included are lists of difficult words to help you discover patterns in the spelling of single words and groups of words.

When you review the principles of good writing, you begin with the study of words and of grammar. This chapter of the book and the next one, therefore, deal with how words are spelled, how grammar applies to good writing, and how words are used in sentences.

You cannot write effectively if you are a poor speller. Poor spelling is the most noticeable of all writing faults. The complaints that schools and colleges hear about the writing of their graduates are mostly concerned with poor spelling.

Improving Your Spelling

Use a dictionary to find the correct spellings of uncommon or difficult words, but you should not need it for common words such as *recommend* or *receive*. You should know words like these, and you should be able to write them as correctly and as effortlessly as you write your own name.

The 400 words most commonly misspelled by college students are found on the following pages. These words are used so frequently that you should begin your review by learning how to spell them.

To study the spelling of a word, take the following steps:

1. **Look at the word carefully and examine its structure.** Does it have a common prefix (*un*necessary, *un*interesting, *dis*appointed, *dis*satisfied) or a common suffix (exist*ence*, differ*ence*, perform*ance*, attend*ance*)?

2. **Pronounce the word correctly**. Many students misspell words such as *government, candidate,* and *library* because they have always mispronounced these words.

3. **Pronounce the word by syllables**. Sounding out the word part by part can help you with its spelling (e.g., "ac-com-mo-date").

4. **Notice the hard spots**. Misspellings almost always occur in the same place within a given word, so watch out for these hard spots (e.g., per*severance*, sep*arate*).

5. **Use memory devices**. The following are helpful memory devices: "Lett*ers* are written on station*ery*," and "*i* before *e* except after *c*."

Write the words you are studying over and over, and practise them until the correct spelling becomes a habit. Learn them any way you can, but *learn* them.

100 TROUBLESOME WORDS

1. success
2. difference
3. pleasant
4. remember
5. finally
6. preferred
7. usually
8. consideration
9. doubt
10. appearance
11. determined
12. decision
13. actually
14. extremely
15. endeavour
16. advisable
17. position
18. basis
19. clothes
20. although
21. February
22. annual
23. partial
24. obliged
25. anxious
26. evidently
27. convenient
28. transferred
29. minimum
30. instruction
31. foreign
32. examination
33. envelope
34. description
35. statement
36. guarantee
37. naturally
38. regretting
39. beautiful
40. practical
41. unnecessary
42. therefore
43. additional
44. inquiry
45. character
46. catalogue
47. impossible
48. superintendent
49. assistance
50. application
51. satisfied
52. completely
53. advertising
54. apparently
55. absolutely
56. information
57. further
58. material
59. purchase
60. ridiculous
61. secretary
62. duly
63. interest
64. mortgage
65. occurred
66. capacity
67. assume
68. equipped
69. double
70. quantity
71. acknowledge
72. criticism
73. occasion
74. especially
75. surprise
76. suggestion
77. explanation
78. authority
79. affectionately
80. cordially
81. situation
82. purpose
83. committee
84. representative
85. necessary
86. probably
87. cancellation
88. regarding
89. tentative
90. recently
91. organization
92. recommendation
93. cancelled
94. bureau
95. government
96. unfortunately
97. commission
98. bulletin
99. attention
100. considerable

► ANOTHER 100 TROUBLESOME WORDS

101. exactly	127. financial	153. Wednesday	179. satisfactory
102. library	128. addressed	154. Saturday	180. practice (n.) practise (v.)
103. studying	129. possibility	155. women	181. exception
104. article	130. sufficient	156. American	182. excellent
105. attached	131. correspondence	157. business	183. replying
106. approval	132. schedule	158. undoubtedly	184. immediately
107. equipment	133. response	159. beginning	185. cooperation (*or* co-operation)
108. hospital	134. exceedingly	160. realize	186. courtesy
109. insurance	135. special	161. imagine	187. appreciation
110. estimate	136. available	162. opportunity	188. requirements
111. memorandum	137. distribution	163. knowledge	189. individual
112. paid	138. sincerely	164. perhaps	190. accordance
113. freight	139. similar	165. experience	191. merchandise
114. remittance	140. arrangement	166. reference	192. various
115. forward	141. disappoint	167. necessity	193. effort
116. convenience	142. remit	168. grateful	194. association
117. earliest	143. judgment	169. general	195. circumstances
118. duplicate	144. extension	170. permanent	196. prompt
119. written	145. particular	171. certificate	197. policy
120. invoice	146. all right	172. temporary	198. customer
121. thoroughly	147. mention	173. difficult	199. assure
122. campaign	148. proposition	174. definite	200. communication
123. benefit	149. planning	175. approximately	
124. community	150. balance	176. opinion	
125. acquaintance	151. shipment	177. specified	
126. familiar	152. either	178. length	

200 FREQUENTLY MISSPELLED WORDS

1. absence	34. cafeteria	67. disease	100. influential
2. accessible	35. calendar	68. division	101. insistence
3. accidentally	36. candidate	69. earnestly	102. intelligence
4. accommodate	37. captain	70. eighth	103. interfere
5. accumulate	38. carrying	71. electricity	104. interrupt
6. accurately	39. catalogue	72. embarrassed	105. invitation
7. achieve	40. certain	73. emphasize	106. laboratory
8. acquainted	41. characteristic	74. essential	107. lightning
9. acquisition	42. chocolate	75. exaggerate	108. literature
10. address	43. choice	76. excitement	109. loneliness
11. advantageous	44. column	77. exercise	110. maintenance
12. agreeable	45. compelling	78. exhausted	111. mathematics
13. allegiance	46. competent	79. extraordinary	112. mechanically
14. almost	47. competition	80. facilities	113. merely
15. already	48. compulsory	81. familiar	114. miniature
16. amateur	49. concentration	82. formula	115. mischievous
17. amount	50. concern	83. generally	116. mysterious
18. apparatus	51. confident	84. grammar	117. negligence
19. appetite	52. conquer	85. gymnasium	118. niece
20. approach	53. conscientious	86. height	119. ninety
21. appropriate	54. continually	87. hindrance	120. noticeable
22. argument	55. controlled	88. humorous	121. obedience
23. associate	56. courteous	89. hurrying	122. occasionally
24. athlete	57. dealt	90. hygiene	123. occurrence
25. athletic	58. deceive	91. illegible	124. o'clock
26. attendance	59. deficiency	92. illiterate	125. omelette
27. aviator	60. definition	93. imagination	126. omitted
28. awkward	61. dependent	94. immensely	127. original
29. bachelor	62. desperate	95. imitation	128. parallel
30. beneficial	63. development	96. inaccuracy	129. paralyze
31. biscuit	64. digestible	97. incidentally	130. pastime
32. bookkeeper	65. dining	98. inevitable	131. perform
33. boundary	66. disappeared	99. independence	132. permissible

> ## 200 FREQUENTLY MISSPELLED WORDS (cont.)

133. perseverance	150. professional	167. rhyme	184. successfully
134. persistent	151. professor	168. rhythm	185. surround
135. perspiration	152. prominent	169. sacrifice	186. technical
136. persuade	153. pronunciation	170. sandwich	187. tenant
137. physically	154. pursuing	171. scarcely	188. tendency
138. physician	155. recipe	172. scissors	189. truly
139. picnicking	156. recognize	173. seize	190. twelfth
140. politics	157. recollect	174. sentence	191. unaccustomed
141. possession	158. recommend	175. separate	192. unanimous
142. practically	159. referred	176. sergeant	193. unusual
143. predicament	160. rehearsal	177. serviceable	194. vacuum
144. prejudice	161. relieve	178. severely	195. valuable
145. preparation	162. religious	179. shining	196. varied
146. presence	163. repetition	180. siege	197. vegetable
147. privilege	164. reservoir	181. specimen	198. villain
148. probability	165. respectability	182. strength	199. weird
149. procedure	166. restaurant	183. succeed	200. wholly

◼ Useful Spelling Rules

Because most of us learn to spell by studying and practising one word at a time, you may find that some spelling rules are more confusing than helpful. But these rules apply to thousands of words and therefore may help you avoid many common difficulties. Four useful rules are set out below.

RULE 1

If a word ends with a *y* preceded by a consonant (as in *copy* or *try*), change the *y* to an *i* before every suffix except *ing*.

$$copy + es = copies$$
$$copy + ing = copying$$
$$worry + ed = worried$$
$$worry + ing = worrying$$
$$try + ed = tried$$
$$try + ing = trying$$
$$lady + es = ladies$$

If the *y* is preceded by a vowel, do not change it (as in *valley* or *honey*).

$$
\begin{aligned}
\text{valley} + \text{s} &= \text{valleys} \\
\text{honey} + \text{s} &= \text{honeys}
\end{aligned}
$$

RULE 2

Write *i* before *e* except after *c* or when sounded as *a*, as in *neighbour* or *weigh*.

i before *e*: brief, piece, belief, chief
e before *i*: receive, ceiling, deceive, freight, weight, sleigh

Exceptions to the rule:

either, neither, seize, leisure, weird

RULE 3

If a word ends with a single consonant preceded by a single vowel (*stop*, *begin*) and you add a suffix beginning with a vowel (*-ed*, *-ing*, *-ance*), double the final consonant in the two situations described below:

1. The word has only one syllable:

$$
\begin{aligned}
\text{stop} + \text{ed} &= \text{stopped} \\
\text{trip} + \text{ed} &= \text{tripped} \\
\text{rub} + \text{ing} &= \text{rubbing} \\
\text{drop} + \text{ing} &= \text{dropping}
\end{aligned}
$$

2. The word is accented on the last syllable:

$$
\begin{aligned}
\text{confer} + \text{ed} &= \text{conferred} \\
\text{begin} + \text{ing} &= \text{beginning} \\
\text{omit} + \text{ing} &= \text{omitting} \\
\text{remit} + \text{ance} &= \text{remittance}
\end{aligned}
$$

Do not double the final consonant if the accent is not on the last syllable (*benefited, profited, exhibited*).

RULE 4

If the word ends with a silent *e* (*bite*, *use*) and you add a suffix, the following rules apply:

1. Drop the *e* if the suffix begins with a vowel.

$$
\begin{aligned}
\text{bite} + \text{ing} &= \text{biting} \\
\text{use} + \text{able} &= \text{usable} \\
\text{desire} + \text{able} &= \text{desirable} \\
\text{gaze} + \text{ed} &= \text{gazed}
\end{aligned}
$$

2. Keep the *e* if the suffix begins with a consonant.

$$
\begin{aligned}
\text{use} + \text{full} &= \text{useful} \\
\text{achieve} + \text{ment} &= \text{achievement} \\
\text{love} + \text{ly} &= \text{lovely} \\
\text{hope} + \text{less} &= \text{hopeless}
\end{aligned}
$$

These rules have two exceptions:

1. Words such as *noticeable* and *courageous* retain the silent *e* to keep the preceding consonant (*c* or *g*) soft.

2. Words such as *truly* and *argument* drop the silent *e* that follows a vowel.

◻ Plurals

With most words, you simply add *s* to form the plural.

bed	beds
book	books
pipe	pipes

Words ending in a sibilant *ch*, *sh*, *s*, *x*, or *z*, however, add *-es* to form the plural.

boss	bosses
box	boxes
bush	bushes
buzz	buzzes
catch	catches
sash	sashes
dress	dresses
fox	foxes

There are two rules for words that end in *y* :

1. If a consonant precedes the *y*, change *y* to *i* and add *es*.

activity	activities
apology	apologies
duty	duties

2. If a vowel precedes the *y*, simply add *s*.

attorney	attorneys
monkey	monkeys
toy	toys

For words that end in *f*, either add *s* or change *f* to *v* and add *es*, depending on the particular case.

belief	beliefs
chief	chiefs
cliff	cliffs
half	halves
life	lives
leaf	leaves
self	selves
loaf	loaves
wife	wives

There are many irregular plurals, some of which are set out below.

ox	oxen
child	children
deer	deer
foot	feet
goose	geese
moose	moose
man	men
woman	women
mouse	mice

There are three types of nouns that end in *o*, and there is a different pluralizing rule for each type.

1. If a vowel precedes the *o*, simply add *s*.

boo	boos
stereo	stereos
radio	radios

2. If the word is a musical term, add *s*.

piano	pianos
solo	solos

3. For all other words ending in *o*, there is no rule. The plurals must be memorized.

echo	echoes
silo	silos
hero	heroes
poncho	ponchos
zero	zeroes
potato	potatoes
tomato	tomatoes

4. Certain plurals derive from their Greek or Latin roots.

crisis	crises
thesis	theses
datum	data
criterion	criteria

EXERCISE 1

FORMING PLURALS

Change the following singular nouns to their correct plural form:

1. attorney _____
2. kiss _____
3. rodeo _____
4. crisis _____
5. foot _____
6. piccolo _____
7. bed _____
8. cargo _____
9. watch _____
10. buzz _____
11. analysis _____
12. canoe _____
13. patio _____
14. man _____
15. latch _____
16. basis _____
17. self _____
18. apology _____
19. zero _____
20. six _____
21. child _____
22. baby _____
23. goose _____
24. try _____
25. box _____

26. dress _____
27. paper _____
28. loss _____
29. chimney _____
30. miss _____
31. mix _____
32. knife _____
33. key _____
34. laugh _____
35. wish _____
36. duty _____
37. tool _____
38. roof _____
39. push _____
40. mouse _____
41. loaf _____
42. wall _____
43. bus _____
44. table _____
45. business _____
46. axe _____
47. belief _____
48. pass _____
49. donkey _____
50. penalty _____

▪ Word Problems

Troublesome words fall into four broad categories:

1. **Homographs**: words that have the same spelling, but have different meanings or uses.

2. **Homonyms**: words that have the same pronunciation, but different spellings and often different meanings.

3. **Synonyms**: words with similar meanings.

4. **Antonyms**: words with opposite meanings.

The following list includes, in addition to words in these categories, a selection of words that are commonly misspelled or misused, and words that are overused.

▶ WORDS FREQUENTLY MISUSED

a, an   These words are *indefinite articles*, used with nouns. *A* is used with nouns that begin with a consonant sound. *An* is used with nouns that begin with a vowel sound.

accede, exceed   To *accede* to something is to go along with it. *To exceed* your limits is to go too far.

accept, except   To *accept* something is to receive it. *To except* something is to exclude it or leave it out. *Except* is also an adverb that means "excluding."

access, excess   *Access* is the way into something. *Excess* means "extra" or "too much."

ad, add   The word *ad* is an abbreviation of *advertisement*. It is best avoided in formal communications. *To add* is to combine or to take a total.

adapt, adept   To *adapt* is to change, either oneself or something else. *Adept* is an adjective meaning "skilled."

addition, edition   *Addition* is the process of adding, or the thing or person added. An *edition* is a version of something, usually a book.

advice, advise   *Advice* is a noun; it is the information that well-meaning people give you when they counsel or *advise* (verb) you.

affect, effect   To *affect* (verb) is to influence, or to put on an act. An *affect* (noun — a psychologists'

jargon word) is an emotion. *To effect* (verb) is to make something happen, and an *effect* (noun) is the result of what happens.

all ready, already   *All ready* means "to be prepared." *Already* means "previously."

all right, alright   Fundamentally, *all right* means "all correct." The expression also has a variety of colloquial meanings. It should not be spelled *alright*.

all together, altogether   *All together* means "as a group." *Altogether* means "entirely." *All together* is also a colloquial expression meaning "rational."

all ways, always   *All ways* means "in every aspect" or "in every direction." *Always* means "forever."

allot, alot, a lot   To *allot* something is to distribute or assign it. *Alot* is a common misspelling of *a lot*, which is an informal way of saying "a great deal" or "a large amount." A *lot* is also a piece of property.

allude, elude   To *allude* to something is to refer to it. *Elude* means "to escape."

allusion, illusion   An *allusion* is a reference to something. An *illusion* is an unreal picture or idea.

aloud, allowed   *Aloud* means "audible, not silent or whispered." *Allowed* means "permitted" or, in some cases, "admitted" or "confessed."

WORDS FREQUENTLY MISUSED (cont.)

altar, alter   An *altar* (noun) is a raised ceremonial area, usually in a church or other place of worship. *To alter* (verb) something is to change it.

alternate, alternative   An *alternate* (noun) is a substitute, or a person or thing that replaces someone or something else. The verb *to alternate* means "to take turns"; as an adjective, *alternate* means "secondary." *Alternative* means "another option."

although   As a conjunction, *although* is synonymous and interchangeable with *though*. *Though* is also used as an adverb. *Tho* and *altho* are not acceptable spellings. *Although* means "in spite of the fact that." For example, "She is happy although she has no money."

among, between   *Among* means "surrounded by." It refers to a position in the midst of several or more. *Between* means "separating," and refers to the situation, or position, of being bounded by two people or things.

amount, number   The *amount* is the quantity, the sum total. It is not the same as *number*, which is the total of all the units.

and/or   *And* means "in addition." *Or* means "one of two." The form *and/or* is grammatically incorrect.

annual, annul   *Annual* is an adverb meaning "yearly." *Annul* (verb) means "to cancel."

anyway, any way   *Anyway* is a colloquial form of "in any event" or "in any case." *Any way* means "any means" or "any path."

appraise, apprise   *To appraise* is to evaluate. *To apprise* is to let someone know something, to inform.

are, our, hour   *Are* is a present tense of the verb *to be*. *Our* means "belonging to us." An *hour* is a time unit of 60 minutes.

as yet   *As yet* often functions as a wordy synonym for *yet*.

assistance, assistants   *Assistance* means "help" or "aid." *Assistants* are those people or things who give help or aid.

attendance, attendants   Your *attendance* means "your presence." *Attendants* are those people who give assistance.

between   See *among*.

born, borne   *Born* means "given birth to" or "created." *To be borne* is to be carried.

brake, break   *To brake* (verb) means "to put a stop to something"; the *brake* (noun) is the device on a car or piece of equipment that makes it stop. *To break* something is to make it come apart or shatter.

canvas, canvass   A *canvas* is a heavy piece of cloth used to cover things, camp under, or paint on. *To canvass* (verb) means "to solicit," as in the case of opinions or money.

capital, capitol   As an adjective, *capital* means "important" or "chief." As a noun, it commonly means "the city in a province, territory, or country that is the centre of government. *Capitol* refers to the building where a legislature meets.

cease, seize   *To cease* is to stop. *To seize* is to take hold of or to capture. Note the spelling of *seize*, which violates the "*i* before *e*" rule.

cite, sight, site   *To cite* means "to refer to" or "to award." *To sight* is to see; a *sight* (noun) is what is seen. *To site* is to locate; a *site* (noun) is a location.

close, clothes   *Close* is a homograph; pronounced one way, and used as an adverb, it means "near" or "in the vicinity." Pronounced another way, and used as a verb, it means "to shut." *Clothes* are the garments you wear.

complement, compliment   *To complement* is to add something that completes or enhances, and a *complement* (noun) is a supply of something. *To compliment* means "to praise," and a *compliment* (noun) is a piece of praise.

> **WORDS FREQUENTLY MISUSED (cont.)**

comprise, consist of, constitute *To comprise* means "to contain." It is used informally to mean *consist of*, which means "made up of." *To constitute* means "to compose" or "to form" or "to create." The phrase *is comprised of* is always grammatically incorrect; use *is composed of* instead.

conscience, conscious Your *conscience* is your inner moral feeling. *Conscious of* means "aware of."

continual, continuous *Continual* means "occurring constantly, again and again." *Continuous* means "happening without interruption."

could of, should of, would of These word combinations are ungrammatical. *Could, should,* and *would* combine with the verb *have*: *could have, should have, would have.*

council, counsel, consul A *council* is a group of advisers, or *councillors. Counsel* means "advice," something a *counsellor* would give. A *consul* is a country's representative, whose office is a *consulate.* In a legal environment, *counsellor* is rarely used. The *counsel* is an outside adviser who is a lawyer.

credible, creditable, credulous Something that is *credible* is something that can be believed. *Creditable* means "praiseworthy." *Credulous* means "easily deceived."

decent, descent, dissent *Decent* means "morally proper" or "adequate." *Descent* (noun) is the act or process of descending, while *dissent* means "disagreement."

desert, dessert A *desert* (noun) is a dry wasteland, while *desert* (verb), pronounced differently, means "to leave without permission." *Dessert* is what is served after the main course of a meal.

device, devise A *device* is "an instrument" or "a means of achieving an end." *Devise* (verb) means "to plan" or "to put together."

discreet, discrete *Discreet* means "tactful" or "inclined to keep things to yourself." *Discrete* means "separate and distinct."

dual, duel *Dual* (adjective) means "consisting of two parts." A *duel* is a single-combat fight between two people.

elicit, illicit *To elicit* something is to extract it or draw it out from some source, as when you ask for information. *Illicit* means "illegal."

elude See *allude.*

emigrate, immigrate To leave a country permanently and live in another country is to *emigrate*; to enter a country and live there permanently is to *immigrate.*

eminent, imminent *Eminent* means "well known" or "famous." *Imminent* means "on the point of arriving."

employ, use *To employ* is to use something or someone in a specified way, usually with the sense of paying someone a wage in return for services.

exceed See *accede.*

except See *accept.*

expand, expend *To expand* is to increase in size. *To expend* is to use up or to spend.

expect See *anticipate.*

farther, further Both *farther* and *further* can indicate physical distance, but *further* is preferable when you mean "also," "to a greater extent," or "in addition to."

feel Avoid the overworked expression *I feel* when you want to render an opinion. Instead use *I believe* or *I think.*

fewer, less *Fewer* means "a smaller number," while *less* refers to quantity and means "a smaller amount."

Firstly An overused adverb, replaceable by *first.*

forth, fourth To go *forth* is to go onward. To finish *fourth* is to arrive after three others.

four, for *Four* is a number; *for* is a conjunction, a connecting word.

> ## WORDS FREQUENTLY MISUSED (cont.)

great, grate   *Great* means "large" or "renowned." A *grate* is a framework of bars, usually criss-crossed pieces of metal or wood.

if, whether   Both words are conjunctions. Use *if* in a conditional situation ("She will work if I pay her"); use *whether* when you are dealing with alternatives ("She will work whether or not I pay her," or "I don't know whether she will work").

illicit   See *elicit*.

illusion   See *allusion*.

incidence, incidents   *Incidence* means "rate of occurrence" ("There was a high incidence of theft"). *Incidents* are events, occurrences.

imply, infer   *To imply* means "to insinuate," "to suggest something without saying it." *To infer* means "to draw a conclusion."

irony, sarcasm   *Irony* involves saying one thing but meaning something else, usually the opposite of what is said, and doing so in a subtle manner so that the real meaning may not be clear. *Sarcasm* is a form of heavy, often bitter irony that leaves no question that the real meaning is opposite to what is being said.

irregardless, regardless   There is no word *irregardless*. Use *regardless* to mean "despite everything," "in any event," or "heedless."

its, it's   *Its* is the possessive form of *it. It's* is the contraction for *it is*.

knew, new   *Knew* is the past tense of *know. New* means "not old."

know, no   *To know* is to understand. *No* expresses negation or refusal.

last, latest, previous   The *last* comes after all the others; the *latest* is the most recent in a series; the *previous* one is the one that went before in time or order.

later, latter   *Later* means "afterwards." The *latter* is the second of two items.

lay, lie   *To lay* means "to put," and always takes an object. For example, "Lay the book down." *Lie*

means "to recline," and never takes an object. For example, "Lie down if you are tired." *To lie* is also a verb meaning "to tell an untruth."

lead, led   *To lead* is to be first, to show the way, to be a distance ahead. The past tense is *led*, pronounced the same as *lead*, a metal.

liable, likely, libel, slander   *Liable* means "legally responsible" or "likely to do something" (usually something undesirable). It is used informally in the sense of *likely*, meaning "probable." A *libel* is a false written statement, damaging to someone's reputation. A *slander* is a false statement, spoken rather than written, that is damaging to someone's reputation. *Libel* and *slander* are not opposites.

like, as   *Like* and *as* are often used interchangeably as connectors ("He is the same as I am"; "He is like me"). *As* can be used as a conjunction or a preposition ("It is as dark as night") while *like* should only be used as a preposition ("She is like her mother"). *Like* is also a verb meaning "feel affection for."

loose, lose   *Loose* means "not tight." *Lose* is an antonym of win, and also means "to misplace."

maybe, may be   *Maybe* is an adverb, synonymous with "perhaps." *May be* is a conjugation of the verb *to be*, expressing possibility.

new   See *knew*.

no   See *know*.

number   See *amount*.

off of   *Off* alone does the job; it doesn't need the *of* ("He jumped off the bike").

pain, pane   A *pain* is something that hurts; a *pane* is a panel, usually of glass.

past, passed   *Past* can be a noun, an adverb, or an adjective ("She lives in the past"; "She ran past the tree"; "She thought of her past loves"). *Passed* is the past tense of the verb *to pass*, meaning "to go by" or "move beyond."

patience, patients   *Patience* means "forbearance" or "endurance." *Patients* are people under medical care.

▶ WORDS FREQUENTLY MISUSED (cont.)

peace, piece   *Peace* is an antonym of war. A *piece* of something is a part of it.

personal, personnel, personally   *Personal* indicates something owned by or affecting a person; something private. Employees are collectively known as *personnel*. The word *personally* is overused as a qualifying word, as in "Personally, I think he was wrong."

plane, plain   A *plane* is a flat surface or a flying machine or a tool for smoothing wooden surfaces. *Plain* means "unattractive" or "unadorned," as well as "a large expanse of usually flat land."

presence, presents   *Presence* means "being in a place" or "attendance." *Presents* are gifts.

principal, principle   *Principal* indicates "most important" or "first." *Principles* are implied rules or ethics.

quiet, quite   *Quiet* means "not noisy," "silent," "unassuming." *Quite* means "entirely" or "to a considerable degree."

raise, rise   *To raise* means "to make something move up" or "to grow," and always takes an object. For example, "I raise the flag." *To rise* means "to stand up" or "to move upward," and never takes an object. For example, "I rise in the morning."

regardless   See *irregardless.*

right, rite, write, wright   *Right* means "the opposite of left" or "a privilege." A *rite* is a ceremony, usually religious. *To write* is to form words on a page. A *wright* is a craftsperson who makes a specified thing ("wheelwright," "playwright").

role, roll   A *role* is a part played by an actor. A *roll* is, among various other things, a list or a bakery product. *Roll* as a verb means "to turn over."

sarcasm   See *irony.*

set, sit   *To set* means "to put something in position," and always takes an object. For example, "Set the book over there." *To sit* means "to take a sitting position," and never takes an object. For example, "Sit in the chair."

should of   See *could of.*

sight, site   See *cite.*

so   Don't use this word as a lone intensive: "She was *so* lucky." Use *very* instead.

stationary, stationery   *Stationary* means "not moving." *Stationery* refers to the materials used for writing, typing; office supplies.

than, then   *Than* is used in comparisons ("bigger than"). *Then* is used in time sequences ("now and then").

their, there, they're   *Their* means "belonging to them." *There* is a place. *They're* is a contraction of *they are.*

though   See *although.*

threw, throw, through, thorough   *Threw* is the past tense of the verb *to throw. Through* is an adverb expressing passage into and out of something, and an adjective meaning "finished." *Thorough* is an adjective that means "exacting," "done with care," "leaving no room for doubt."

to, too, two   *To* is, among other things, a preposition indicating a direction or destination. *Too* means "excessively" or "also." *Two* is a number.

weak, week   *Weak* means "not strong." A *week* is seven days.

weather, whether   The atmospheric condition is what we call the *weather.* We use *whether* to indicate a choice between, or a question involving, alternatives. ("He didn't know whether to buy the blue one or the grey one.") See also *if.*

who's, whose   *Who's* is a contraction of *who is. Whose* is the possessive form of "who" and can function either as an adjective ("Whose coat is that?") or as a pronoun ("Whose is that?").

would of   See *could of.*

write   See *right.*

your, you're   *Your* is an adjective, the possessive form of *you,* meaning "owned by you." *You're* is a contraction of *you are.*

EXERCISE 2

DISTINGUISHING HOMONYMS

Correct the following sentence:

Weather the weather be cold, or weather the weather be hot, we'll weather the weather whatever the weather, weather we like it or not.

EXERCISE 3

CHOOSING THE CORRECT SPELLING

Correct the following passage:

When going for an interview, your wise too exercise patients. Be prepared. Find out about the personal of the firm, than any other peace of information your likely to need if your asked about the firm. Find out whose in charge. Be through in your answers. Your more liable to be considered if you no the amount of employees. Perhaps the boss is an imminent person in the community. Go further in your analysis of questions than expected; the less number of things you know about the firm, the less likely youll feel grate about the interview. Irregardless, its important that you do your best and ask for assistants if you can't answer a question. Sight any awards you know the firm has received, and complement the firm for its successes. Appear credulous to your interviewers, present yourself as a descent person, use whatever devises you need to make your points, and don't forget — wear proper close.

EXERCISE 4

SELECTING THE RIGHT WORD

Choose the correct word in each of the following sentences:

1. Counsel for the defendant has (acceded, exceeded) to our request for partial settlement.

2. The judge prefers statements of claim not to (accede, exceed) 10 pages.

3. The court documents will be delivered this afternoon. Please (accept, except) them on my behalf.

4. Everything is in the file (accept, except) the agreement of purchase and sale.

5. The divorce settlement awarded custody of the children to the wife, but the husband has (access, excess) to them on weekends.

6. If he drinks to (access, excess), however, he will lose this privilege.

7. Sometimes it seems that more television time is devoted to (ads, adds) than to programs.

8. The figures in this bill are wrong. Please (ad, add) them up again.

9. Law clerks and legal assistants must (adapt, adept) their work styles to suit their lawyers.

10. As a professional law clerk, you need to be (adapt, adept) at placating upset clients.

11. Is this new task an (addition, edition) to my regular duties?

12. Please order the latest (edition, addition) of the *Globe and Mail Stylebook*.

13. The client is going to seek the (advice, advise) of counsel in this matter.

14. I strongly (advice, advise) you not to be late for your court hearing, as this judge is known to be impatient.

15. The new insurance regulations will (affect, effect) your premium for next year.

16. At the examination for discovery, the defendant displayed a confused (affect, effect).

17. The new manager is (affecting, effecting) many changes in procedure.

18. Poor communications skills will have a negative (affect, effect) on your legal career.

19. Mrs. Smith's will (allots, a lots, alots) various sums of money to all her beneficiaries.

20. We don't have (allot, alot, a lot) of time to prepare all of the documents for closing next week.

21. We expect (allot, a lot) of donations to the firm's holiday fund.

22. We are (all ready, already) for the meeting (all ready, already).

23. I have (all ready, already) finished preparing the statement of claim in the matter of *Robertson v. Marco*.

24. The documents are (all together, altogether) on my desk.

25. I'm not (all together, altogether) sure that this is true.

26. We agree in (all ways, always) that matter.

27. I will (all ways, always) remember my first job.

28. Rehearse your presentation (aloud, allowed) to determine how it sounds.

29. Driving without a licence is not (aloud, allowed) by law.

30. The judge (alluded, eluded) to the defendant's previous offences when she sentenced him.

31. They won't be able to (allude, elude) justice for long.

32. The speaker made constant (allusion, illusion) to the news of the day.

EXERCISE 4 (cont.)

33. I was under the (allusion, illusion) that this would be an easy job, but I was wrong.

34. Too often, principles are sacrificed on the (altar, alter) of profit.

35. Put red check marks where you want me to (altar, alter) the factum.

36. Each director appoints an (alternate, alternative) in case he or she cannot attend a meeting.

37. The classes (alternate, alternative) between Mondays and Wednesdays.

38. I took the (alternate, alternative) route because of construction on the highway.

39. The evidence left the jury no (alternate, alternative) but to convict.

40. (Though, Although) Joan writes excellent research reports, it's not her favourite part of the job.

41. The firm had to choose (between, among) three excellent candidates.

42. Just (between, among) the two of us, I'm looking for a new job.

43. A huge (amount, number) of accidents take place on this corner every year.

44. The large (amount, number) of snow that fell overnight made it difficult to drive to work this morning.

45. The association holds its (annual, annul) conference in June.

46. I'm afraid you don't have grounds to (annual, annul) the contract.

47. (Lie, lay) the petition on his desk.

48. (Rise, raise) the table a bit to put this book under the broken leg.

49. I don't have much chance of winning the race, but I'll enter it (anyway, any way).

50. I want you to be successful and I will help you in (anyway, any way) I can.

51. You need to have your property (appraised, apprised) early in the process of selling it.

52. As a legal assistant, you should keep your lawyer (appraised, apprised) of any contact you have with the client.

53. We (are, our, hour) expecting to arrive at (are, our, hour) destination in an (are, our, hour).

54. The articling student requested (assistance, assistants) with the special assignment.

55. Arthur is such a busy lawyer that he needs not one but two (assistance, assistants).

56. Your (attendance, attendants) at the meeting is essential.

57. The bride and her (attendance, attendants) looked radiant.

58. Please complete the application form by inserting the year you were (born, borne).

59. My belief in his innocence was (born, borne) out by the evidence presented.

60. This candy is hard enough to (break, brake) my teeth.

61. The accident happened when the car's (breaks, brakes) failed.

62. The team worked six hours without a (break, brake).

63. The new tents are much lighter than the old (canvas, canvass) ones.

64. I will (canvas, canvass) the partners to see what they think of casual Friday attire.

65. The (Capitol, capital) is one of the main attractions in Washington, the (capitol, capital) of the United States.

66. The court ordered the company to (cease, seize) violating its competitor's copyright.

67. His assets were (ceased, seized) when he declared bankruptcy.

EXERCISE 4 (cont.)

68. The lawyer (cited, sighted, sited) several precedents in her argument for the defence.

69. For the exhausted marathon runners, the finishing line was a welcome (cite, sight, site).

70. We have chosen an excellent (cite, sight, site) for our new cottage.

71. The course in English grammar (complements, compliments) the writing program I took last year.

72. The corporation was represented in court by a formidable (complement, compliment) of seven lawyers.

73. The client (complemented, complimented) David on the fine job he did on the file.

74. The new firm (comprises, constitutes) 50 lawyers.

75. The thief showed no signs of a guilty (conscience, conscious).

76. Rebecca was very (conscience, conscious) of the importance of her job.

77. I can't rely on an assistant who (continually, continuously) arrives late for work.

78. Our softball team held the league championship (continually, continuously) for 10 years.

79. The new town (council, counsel, consul) has vowed to clean up the streets.

80. This is a complex legal matter on which we must seek the advice of (council, counsel, consul).

81. If you should find yourself in trouble in a foreign country, seek help from the Canadian (council, counsel, consul) there.

82. He presented a great deal of evidence, very little of which was (credible, credulous).

83. He is so (credible, credulous) that he believes what he sees on television commercials.

84. Although he lost the race, he gave a (decent, descent, dissent) effort.

85. We are beginning our (decent, descent, dissent) into Toronto's Pearson International Airport.

86. Freedom of speech can result in loud expressions of (decent, descent, dissent).

87. Much of the land that is now (dessert, desert) was covered in water millions of years ago.

88. They say rats always (dessert, desert) a sinking ship.

89. Since I am on a diet, I won't have (dessert, desert).

90. A restraining order is a legal (device, devise) to keep offenders away from their victims.

91. Ms. Wilson (deviced, devised) a brilliant defence strategy.

92. The nature of their work demands that law clerks and legal assistants be very (discrete, discreet).

93. A share purchase agreement can be a complex document, with many (discrete, discreet) elements.

94. Since he has (dual, duel) citizenship, my father carries two passports.

95. Fortunately, arguments are no longer settled by a (dual, duel) at dawn.

96. Law clerks need good interviewing skills in order to (illicit, elicit) needed information from clients.

97. The police discovered an (illicit, elicit) gambling operation in the basement of the old building.

98. Canada owes much of its development to the work of (emigrants, immigrants).

99. I left my home and (emigrated, immigrated) to Canada.

EXERCISE 4 (cont.)

100. Everyone was pleased when an (eminent, imminent) lawyer joined the firm.

101. Final agreement was held up pending an (eminent, imminent) change in the regulations.

102. The firm continues to (expend, expand), with the addition of three new lawyers.

103. Tom (expends, expands) a great deal of energy in his morning workout.

104. (Farther, Further) to our previous correspondence, I can now give you the closing date for the sale of the property.

105. Our destination is just a little bit (farther, further) along the highway.

106. We hired back (less, fewer) articling students this year than usual.

107. Although there were more accidents on this street last year, there was (less, fewer) loss of life.

108. Go (fourth, forth) proudly and accept your award.

109. The sprinter came in (fourth, forth), so he did not win a medal.

110. His (great, grate) powers of oratory made him formidable in court.

111. The sound of that squeaky door (greats, grates) on my nerves.

112. There was too great an (incidents, incidence) of this error for it to be accidental.

113. An unfortunate (incident, incidence) occurred when the two parties met outside the courtroom.

114. The client (implied, inferred) that he was going to change lawyers.

115. From the preliminary client discussion, the clerk (implied, inferred) that this matter would be complicated.

116. He displayed a fine sense of (sarcasm, irony) by wishing her happy birthday as he served her with divorce papers.

117. His use of (irony, sarcasm) is so continuous that it's hard to tell what he really means.

118. When you have everything in (it's, its) place, (it's, its) easy to find what you need.

119. Jennifer, the (new, knew) legal assistant, certainly knows about real estate law.

120. I always like to get my favourite author's (last, latest) book as soon as it's published.

121. Her answer to the (last, latest) question in the text was wrong.

122. Jonathan and Christina are both excellent law clerks, but the (later, latter) deals particularly well with clients.

123. The meeting went longer than planned, so I had to catch a (later, latter) train.

124. Our firm (lead, led) the way in hiring women for managerial positions.

125. Seepage of (led, lead) into the drinking water has (lead, led) to lawsuits against the company.

126. If you lose the lawsuit, you will be (libel, slander, liable) for court costs.

127. The front page story resulted in a (libel, slander, liable) action against the newspaper.

128. The president gave incorrect information to a reporter, resulting in a (libel, slander, liable) action against the company.

129. If we (lose, loose) this case, it will do great damage to the firm's reputation.

130. I don't like having papers (lose, loose) in a file; it's too easy to (lose, loose) them.

131. (Maybe, May be) I'll try that new restaurant for lunch today.

132. It (maybe, may be) worth taking your complaint to a higher level.

EXERCISE 4 (cont.)

133. The (pain, pane) of glass shattered, causing me great (pain, pane).

134. Elizabeth (past, passed) the position of company president on to her successor at the annual meeting. Elizabeth is now the (past, passed) president.

135. Proofreading a long legal document requires much (patience, patients).

136. Although he has been a doctor for only two years, Jack has already treated hundreds of (patience, patients).

137. In a democracy, the state does not interfere with (personnel, personal) religious beliefs.

138. The department that handles staff was once called (Personnel, Personal), but it's now known as Human Resources.

139. What he said may be hard to accept, but it's the (plane, plain) truth.

140. Use a (plane, plain) to level out the bumps in the wood.

141. He was such a charismatic leader that his (presents, presence) seemed to fill the room.

142. The firm has a policy against accepting (presents, presence) from clients.

143. The presumption of innocence is a basic (principal, principle) of our legal system.

144. I was proud of my son when he took the (principal, principle) role in the school play.

145. Business tends to be (quite, quiet) in the summer, but it picks up (quite, quiet) a bit in September.

146. Even a criminal has certain (rights, writes, rites, wrights) under the law.

147. The high-school prom is a traditional (right, write, rite, wright) of passage out of adolescence.

148. A famous (playright, playwrite, playrite, playwright) asked us for a legal opinion about his (copyright, copywrite, copyrite, copywright).

149. The law clerk's (role, roll) often is to act as liaison between client and lawyer.

150. Each morning at camp began with a (role, roll) call.

151. He stood as (stationary, stationery) as a rock while the tornado passed.

152. The firm's new (stationary, stationery) is very elegant.

153. Where are (they're, their, there) law books? (They're, Their, There) over (they're, their, there).

154. After a (threw, through, thorough) cross-examination, their witness was excused.

155. The professional basketball player (threw, through, thorough) the ball (threw, through, thorough) the hoop with amazing accuracy.

156. I wanted (too, to, two) go (too, to, two), but one taxi was (too, to, two) small to take us all, and we had to order (too, to, two).

157. It doesn't matter (weather, whether) you like the job or not; you're stuck with it.

158. The lawyer for the prosecution presented a (weak, week) case in court.

159. (Whose, Who's) turn is it to make the coffee?

160. You will (loose, lose) your footing on the ice if you're not careful.

EXERCISE 5

EXPANDING YOUR VOCABULARY

Be able to spell and define the following words:

1. abrasion	24. calibre	47. extenuating	70. perpetrator
2. accelerate	25. cartridge	48. fabricate	71. pertinent
3. accessory	26. circumstantial	49. felon	72. plaintiff
4. accomplice	27. civilian	50. fugitive	73. preliminary
5. accused	28. collision	51. grievous	74. provocation
6. acquit	29. complainant	52. habitual	75. recidivist
7. adjourn	30. concurrent	53. homicide	76. refute
8. adjudicate	31. condemn	54. incarcerate	77. reprieve
9. admissible	32. confession	55. incorrigible	78. resuscitate
10. affidavit	33. confiscate	56. inquest	79. supplementary
11. aggravate	34. corroborate	57. interrogate	80. surveillance
12. alcohol	35. credibility	58. judicial	81. tactical
13. alleged	36. culpable	59. jurisdiction	82. testimony
14. altercation	37. defendant	60. laceration	83. trajectory
15. analyze	38. delinquent	61. lenient	84. trauma
16. anonymous	39. deposition	62. litigant	85. truancy
17. apprehend	40. detention	63. malicious	86. velocity
18. arraign	41. deterrent	64. mandatory	87. verdict
19. assailant	42. disperse	65. mitigating	88. vicious
20. assault	43. embezzle	66. negligence	89. waiver
21. attorney	44. enforceable	67. nuisance	90. warrant
22. bailiff	45. evidence	68. occurrence	
23. boulevard	46. exhibit	69. pedestrian	

EXERCISE 6

LEARNING LEGAL VOCABULARY

The following words are particular to the legal and law clerk professions. Be able to spell and define these words:

1. abeyance	15. citation	28. precedent
2. abscond	16. civil	29. *prima facie*
3. acquittal	17. codicil	30. proceeding
4. action *in rem*	18. contributory negligence	31. recognizance
5. action *in personam*		32. *regina*
6. ad hoc	19. defeasance	33. *res gestae*
7. admissible evidence	20. disposition	34. retainer
8. amendment	21. exhibit	35. solicitor
9. appeal	22. grievance	36. specimen
10. arbitration	23. *habeas corpus*	37. statute
11. boycott	24. indictable	38. subrogation
12. brief	25. injunction	39. tort
13. case law	26. *mens rea*	40. waive
14. *caveat emptor*	27. preamble	

■ Summary

The English language is complicated. While spelling rules apply to many words, there are certain words that, especially in their verb tenses and plural forms, do not follow these rules, and such words must be learned individually. Knowing how to spell is important, but you should also understand the meanings of words; it is of little value to be able to spell a word without knowing its meaning. Law clerks and legal assistants can make themselves more effective by learning the vocabulary that applies to the legal profession.

SPELLING AND DEFINITIONS

Be able to spell and define the following words:

accessible	ceiling	evidence	pamphlet
accuracy	conspicuous	government	stomach
acquaintance	description	identity	tangential
affirmative	disabled	liable	valuable
aggravated	disastrous	loitering	vigilance
analysis	eliminate	memorandum	youthful
belligerent	evasive	miscellaneous	

CHAPTER 3

Grammar Skills

Learning Objectives

After completing this chapter, you should be able to

- Identify parts of speech in a sentence.
- Identify the purpose of a sentence.
- Correct common grammar errors.
- Recognize different kinds of phrases and clauses.
- Identify common punctuation marks and their uses.

Introduction

Correct grammar is important because it helps people understand each other in the communication process. Conversely, poor grammar can be a significant barrier to communication, especially when it leads to misunderstanding and misinterpretation.

In the legal field, misunderstanding and misinterpretation must be avoided at all costs. Grammar is one of the essential tools of the trade for law clerks and legal assistants, whose ability and efficiency are directly related to their competence with grammar. Both lawyers and clients will form an opinion of your professionalism on the basis of your use of language. After all, if you can't be trusted to use language correctly, what can you be trusted with? Letters, memos, and forms can become legal documents, and if these written communications contain errors in grammar and punctuation, an entirely different meaning from the one intended can result.

Learn to use grammar and punctuation correctly. Misuse of language can have significant consequences for you, your firm, and the client.

To begin this chapter, complete the following pre-test to check your knowledge of grammar usage. Doing so will help you locate your areas of weakness.

GRAMMAR PRE-TEST

EXERCISE 1

FINDING SUBJECTS AND VERBS

Underline the subject with one line and the verb(s) with two lines in the following sentences:

1. Law clerks are becoming more knowledgeable in the law than ever before.

2. In the modern law firm, the role of legal assistant has evolved to a high level.

3. Many reasons are given for the fact that mainly baby boomers are retiring.

4. There has not been much attention given in the past to the impending personnel shortage.

5. Now law clerks can choose from several different work environments while still making use of their specialized skills.

EXERCISE 2

CORRECTING SENTENCE FRAGMENTS

Change the following sentence fragments into complete sentences. One of the examples is already a complete sentence.

1. While preparing for her court appearance.

2. The partner's assistant received a call from the client about a problem with the contract.

3. A new property on the market.

4. At Osgoode Hall.

5. Was called to the Bar in 2005.

EXERCISE 3

USING SUBORDINATION AND COORDINATION

Use subordination or coordination correctly to combine each of the following pairs of sentences. One of the sentences is already correct.

1. In proofreading the contract. The assistant found a major error.

2. We all worked overtime on the contract; the closing date had been advanced by a month.

3. Many groups of lawyers are leaving big firms to start boutique firms, it seems to be a trend.

4. Sharon had been an assistant to many lawyers during her career; and was highly regarded by them all.

5. Working in a busy downtown law firm is exciting. And challenging too.

EXERCISE 4

RECASTING RUN-ON SENTENCES

Correct the following run-on sentences. One of the sentences is correct as it is.

1. I was asked to take photographs of striking workers I decided to do so.

2. Strong competition exists among litigation firms they are each trying to build up their business.

3. Janet wanted to become a law clerk she didn't realize how hard she would need to study.

4. It's important to address clients with respect it's their business that pays your salary.

5. The information you need to complete the documentation for a real estate transaction can be found using online research tools.

EXERCISE 5

USING COMMAS

Correctly punctuate the following sentences with commas. One of the sentences is correct as it is.

1. White-collar criminals dishonest employees and Internet scam artists are surfacing in growing numbers.

2. Recent arrests especially among technology manufacturers have been making headlines.

3. Even owners of sports franchises have been charged.

4. Small fines short prison terms or absolute discharges have not been effective.

5. Corruption reduces public trust in business corporations affects the stock market and has an overall negative effect on the economy.

EXERCISE 6

USING OTHER PUNCTUATION MARKS

Place punctuation marks (colons, semicolons, quotation marks) where they belong in the following sentences. One of the sentences is correct as it is.

1. He was advised to plead guilty the evidence was stacked against him.

2. The key term, say his lawyers, is plea bargain.

3. The *Highway Traffic Act* regulates the following motorists, passengers, and pedestrians.

4. There are three areas of specialty in the firm wills and estates real estate and family law.

5. We do business according to the following rule: "The client's needs are paramount."

EXERCISE 7

ENSURING SUBJECT–VERB AGREEMENT

Correct the errors in subject–verb agreement in the following sentences. One of the sentences is correct as it is.

1. The history of jurisprudence go back thousands of years.

2. Some writers from ancient Rome has described a system of law enforcement in that city.

3. Laws were modified so that the people could understand them.

4. Each group of explorers who went to America were surprised at the codification of laws in certain cultures.

5. The Iroquois Confederacy were able to formalize rules of behaviour.

EXERCISE 8

ESTABLISHING PARALLEL STRUCTURE

All but one of the following sentences lack parallel structure. Revise to create parallel structure.

1. In the early days of the profession, law clerks were expected to be male, have a university education, and well dressed.

2. Having women in the majority of law clerk positions offers many advantages, and to have them achieve senior positions is better yet.

3. With good planning and lucky, law clerks and legal assistants can retire with substantial compensation packages.

4. Report writing, research, and listening are more common activities than those depicted as occurring in the intrigue-filled law firms on television.

5. She was a good assistant, an intelligent woman, and she worked hard.

EXERCISE 9

EDITING SENTENCES FOR ERRORS

Each of the following sentences contains an error in grammar or punctuation. Revise each sentence so that it is complete and correct.

1. These sort of experiences are helpful when applying for promotion.

2. No one wants to spend all their time writing reports.

3. I haven't kept the record up to date however I know I'm going to need it for court.

4. The Breathalyzer technician plan to come during the next shift.

5. All of my partners is very friendly.

6. The *Criminal Code* is long complicated and important.

7. Guns are dangerous they can cause a lot of trouble.

8. The siren wailed and we covered our ears loudly.

9. The files were lost for three weeks before the assistant found it.

10. Is a great advocate.

■ Grammar Essentials: Sentences

A sentence is a group of words that contains a complete thought. Every sentence must contain a **subject** and a **verb**.

SUBJECT

The subject of a sentence is the word or group of words that the sentence is about or that the sentence concerns.

> Fred is a lawyer.

The subject here is *Fred*. Fred is who the sentence is about. If you wrote *Is a lawyer*, you wouldn't know that the sentence is about Fred. This type of subject is called a **simple subject**.

The simple subject may be a noun (Fred), a pronoun (he), or a word ending in -*ing*, also known as a *gerund* or *verbal noun*.

> Reading is her favourite hobby.

In this sentence, *reading* is what the sentence is about, or the focus of the sentence. The subjects in the following sentences are italicized.

> *I* am in my second semester at college.

> *Driving* is a chore.

The *tree* fell in the storm.

The *store* was robbed last night.

She became a legal assistant.

Bill is in jail.

A subject can consist of more than one word, in which case it is called the **complete subject**. The complete subject contains the simple subject.

The man on the jury seems to be asleep.

Here, *man* is the simple subject, and *the man on the jury* is the complete subject. The complete subject describes the simple subject by distinguishing the particular man from all other men in the courtroom. In the following sentences, the simple subject is italicized, and the complete subject appears in parentheses:

(*Pat* and *René*) are partners.

(*Lawyers* and *law clerks*) attended the seminar.

(*To run or to surrender*) are his only options.

(*Meeting new clients* and *seeing a file through to completion*) are my favourite parts of my job as a law clerk.

In every case, remember that for a sentence to be complete, it must have a subject or subjects. Without a subject, a sentence is called a sentence fragment, which will be discussed later in this chapter.

EXERCISE 10

ADDING COMPLETE SUBJECTS

Add complete subjects to turn the following fragments into sentences:

1. is responsible for court documentation.
2. were my favourite courses at college.
3. teaches law and securities courses at the college.
4. takes emergency calls from the public.
5. manages the accounting department.

VERB

The verb is the action word in a sentence. Every sentence must have a verb; otherwise, as in the case of a sentence without a subject, a sentence fragment occurs, which is a grammar error.

The verb in the following sentence is italicized:

The attorney *impresses* the jury with her argument.

The subject of this sentence (*the attorney*) does something, or causes an action to take place (*impresses*). Therefore, *impresses* is the verb.

> Ming *operated* the radio.

> She *arrested* the offender.

> Jane *questioned* witnesses on the stand.

> The human resources officer *orients* the new articling students.

The **tense** of a verb indicates when the action took place (past), is taking place (present), or will take place (future).

> *Past:*   I *walked* to work every day.

> *Present:*   I *walk* to work every day.

> *Future:*   I *will walk* to work every day.

Many verbs in the English language are known as **regular verbs**; these can be changed from present to past tense by adding *-ed* to the present form of the verb. This is not true of **irregular verbs**, which are dealt with below.

Changing the present tense to the future tense usually involves adding a word such as *will* or *shall* to the verb:

> I *will apply* to a small law firm.

> She *shall obtain* her diploma.

There are some verbs that don't appear to be "action" words; the action isn't obvious. These verbs are called **linking verbs** because they link subjects to other parts of the sentence. They are as much verbs, however, as any action word. The most common linking verbs are various forms of the verb *to be*: *is, am, are, was*, and *were*.

> The lawyer *is* efficient.

> I *am* an employee of a corporate legal department.

> They *are* guilty as charged.

> The officers *were* on patrol.

These forms of the verb *to be* are irregular because they don't take the forms of most regular action verbs. For instance, instead of adding *-ed* to the present form of *to be* to form the past tense, use the following forms:

Present	Past
I *am*	I *was*
You *are*	You *were*
He, she, it *is*	He, she, it *was*
We, you, they *are*	We, you, they *were*

The various tenses of the irregular verb *to be* may combine with an *-ing* word, or present participle, to produce the progressive verb tense.

I *am* running.

He *was* training.

They *will be* exercising.

These present participles, ending in *-ing*, form part of the complete verb; in the examples above, *am running*, *was training*, and *will be exercising* are complete verbs.

Another irregular verb is *to have*. Note that *to be* and *to have* are called **infinitives**. The infinitive is the "to" form of the word — the basic verb form, without inflections to show person, number, or tense.

Present	Past
I *have*	I *had*
You *have*	You *had*
He, she, it *has*	He, she, it *had*
We, you, they *have*	We, you, they *had*

Below is a list of some irregular verbs in their infinitive, present tense, and past tense forms.

Infinitive	Present	Past
to break	break	broke
to catch	catch	caught
to do	do	did
to drive	drive	drove
to eat	eat	ate
to give	give	gave
to go	go	went
to know	know	knew
to see	see	saw
to sit	sit	sat
to speak	speak	spoke
to take	take	took
to write	write	wrote

A final point to keep in mind is that there can be more than one verb in a sentence.

EXERCISE 11

CHANGING VERB TENSE

Underline the complete verbs in the following passage. Then rewrite the passage, changing the verbs from the present to the past tense.

The injury occurs on November 3, 2005 at the Plaintiff's property located at 123 Manchester Avenue, Anytown, Ontario. The Plaintiff is using an electric device to trim the hedge at the front of his garden when the Defendant walks past with his dog. The dog, a large German shepherd, suddenly leaps toward the Plaintiff, who is startled. His grip loosens and the machine slips and severs the Plaintiff's left thumb. The Defendant claims it is not his responsibility as the dog is on a short leash and cannot possibly reach the Plaintiff, so the Plaintiff is in no danger from the Defendant's dog.

SUBJECT–VERB AGREEMENT

Subjects and verbs must agree in their person and their number. Follow the "rule of *s*." Put an *s* on the end of either the subject or the verb, but not both at once:

> Cars speed.
> A car speeds.

When trying to ensure that your subjects and verbs agree, take particular care in the following situations:

1. *Words intervening between simple subject and verb.*

   One of the pictures *shows* the firm's founding partner.

   The *suspect* in the robberies *was* arrested yesterday.

2. *Subject following verb.*

   Have John and Solly started a new firm?

   Around the corner *ride the cyclists.*

3. *Two or more singular subjects joined by* or *or* nor.

   John *and* Bill *work* in litigation. [Compound subject takes plural.]

   John *or* Bill *works* in litigation. [One of John or Bill, but not both, works there.]

4. *Collective noun (group word) subject.*

   The jury *is* ready with its verdict. [The entity is acting as a single unit.]

   The jury *were* not in agreement. [Individual actions within the whole entity are meant to be considered.]

5. *Nouns plural in form but singular in meaning.*

   The news *is* reporting that the bank was robbed.

   The West Indies *is* a group of islands.

   Politics *is* of no concern to the law.

6. *Periods of time, fractions, weights, amounts of money.*

    Three days *is* a long time to spend on a cross-examination.

    Three-quarters of the stash *was* seized.

    Fifty pounds of contraband *is* in that car.

    A hundred dollars *is* the fine for the bylaw infraction.

If a fraction refers to a quantity ("three-quarters of the membership"), it is treated as singular; if it refers to a number, it is treated as plural ("three-quarters of the pencils").

7. *Relative pronouns.* These pronouns (*who, which, that*) agree with their antecedent (the word to which they refer or the word that they replace) in number.

    These are the *employees who are* always reliable. [The antecedent of *who* is *employees.*]

    Bill is one of the *employees who are* always reliable. [*Employees* is the antecedent of *who*, requiring the plural verb *are.*]

    George is the *only one* of the clerks *who is* on vacation. [*Only one* is the antecedent of *who*, requiring the singular verb *is.*]

    Lian is one of the *women who work* in the firm's library. [*Women* is the antecedent of *who.*]

8. *Indefinite pronouns.* The following indefinite pronouns are always singular: *one, each, anybody, anyone, somebody, someone, everybody, everyone, nobody, no one, either,* and *neither.*

    One *is* not obliged to purchase a raffle ticket.

    Each of the students *has* an assignment.

    Anybody who works with him *knows* he couldn't have done it.

    Anyone who *wants* to join may do so.

    Somebody up there *likes* me.

    Someone *is* following them.

    Everybody *is* going to the staff picnic.

    Everyone in the room *is* dancing.

    Nobody *cares* about that.

    No one *has* a salary increase.

    Either suspect *fits* the description.

    Neither Joe nor Dave *has* a girlfriend.

    The following indefinite pronouns are always plural: *both, many, few,* and *several.*

    Both of the cars *were* blue.

    Many of the students *speak* French.

    A few of the officers *are* at the scene.

    Several of the people *were* victims of the scam.

The following indefinite pronouns are singular for quantity and plural for number: *all, any, most, none,* and *some.*

Quantity (Singular)	Number (Plural)
All of the parking lot *was* full.	All of the parking spots *were* taken.
Any time *is* good for me.	Any days *are* good for me.
Most of the audience *likes* the show.	Most of the people *like* the show.
None of the laundry *feels* dry.	None of the clothes *feel* dry.
Some of the food *was* spoiled.	Some of the eggs *were* spoiled.

9. *Compound subjects that do not agree in number.* In a compound subject, where one subject is singular and one is plural, make the verb agree with the *nearest* subject.

Either the manager or the *assistants are* at the workshop.

Either the assistants or the *manager is* at the workshop.

EXERCISE 12

REVISING: SUBJECT–VERB AGREEMENT AND PRONOUNS

1. Correct the errors in subject–verb agreement and any pronoun errors in the following passage:

    The correspondence in my files indicate that Joan Bennett has liabilities of approximately $1,000,000. These amount include an estimated additional accruals of rental to my client of approximately $25,000. Ms. Bennett also have realizable assets of less than $35,000, which mean that a division of sale of her assets among her creditors result in a realization of less than four cents on the dollar. From this amounts also come the fees of a trustee and other realization costs.

2. Complete the following sentences, using the correct present tense of the verb *to be*:

    a. Anyone _____ .

    b. Each _____ .

    c. Somebody _____ .

    d. Neither _____ .

    e. Either _____ .

    f. No one _____ .

    g. Something _____ .

    h. Much _____ .

    i. Anybody _____ .

    j. Everyone _____ .

SENTENCE FRAGMENTS

Since every complete sentence must have a subject, must have a verb, and must make a complete thought, any group of words without one of these three characteristics is a **sentence fragment**.

> She reads a training manual.

This is a complete sentence: It has a subject (*she*) and a verb (*reads*), and it is a complete thought; it makes sense, and it's understandable. However, if the subject were left out, the remaining words would be

> Reads a training manual.

This is a sentence fragment because the sentence now has no subject. Who reads a training manual? A subject is needed.

Examples of different kinds of sentence fragments are set out below.

> Parked in the centre of town. [What or who parked in the centre of town?]

> My research report on my boss's desk. [What about the report on the desk?]

> With only my jacket. [What happened with the jacket?]

> Waiting for the shipment. [Who was waiting?]

Adding a subject and verb to these fragments makes them into complete thoughts.

> I parked in the centre of town.

> My research report is on my boss's desk.

> With only my jacket, I fought off a swarm of bees.

> The mailroom clerk was waiting for the shipment.

Any group of words that contains a subject and a verb is called a **clause**. A sentence is a clause in most cases, but not always. There are two types of clauses: independent and dependent.

An **independent clause** contains a subject, a verb, and a complete thought; therefore, independent clauses are also sentences.

> He will answer for his crimes.

A **dependent clause** contains a subject and a verb, but it does not express a complete thought. It is a fragment that needs something else to complete it.

> Because he was caught.

He is the subject, *was caught* is the verb, but the clause does not explain what happened because he was caught. Therefore, this group of words does not contain a complete thought and is a sentence fragment.

> Because he was caught, he will answer for his crimes.

As shown here, a dependent clause at the beginning of a sentence must be followed by a comma. If the dependent clause falls at the end of a sentence, the comma is not needed.

> He will have to answer for his crimes because he was caught.

Another type of sentence fragment to be considered is the "list" fragment.

Law clerks must be. Intelligent, resourceful, and cautious.

Both of these fragments are dependent. The first fragment has a subject and a verb, but it needs the list ("intelligent, resourceful, and cautious") to complete its meaning. The list doesn't have a subject or a verb. The straightforward solution is to combine the two:

Law clerks must be intelligent, resourceful, and cautious.

Two further examples of common sentence-fragment errors are set out below, along with their corrected forms.

> *Fragment:*   I like card games. Such as euchre, poker, and blackjack.
>
> *Complete:*   I like card games, such as euchre, poker, and blackjack.
>
> *Fragment:*   We went to court. Saw the judge, the bailiff, and the lawyer.
>
> *Complete:*   We went to court, where we saw the judge, the bailiff, and the lawyer.

Finally, be aware that commands, brief though they usually are, do not qualify as sentence fragments.

Stop!

The subject *you* is implied here, so the sentence is complete.

Remember, too, that an *-ing* word, also known as a present participle (e.g., *running, shooting*), can never be the complete verb in a sentence.

> *Fragment:*   I running to keep in shape.
>
> *Complete:*   I am running to keep in shape.

EXERCISE 13

CORRECTING FRAGMENTS

Form the following fragments into complete sentences:

1. I worked hard. So that I could get a promotion.

2. We went into law. Because we love helping people.

3. Tell me the truth. If you know it.

4. He was arrested; because he was drinking and driving.

5. I love facing danger. Wherever I find it.

6. You will find your shirt. In the drawer. Where you keep your socks.

7. Because the traffic was heavy.

8. If they get their act together.

9. While running for the bus.

10. Litigation, corporate, intellectual property.

RUN-ON SENTENCES

The **run-on sentence** is the opposite of the sentence fragment. While the fragment is part of a sentence, the run-on is two complete sentences or independent clauses that have been joined together in an inappropriate way.

> **I always stop here for doughnuts it is my favourite place.**

The sentence can be corrected in four ways. You could use two sentences.

> **I always stop here for doughnuts. It is my favourite place.**

You could use a conjunction.

> **I always stop here for doughnuts because it is my favourite place.**

You could use a semicolon.

> **I always stop here for doughnuts; it is my favourite place.**

You could use a dependent clause.

> **Since it is my favourite place, I always stop here for doughnuts.**

Keep in mind that an independent clause contains a complete thought, but only one complete thought. The run-on expresses more than one thought with no division between the thoughts.

Another type of run-on is the **comma splice**.

> **There is a leash law, no one obeys it.**

In this case, the comma is misplaced; two independent clauses can't be separated by a comma without a conjunction or linking word. A comma splice can be corrected in the same four ways as any other run-on. You can use two sentences.

> **There is a leash law. No one obeys it.**

You can use a conjunction.

> **There is a leash law, but no one obeys it.**

You can use a semicolon.

> **There is a leash law; no one obeys it.**

You can use a dependent clause.

> **Although there is a leash law, no one obeys it.**

EXERCISE 14

CORRECTING RUN-ONS

1. Correct the following run-on sentences:

   a. Just let me do the talking you'll get us a ticket if you don't keep quiet.

   b. The cabin was cold however it had a wood stove.

   c. A strong wind was blowing the boat from the yacht club nearly sank.

   d. Most people have 20/20 vision that is a requirement for a job here.

   e. Career opportunities are good for students in the law clerk program some employers also demand experience.

2. Remove the run-on sentences from the following paragraph:

   Thank you for your attention to this matter if I can be of any assistance to you in collecting the necessary documents please contact me I will do what I can to expedite the process it is important that this be completed as soon as possible if any of the documents are missing your case could be dismissed you would still be liable for court costs.

MODIFIERS

A modifier is a word or phrase that refers to, describes, or explains another word in a sentence. Modifiers must be placed as close as possible to the word or words they modify. There are two types of sentence errors involving modifiers: **misplaced modifiers** and **dangling modifiers**.

Misplaced Modifiers

Misplaced modifiers are modifiers that are placed within a sentence in such a way that it is unclear what word they apply to.

> The audience cheered when we graduated from law school excitedly.

The modifier *excitedly* is misplaced here because it is unclear whether it modifies *graduated* or *cheered*.

Consider these other examples, in which the misplaced modifiers are italicized:

> He protested at the noise of the siren wailing *angrily*.

> The police officer approached the hostile-looking dog *with a hockey glove on*.

> Our lawyer rated our chances of winning *without much enthusiasm*.

To correct the sentences, place the modifiers closer to the words they modify.

> He angrily protested at the noise of the siren wailing.

> With a hockey glove on, the police officer approached the hostile-looking dog.

> Without much enthusiasm, our lawyer rated our chances of winning.

EXERCISE 15

CORRECTING MISPLACED MODIFIERS

Correct the misplaced modifiers in the following sentences:

1. The woman was stopped for speeding with the hat.
2. He made cookies for his friends with chocolate chips in them.
3. The lawyer being recruited fervently believed it was time for a change.
4. The police chief led the parade in full dress uniform.
5. Customs officers intercepted the smugglers guarding the coast line.
6. The criminal laughed when she was almost convicted maliciously.
7. The man escaped before the fire spread barely.
8. We planned to start work early Christmas Eve a long time ago.
9. The defendant stood in the dock without any signs of cracking.
10. The suspect said he was at home with a bow tie.

Dangling Modifiers

The other form of modifier fault is the dangling modifier. A dangling modifier is one that doesn't logically modify anything in its sentence.

> Crossing the border, my bags were searched.

> Expecting a lot of work, extra help was requested.

In both of these cases, the modifier is dangling. In the first case, who was crossing the border? *My bags*? In the second sentence, *who* is expecting a lot of work? Correct the sentences as follows:

> When I was crossing the border, my bags were searched.

> Expecting a lot of work, we requested extra help.

To fix a dangling modifier, add a word to which the modifier refers, and put the modifier as close to that word as possible.

EXERCISE 16

CORRECTING DANGLING MODIFIERS

Correct the dangling modifiers in the following sentences:

1. Risking her life, the accident victims were rescued by the lifeguard.
2. Crossing the street, my hat blew away.
3. To pass the Law Clerk course, one essay every week is required.
4. Driving through the suburbs, several luxury vehicles were seen.
5. Jogging through the park, a dog bit me.
6. On receiving an offer of employment, tears filled his mother's eyes.
7. When learning legal terminology, memorizing is often used.
8. Driving at night, his mind began to wander.
9. Being a qualified legal assistant, a framed certificate was proudly displayed.
10. While attending the theatre, the apartment was looted.

PRONOUN REFERENCES

A pronoun is a word that replaces a noun. It may be used as the subject of a sentence (the word that indicates who or what performs an action). A pronoun may also be the object of a sentence (the word that indicates upon whom or what an action is performed).

Noun:	Roy works in corporate litigation.
Pronoun:	*He* works in corporate litigation.

Noun:	Sylvie and Ruth handle complete real estate files.
Pronoun:	Sylvie and Ruth handle *them*.

Pronouns may also be used as both the subject and the object of a single sentence.

Nouns:	Joe writes his report.
Pronouns:	*He* writes *it*.

Joe is the subject of the sentence, which is replaced with the pronoun *he*. The thing being written, *his report*, is the object of the sentence, which is replaced with the pronoun *it*.

When replacing a subject, use the following personal pronouns:

Singular	Plural
I	we
you	you
he, she, it	they

When replacing an object, use the following personal pronouns:

Singular	Plural
me	us
you	you
him, her, it	them

Note the use of both subjective and objective personal pronouns in the following examples:

Nouns:	Rex ran away from the intruders.
Pronouns:	*He* ran away from *them.*
Nouns:	The police officer told Fred to move the van.
Pronouns:	*She* told *him* to move *it.*

Pronouns and Case

The case (subjective, objective, or possessive) of a personal pronoun is determined by the function it serves in a sentence. Pronouns can be subjects or subject complements (subjective case); they can be direct objects, indirect objects, or objects of prepositions (objective case); or they can indicate ownership (possessive case).

Subjective pronouns	Objective pronouns	Possessive pronouns
I	me	my (mine)
you	you	your (yours)
he	him	his
she	her	her (hers)
it	it	its
who	whom	whose
we	us	our (ours)
they	them	their (theirs)

He (*subject*) made the donation for me (*object*).

With whom (*object*) did I (*subject*) see you last night?

Her (*possessive*) litigation caseload is much heavier than his (*possessive*).

A subject complement following a linking verb (*to be* [am, is, are, was, were, have been], *to act, to appear, to become, to feel, to grow, to seem, to look, to taste*) takes the subjective case; for example, "It was I who opened the file."

EXERCISE 17

USING PRONOUNS

Underline the correct pronoun in parentheses in each of the following sentences:

1. We expect you and (they, them) at the meeting.
2. Wait for my partner and (I, me).
3. (He, Him) and Amad worked together.
4. The receptionist told you and (her, she) to stay here.
5. Everyone was at the party except (we, us).
6. You and (I, me) are both in line for promotion.
7. Professionals such as you and (he, him) should help younger employees.
8. Was it (she, her) that you saw?
9. I think that the shoplifter was (he, him).
10. It could have been (they, them) who won the race.

Ambiguous and Indefinite Pronoun References

It is important to eliminate ambiguity in pronoun references.

> **When Rebecca saw Jane, she was angry.**

Which woman was angry? To indicate that it was Rebecca and not Jane who was angry, the sentence can be recast as follows:

> **Rebecca was angry when she saw Jane.**

To indicate that Jane was the angry one, recast the sentence as follows:

> **When Rebecca saw her, Jane was angry.**

Use a pronoun to refer to a single noun, not a group of words.

> **He admitted that he defrauded the client. This was welcome news.**

Does *this* refer to the fact that he defrauded the client, or to his admission of the fact? Rewrite the sentence to remove this ambiguity:

> **He admitted that he defrauded the client. His admission was welcome news.**

Avoid the indefinite use of *it* and *they*.

> **They say automation is a growing factor in legal proceedings.**

Who is *they*? Rewrite the sentence to give *they* a face:

> **The Law Society says that automation is a growing factor in legal proceedings.**

EXERCISE 18

REMOVING AMBIGUOUS AND INDEFINITE PRONOUN REFERENCES

Correct the pronoun errors in the following sentences:

1. They did not see the Smiths arrive because they were having lunch.

2. I don't know what he said to him, but he was angry.

3. The girl's mother studied law, and she is going to be one when she grows up.

4. He began his career as a private investigator, which was terminated by his death.

5. In my first job, I learned to change a toner cartridge without getting it all over me.

6. I let my relatives help me with the new cars although they were rather dirty.

7. The assistant told her manager that whatever she did she could not please her.

8. They say that crime is decreasing in the city.

9. He fell while addressing the jury, which was embarrassing.

10. They have good traffic laws in Ontario.

PARALLEL STRUCTURE

Parallel structure involves joining similar structures together in a sentence.

> writing, listening, speaking

These *-ing* words all refer to forms of communication, and they are parallel in structure because they all end in *-ing*.

> Svetlana is intelligent, witty, and charms people.

This sentence does not use parallel structure. To obtain parallel structure, you must rewrite the sentence as follows:

> Svetlana is intelligent, witty, and charming.

Parallel structure should be used when phrases, clauses, or infinitives are connected by conjunctions:

Two phrases:	up the hill and down the valley
Two clauses:	that he is a thief and that he is in jail
Two infinitives:	to go or to stay

CORRELATIVES

Correlative conjunctions are specific sets of words that require parallel structure when used together. Some common correlative conjunctions are the following:

> either . . . or
>
> neither . . . nor
>
> not . . . but
>
> not only . . . but also
>
> both . . . and

These groups of words don't have to be used if there is no parallel structure involved in the sentence:

> The job required *both* concentration *and* speed.
>
> I like both colours.

EXERCISE 19

USING PARALLEL STRUCTURE

Correct the parallel structure faults in the following sentences:

1. Fish or a steak meal is fine by me.
2. I don't enjoy jogging when it is raining or it snows.
3. He learned juggling and to type.
4. I knew all the dangerous areas of the city and to avoid them.
5. He didn't know the bylaw or the *Highway Traffic Act*.
6. Catherine taught us minute taking, writing reports, and how to do summaries.
7. Every legal assistant is taught the value of following instructions and how to think independently.
8. The supervisor is influential and a popular person.
9. He is not happy nor satisfied with his job.
10. My dream is to have a job with a major law firm in a warm climate, a family, and buy a house.

■ Grammar Essentials: Punctuation and Capitalization

COMMAS

As a rule of thumb, fewer commas are better than many. Don't use a comma if you're not sure you need one. However, there are certain rules for comma use that should be followed.

1. Use a comma to separate three or more items in a series.

   The warrant was signed, sealed, and delivered.

   Some people prefer not to use a comma before the word *and* in a series. The only firm rule is, Be consistent.

2. Use a comma between two independent clauses separated by the coordinate conjunctions *and, but, or, nor, yet*, and *so*, especially if the subject changes in the second clause.

   He was a kind man, and his life was an inspiration to many.

3. Use a comma after a long introductory element.

   After 10 years with the company, Tom became president.

4. Do not use a comma if such an expression is put at the end of the sentence.

   Tom became president after 10 years with the company.

5. Use commas to separate "interrupters" from the rest of the sentence. Interrupters are words or phrases that are not essential to the meaning of

the sentence. Taking interrupters out of the sentence does not change the meaning of the sentence.

I knew, *of course,* **that I would be caught.**

6. Use commas to surround material that is not essential to the sentence. The difference between this rule and the preceding one is that, in this case, the information surrounded by commas adds some substance to the meaning of the sentence.

   Lawyers, no matter how talented, cannot function without efficient assistants.

7. Use a comma to separate different parts of addresses and dates.

   198 Queen Street South, Hamilton, Ontario L8P 3S7
   November 10, 2002

8. Do not use commas unnecessarily in addresses and dates.

   198 Queen Street South, Hamilton, ON L8P 3S7 [A comma is not needed between the province and the postal code.]
   10 November 2002

9. Do not use commas with the 24-hour clock or when dates are written as numerals.

   1320 (1:20 p.m.)
   44.05.31 (31 May 1944)

10. Use commas before or after a direct quotation.

    She said, "I'm here for the written communication test."

    "I'm here for the written communication test," she said.

    He answered, "You must be joking!"

EXERCISE 20

USING COMMAS

Insert commas where necessary in the following sentences:

1. Her excuse of course was completely ridiculous.

2. By the way you have been promoted.

3. The elderly man coughed staggered and fell to the ground.

4. She smuggled drugs was caught as she left the plane and now has to pay for the crime.

5. The court date is set for August 8 2004.

6. I live at apartment 5 216 Bold St. Toronto ON.

7. Tomorrow July 31 is the anniversary of the day I was hired.

8. That's the best way I think to take creases out of your uniform.

9. I said "Your last statement isn't the truth."

10. You have to comply with the court order or you'll be arrested.

APOSTROPHES

The apostrophe shows possession. It is also used in contractions.

> *Possession:*   John's [belonging to John]
> *Contraction:*   Didn't [did not]

Possessives

The possessive indicates ownership or affiliation. Most possessives can be written by adding an apostrophe and an *s* to a singular noun.

> *Possession:*   Theo's whistle [Theo owns the whistle.]
> *Affiliation:*   Manny's club [Manny is a member of the club.]

It often helps in determining possessives to rephrase a sentence using the word *of* to show possession.

> The whistle of Theo.

When forming the possessive of plural nouns ending in *s*, add the apostrophe after the noun.

> The cars' noise [More than one car is making noise.]

Compare this to the singular possessive.

> The car's noise [One car is making noise.]

A review of various forms of the word *car* is provided below.

Word	Part of speech
car	singular noun
car's	possessive singular noun [belonging to one car]
cars	plural noun
cars'	possessive plural noun [belonging to more than one car]

The following rules will assist you in creating possessive nouns:

1. If a singular word ends in *s*, add *s* to the final letter.

   My boss's office [There is one boss with one office.]

2. Words that are already plural take an apostrophe followed by an *s*.

   My children's toys

3. Statements relating to time need apostrophes in certain situations.

   I am eligible for a week's vacation [a vacation of one week].

   I am eligible for three weeks' vacation [a vacation of three weeks].

4. Never use an apostrophe with the following pronouns:

my	your	yours	his
whose	their	theirs	her
its	our	ours	hers

Note that *it's* is a contraction meaning "it is"; it does not show ownership or affiliation.

Contractions

Contractions are formed from a combination of two words. Both contractions and possessives use apostrophes, but contractions do not show ownership or affiliation. The contraction is formed by replacing a letter or group of letters with an apostrophe.

I am becomes *I'm.*

You are becomes *you're.*

It is becomes *it's.*

Common contractions include the following:

I'm (I am)	they're (they are)
I'd (I had/I would)	they'd (they had/they would)
I'll (I will)	they'll (they will)
I've (I have)	we're (we are)
you're (you are)	we'd (we had/we would)
you'd (you had/you would)	we'll (we will)
you'll (you will)	who're (who are)
you've (you have)	who'd (who had/who would)
he's (he is/he has)	who'll (who will)
he'd (he had/he would)	it's (it is)
he'll (he will)	it'd (it had/it would)
she's (she is/she has)	it'll (it will)
she'd (she had/she would)	let's (let us)
she'll (she will)	isn't (is not)
aren't (are not)	hadn't (had not)
wasn't (was not)	wouldn't (would not)
weren't (were not)	would've (would have)
don't (do not)	couldn't (could not)
doesn't (does not)	could've (could have)
didn't (did not)	shouldn't (should not)
hasn't (has not)	should've (should have)
haven't (have not)	

EXERCISE 21

USING APOSTROPHES

Use apostrophes correctly in the following sentences:

1. Junes mother works for the Ministry of the Attorney General.
2. Those are the employees [plural] records we seized.
3. The clerks salaries were up for review.
4. The rooftops slant made it difficult to repair the tiles.
5. Is that Carlos desk?
6. We will be there in about a minutes time.
7. The ropes mark on the corpse was a clue.
8. Jeff Saunders daughters will be married next week.
9. The lawyers offices had to be cleaned.
10. Tobaccos high cost is leading to more smuggling.
11. Its against the law.
12. Theyre coming with their lawyers this afternoon.
13. Youre going to be promoted.
14. Whos going to pay for the damage?
15. Its Russs car that was involved in the accident.
16. Weve been working late every night.
17. Thats the managing partners problem.
18. Theyve got a chance to win the law league softball championship.
19. Youll never get hired with that attitude.
20. Whats the problem?

PERIODS

1. Use a period at the end of a sentence.

   We had a quiet evening at home.

2. Use a period after most abbreviations.

   Mr. (Mister)
   Oct. (October)

3. Note that *Ms* is not an abbreviation. A period is therefore unnecessary.

4. Note that certain organizations do not use periods in their abbreviated names.

   RCMP (Royal Canadian Mounted Police)
   CSIS (Canadian Security Intelligence Service)

5. Note that the names of most provinces have alternative abbreviations, some of which do not contain periods.

> Ont. or ON (Ontario)
> Alta. or AB (Alberta)

QUESTION MARKS

1. Use a question mark after a direct question.

> She asked, "Are you writing the legal research examination?"

2. Do not use a question mark in an indirect question.

> She asked whether I was writing the legal research examination.

EXCLAMATION POINTS

Use an exclamation point after an emphatic statement or command.

> Stop, or you'll go off the road!

QUOTATION MARKS

1. Use quotation marks to enclose the exact words of a speaker.

> I said, "I'm going on vacation next week."

2. Do not use quotation marks around an indirect quotation.

> I said that I'm going on vacation next week.

3. After quotation marks, use a capital letter unless the quotation is split.

> "I'm going on vacation," I said, "next week."

4. Use quotation marks to enclose the titles of short works. Short works include poems, essays, articles, short stories, songs, and radio or television programs. (Longer works, such as novels, are underlined or italicized.)

> I read the pamphlet "Better Reports" before my test.

SEMICOLONS

1. Use a semicolon to indicate connection between two independent clauses. In the following example, the two independent clauses can be either separated by a period or, if you want to stress the connection between the two statements, joined with a semicolon:

> I witnessed the accident. I will testify in court.

> I witnessed the accident; I will testify in court.

2. Certain conjunctions need to be preceded by a semicolon and followed by a comma. These conjunctions are the following:

however	otherwise	nevertheless
moreover	therefore	nonetheless

> I did not see the accident; however, I was asked to testify in court.

> He was not happy with his allocation; nonetheless, he stayed with the firm.

3. Do not use a semicolon with the coordinate conjunctions *and, but, or, nor, yet,* and *so.* When these coordinate conjunctions separate two independent clauses, a comma is used in preference to a semicolon.

   I witnessed the accident, but you will testify in court.

COLONS

1. Use a colon after an independent clause to introduce a list of particulars.

   I have three favourite career choices: law clerk, legal assistant, and circus performer.

2. The introductory clause may often conclude with the terms *the following* or *as follows.*

   The thieves stole the following: a camera, a television, and a computer.

CAPITAL LETTERS

1. Capitalize the first word in a sentence.

   Capitalize the first word in a sentence.

2. Capitalize the first, last, and important words in a title.

   Communications for Legal Professionals

3. Capitalize the names of specific persons, places, languages, nations, and nationalities.

   Mayor Huang
   Hamilton
   French
   Canada
   Canadian

4. Capitalize the names of days, months, and holidays. Do not capitalize the seasons.

   Monday
   November
   Labour Day
   summer

5. Capitalize the first word in a direct quotation.

   I told her, "There is no charge for these services."

6. Capitalize the word *I.*

   I mean what I say.

7. Capitalize the names of specific academic courses. Do not capitalize general words that refer to a course.

   I am taking Communications I.

   I am taking a communications course.

EXERCISE 22

APPLYING GRAMMAR RULES

Correct the errors in the following sentences:

1. Mrs Ames appeared to be ready to settle her lawsuit.

2. If I had to do it over.

3. Get away from me he yelled.

4. I warned my sister to "drive slowly on icy roads."

5. Stop you're going to hit that pole.

6. The first chapter of this book is entitled effective listening.

7. I have read: a book, a poem, and a short story.

8. I lost the following from my wallet; my money, my identification, and my credit cards.

9. There's 200 students enrolled in the legal program.

10. Prof Brown is the director of the law clerk program at the college.

11. He failed the grammar, and the spelling part of the communications course.

12. The instructor said both him and I should pass the course.

13. When I suddenly heard a car door slam and the sound of many voices.

14. The hearing was supposed to begin at noon yet however the witness had not arrived.

15. She was employed by a woman who owned a van named Mary.

16. They're are the children who were called to the principals office.

17. That's the forth traffic ticket I've received.

18. Each of the lawyers owns their own house.

19. Neither the defendant nor the witness impress the inspector.

20. I don't mind postponing the trial. Because that's my time for vacation.

■ Voice

Voice is the form of a verb that indicates whether the subject of a sentence is the instigator of the action or the receiver of the action. There are two voices: active and passive. A sentence is in the active voice when the subject of the sentence initiates the action.

> He *sued* his former employer.
> Our client *cannot sell* his property because of liens against it.

A sentence is in the passive voice when the subject receives the action. When an active verb is made passive, a form of the verb *to be* is used.

> He *was sued* by his former employer.
> Property with liens against it *cannot be sold.*

The active voice is more forceful and direct than the passive voice, and should be used in most legal writing when possible. However, when it is the action itself that is important, and the person initiating the action is less important (or indefinite or even unknown), or when you wish to emphasize the receiver of the action rather than the person initiating the action, use the passive voice.

EXERCISE 23

USING PUNCTUATION

The following passages from various legal documents have been stripped of all punctuation, including paragraph breaks. Read each passage carefully until you are sure you understand it. Then, punctuate the passage so that the sentence structure is correct and the meaning is as clear as possible. After you have punctuated the passages, discuss in class your understanding of their meaning.

Passage from a Will

I nominate my brother Arthur Robert Hutchison to serve as executor of my estate if my brother Arthur Robert Hutchison fails or is unable for any reason to serve as executor of my estate I nominate my cousin Martha Goldman as the alternate executor of my estate in addition to any powers or elective rights conferred by federal or provincial law or by other provisions of this will I grant my executor the full power and authority to administer my estate except that the executor shall first obtain court authority before selling leasing encumbering trading or otherwise disposing of real property of my estate

Passage from a Power of Attorney

Without restricting its generality in any way the following powers are specifically included within the general powers described in this document real estate matters to sign all documents on my behalf concerning lands which may be registered under land titles legislation real property legislation or such other legislation of all the provinces and territories of Canada such power to include the ability to purchase sell rent mortgage charge manage or otherwise deal with real estate and any interest therein in any way shape or form required for any legitimate purpose as envisioned by this document

Passage from a Confidentiality Agreement

This agreement constitutes the entire agreement between the two parties hereto with respect to the subject matter hereof and cancels and supersedes any prior understandings and agreements between the parties hereto with respect thereto if in any jurisdiction any provision of this agreement or its application to any party or circumstance is restricted prohibited or unenforceable such provision shall as to such jurisdiction be ineffective only to the extent of such restriction prohibition or unenforceability without invalidating the remaining provisions of this agreement and without affecting the validity or enforceability of such provisions in any other jurisdiction or without affecting its application to other parties or circumstances

Summary

Studying grammar will help you understand that there are different ways of expressing yourself. While there may be more than one correct method of writing, grammar rules must be followed. Correct grammar helps you to write with clarity and to eliminate potential misunderstandings and ambiguities.

SPELLING AND DEFINITIONS

Be able to spell and define the following words:

awkward	enough	obstructed	signature
confidentiality	flexible	occurrence	statute
courteous	grievance	personnel	subpoena
disappear	implement	preamble	supersede
disposition	legible	qualification	truncation
dissent	master	questionnaire	vehicle
disturbance	nevertheless	receive	
domestic	objectively	regulations	

CHAPTER 4

Writing: Letters, Memos, Reports, and E-mail

Learning Objectives

After reading this chapter, you should be able to

- Write effective letters, memos, reports, and e-mail.

- Edit your written messages for clarity and conciseness.

- Understand the purpose, form, and layout of the memorandum of law.

Introduction

As a law clerk or legal assistant, you will spend a great deal of your time writing. In the legal environment, possibly even more than in other businesses, everything that takes place must be carefully recorded in writing so that all facts and information are available for future reference. Although you may be involved with contracts or other documents, your writing will often consist of:

- letters,

- memos,

- reports, and

- e-mail.

The main difference between the first two is that letters are traditionally written to people outside the organization, while memos are more often used for internal communication. Reports can be in either letter or memo format. E-mail is a quick and convenient medium for sending your message, so both letters and memos may be sent via e-mail. Therefore, we will examine the actual writing of only letters and memos, and then look at some related issues regarding e-mail.

You might use letters to

- send information to a client,
- exchange information with lawyers in other firms, or
- correspond with government departments and other bodies from whom you must obtain information.

You might use memos to

- convey messages to individuals or groups within your firm or company,
- deliver information you have obtained through research,
- update others on the progress of a legal matter,
- confirm arrangements for meetings and other activities, or
- record information for a file.

Writing Strategies

A letter can be written in either direct or indirect order, depending on the purpose of the document.

DIRECT ORDER

The direct order letter is a short, three-section document that conveys good news or a neutral message, or requests information. You expect that your message will get a positive, or at least a neutral, response. This type of message takes the "good news" approach:

Section 1 State the news or the information you are conveying, or the request you are making.

Section 2 Explain the reason for the message or the request. Use a list form if appropriate.

Section 3 Conclude with a goodwill closing paragraph, providing necessary details, requesting additional information, or requesting action.

For example:

> The purchase of your property at 123 King Street is closing Friday, November 12. We need additional documentation to complete the closing.
>
> We need copies of the following for the year 2005:
>
> 1. Water bills
>
> 2. Hydro bills
>
> Please have these items delivered to this office no later than Wednesday, November 10. Thank you for your attention to this matter.

INDIRECT ORDER

An indirect order letter is more difficult to write than a direct order message because you expect it will meet with some resistance or negativity, or with indifference. This type of message takes the "bad news" approach.

The indirect order message has four sections, and you put off the point of your message until the third section. If you have a subject line in your letter, it should be general in nature, because your audience might ignore or discard the message if the subject line promises uninteresting or unpleasant news. The sections are as follows:

Section 1   Start with a goodwill opening in which you introduce the general subject of your message, but do not make a request, refusal, or complaint.

Section 2   Give reasons for the message that will follow in the next section. Do not state the message as such, though you can imply it.

Section 3   State your request, refusal, or complaint, and attempt to show how your message is of benefit to the reader.

Section 4   Conclude with a goodwill closing in which you offer alternatives to your message or request that some action be taken.

The following letter by the president of Smith, Jones to her employees provides an example.

> As you know, the Canadian Cancer Society has made a significant contribution toward lowering the rate of cancer deaths in Canada over the past number of years. You may even know someone who has been helped by the Society. You may also know, then, that private contributions are the Society's main source of revenue.
>
> Employees of Smith, Jones have contributed a great deal of money in the past to the Canadian Cancer Society, entirely through voluntary donations. However, over the past five years, contributions have dropped from an average of over $20 per person to just over $10. Smith, Jones would like to make a more significant contribution to the Society's very important work.
>
> In order to increase our commitment to the Canadian Cancer Society, we have arranged to deduct a small weekly contribution from your payroll deposit for the Society. This will result in a total contribution of $30 per employee over the course of the year. We urge you to sign the payroll forms authorizing this deduction. Smith, Jones will match all employee contributions. Your contribution is tax-deductible.
>
> Please fill out the appropriate forms by February 15. These forms will be sent to each employee by interoffice mail. The contribution you make will have a significant impact on the fight against cancer in Canada.

Letters

FORMATS

The basic business letter format is reproduced in outline form in figure 4.1. There are three formats that can be developed from the outline shown in this figure: the modified block style, the traditional style, and the full block style. In addition, there are three different types of punctuation that can be used: modified open punctuation, closed punctuation, and open punctuation. These styles are outlined in figures 4.2, 4.3, and 4.4.

Figure 4.1   Basic Business Letter Format

```
Letterhead

Date

Receiver's name and address [sometimes called the inside
address]

Salutation

Subject line

Body of letter

Complimentary close
```

Figure 4.2   Modified Block Style with Modified Open Punctuation

SMITH, BROWN AND MARTINO, LLP
Barristers & Solicitors
4700 Arbuthnot Street, Suite 2700
Naismith, ON N0P 1V0

July 16, 2006

Mr. William Wilton
22 Penny Lane
Naismith, Ontario   N0P 1V0

Dear Mr. Wilton:

RE: xxxxxxxxx xxx xxxxxxx xxx

XXX XXXXXXXXXXXXXX XXXXXX XXXXXXXXXXXX XXXXXXX XXXXXX
XXXXX XXXXXXXXXX.

XXX XXXXXXXXXXXXXX XXXXXX XXXXXXXXXXXX XXXXXXX XXXXXX
XXXXX XXXXXXXXXX. XXX XXXXXXXXXXXXXX XXXXXX XXXXXXXXXXXX
XXXXXXX XXXXXX XXXXX XXXXXXXXXX.

XXX XXXXXXXXXXXXXX XXXXXX XXXXXXXXXXXX XXXXXXX XXXXXX
XXXXX XXXXXXXXXX.

Yours sincerely,

SMITH, BROWN AND MARTINO, LLP

Robert Martino

cc: XXXXXXX XXXXXXXXXX XXXXXXXX

Enc.

Note: Use punctuation between items (such as city and province) within a line and within the body of the letter. End the salutation with a colon, and end the complimentary close with a comma. Do not indent paragraphs.

Figure 4.3   Traditional Style with Closed Punctuation

SMITH, BROWN AND MARTINO, LLP
Barristers & Solicitors
4700 Arbuthnot Street, Suite 2700
Naismith, ON N0P IV0

July 16, 2006

Mr. William Wilton
22 Penny Lane
Naismith, Ontario   N0P 1V0

Dear Mr. Wilton:

RE: xxxxxxxxx xxx xxxxxxx xx xxx xxxxxxxxx

    xxx xxxxxxxxxxxxxxx xxxxxx xxxxxxxxxxxxx xxxxxxx
xxxxxx xxxxx xxxxxxxxxxx.

    xxx xxxxxxxxxxxxxxx xxxxxx xxxxxxxxxxxxx xxxxxxx
xxxxxx xxxxx xxxxxxxxxxx. xxx xxxxxxxxxxxxxxx xxxxxx
xxxxxxxxxxxx xxxxxxx xxxxxx xxxxx xxxxxxxxxx.

    xxx xxxxxxxxxxxxxxx xxxxxx xxxxxxxxxxxxx xxxxxxx
xxxxxx xxxxx xxxxxxxxxxx.

    xxx xxxxxxxxxxxxxxx xxxxxx xxxxxxxxxxxxx xxxxxxx
xxxxxx xxxxx xxxxxxxxxxx.

Yours sincerely,

SMITH, BROWN AND MARTINO, LLP

Robert Martino

cc: xxxxxxxx xxxxxxxx xxxxxxxxxxxxx xxxxxx

Enc.

Note: Indent paragraphs.

Figure 4.4   Full Block Style with Open Punctuation

SMITH, BROWN AND MARTINO, LLP
Barristers and Solicitors
4700 Arbuthnot Street, Suite 2700
Naismith, ON N0P IV0

16 July 2006

Mr. William Wilton
22 Penny Lane
Naismith, Ontario N0P 1V0

Dear Mr. Wilton

RE: xxxxxxx xxx xx xxxxxxxxx xxx xxxxxxxxx

XXX XXXXXXXXXXXXXX XXXXXX XXXXXXXXXXXX XXXXXXX XXXXXX
XXXXX XXXXXXXXXX.

XXX XXXXXXXXXXXXXX XXXXXX XXXXXXXXXXXX XXXXXXX XXXXXX
XXXXX XXXXXXXXXX. XXX XXXXXXXXXXXXXX XXXXXX XXXXXXXXXXXX
XXXXXXX XXXXXX XXXXX XXXXXXXXXX.

XXX XXXXXXXXXXXXXX XXXXXX XXXXXXXXXXXX XXXXXXX XXXXXX
XXXXX XXXXXXXXXX.

XXX XXXXXXXXXXXXXX XXXXXX XXXXXXXXXXXX XXXXXXX XXXXXX
XXXXX XXXXXXXXXX.

Yours sincerely

SMITH, BROWN AND MARTINO, LLP
Barristers and Solicitors

Robert Martino

CC: XXXXXXXXXX XXXXXXXXX

Enc.

Note: No punctuation is used within the date line, at the end of the salutation, or at the end of the complimentary close. Use punctuation within the body of the letter.

STYLE

When you are writing letters, be aware that there are certain stylistic conventions governing the format of the date, the inside address, the attention line, the salutation, the subject line, and the complimentary close. Generally speaking, avoid abbreviations such as *St.* for *Street*, not only in your headings but also in other parts of your letter (with the exception of titles such as *Dr.* for *doctor* in your salutation). Abbreviations indicate a certain carelessness on your part, or a desire to get through the letter quickly.

Now let's look at all the individual parts of a letter.

Date

The chronological order of everything that happens in a legal matter is important, so it is vital that your letters are dated. The date line is typically the first line you typed after the letterhead. In Canada, the usual form is month followed by day, then a comma and the year in full:

```
May 25, 2006
```

"Without Prejudice"

This term is used in letters in which a lawyer wants to put forward a position that has the potential to prejudice his or her client's position at law or under a contract. When the term is used, the contents of the letter may not be used in evidence at any future time without permission of the lawyer and client. The words are typed in block capitals, underlined, and placed either immediately above the inside address or before the date line. Both forms are used, so you should follow the convention of your firm.

```
WITHOUT PREJUDICE
```

Inside Address, Attention Line, and Salutation

A typical inside address presents address information—personal or organization name, street address, and city, jurisdiction, and postal code—on separate lines. For example:

```
Smith, Brown and Martino, LLP
4700 Arbuthnot Street, Suite 2700
Naismith, Ontario   N0P 1V0
```

Note that the inside address uses very little punctuation, with the following exceptions:

- Periods are used in abbreviations such as "Mr." and "Mrs."

- If a firm name uses commas, the inside address uses them as well.

- A comma follows the street name if a suite number appears on the same line. No comma is used if the suite number is placed on its own line.

- A comma follows the city name, separating it from the jurisdiction name.

> ### CANADA POST GUIDELINES
>
> Canada Post has a preferred format for addressing envelopes. The name and address are typed in upper case, with no punctuation at the end of a line. The postal code appears on the same line as the city and jurisdiction symbol, with two spaces between the jurisdiction symbol and the postal code. For example:
>
> ```
> MR. ROBERT MARTINO
> SMITH, BROWN AND MARTINO, LLP
> 4700 ARBUTHNOT STREET, SUITE 2700
> NAISMITH ON  N0P 1V0
> ```
>
> The two-letter symbols for the provinces and territories are as follows:
>
> | | |
> |---|---|
> | Newfoundland and Labrador | NF |
> | Nova Scotia | NS |
> | New Brunswick | NB |
> | Prince Edward Island | PE |
> | Quebec | QC |
> | Ontario | ON |
> | Manitoba | MB |
> | Saskatchewan | SK |
> | Alberta | AB |
> | British Columbia | BC |
> | Yukon | YT |
> | Northwest Territories | NT |
> | Nunavut | NU |

The form of the inside address depends on whether you are addressing the letter to a business entity, such as a company or firm, or to an individual within that firm. This choice also governs the attention line and the salutation. As a rule of thumb, the first line of the inside address should "match" the salutation.

If you are addressing the letter to a company, you still need to show someone's name so that the mailing department will know where to deliver the letter. In that case, you need an "attention line." This goes beneath the inside address, separated by one line space. It is important to note that, because you are addressing the company, the salutation should reflect this fact and should not mention the person's name.

You can "salute" the company in one of two ways:

```
The Provincial Bank
123 Main Street
Royston, Ontario  R8H 2Y7


Attention: Robert Brown


Dear Sirs/Mesdames:
```

or

```
Ladies and Gentlemen:
```

If your letter is addressed to Mr. Brown, you do not need an attention line and you should "salute" Mr. Brown as follows:

```
Mr. Robert Brown, Vice-President
The Provincial Bank
123 Main Street
Royston, Ontario  R8H 2Y7

Dear Mr. Brown:
```

In this example, the recipient of the letter, Robert Brown, has the business title of vice-president. It is customary to show such a title in the inside address. The title can be placed on the same line as the name, separated by a comma as shown, or on its own line, below the name, without a comma.

You can use the recipient's given name or a number of courtesy titles (Ms, Miss, Mrs., Mr., or Dr.) in the salutation. Much will depend on how the person wishes to be addressed. When writing to someone for the first time, always use a courtesy title and the last name. For example, if you receive a letter signed "Mrs. Edna Jones," send a reply to "Mrs. Edna Jones" with the salutation "Dear Mrs. Jones." Otherwise, *Ms* is the standard courtesy title for women. If the person has a gender-neutral name, such as Jean or Terry, call the organization and find out whether you are addressing a man or a woman so that you can use the correct courtesy title. See "Titles and Forms of Address" for information on correct forms of address.

Subject Line

The subject line prepares your reader's mind for the information in your letter, so it's important to make it as clear and useful as possible. In legal writing, the line usually begins with *RE:* (short for *regarding*), which is why it is sometimes called the "Re Line." Some firms have a standard format for subject lines, which, of course, you will follow. Here are some possibilities:

<u>RE: Bartholomew v. Nicodemus</u> [*a litigation matter between Bartholomew and Nicodemus*]

<u>RE: Bartholomew ats. Nicodemus</u> [*Bartholomew "at the suit of" Nicodemus; Nicodemus is suing Bartholomew*]

<u>RE: Bartholomew v. Nicodemus, Our File ZZ00236</u> [*when writing to another law firm, you might include their file number also for their convenience*]

<u>RE: Purchase and sale agreement dated November 21, 2005, between Alfred Bartholomew (Purchaser) and George Nicodemus (Seller)</u>

<u>RE: 23 Smith Road located at the NW corner of Smith Road and West Street and being that Part of Lot 13, Concession 20, City of Brampton, Regional Municipality of Peel</u> [*long-form description of real estate*]

When citing the names of the parties in a subject line, always put your firm's client first. So, in a letter from another law firm with the subject line

<u>RE: Bartholomew v. Nicodemus</u>

TITLES AND FORMS OF ADDRESS

People with a professional title or academic degree(s) often append the title or degree abbreviation(s) to their name. The title or abbreviation appears on the same line as the person's name, and is separated from the name by a comma. For a person with an advanced academic degree, such as a Ph.D. (doctor of philosophy) or J.D. (doctor of jurisprudence), the usual courtesy title (Mr., Ms, Miss, Mrs.) is omitted from the inside address. The courtesy title "Esq." (esquire) is sometimes used by male lawyers, and appears after the name and before the title or degree. The form of the salutation depends on the degree or title. Some common titles and degrees and their use in the inside address and salutation are shown below.

Degree/title	Inside address form	Salutation
J.D. (doctor of jurisprudence)	Paula Szacki, J.D.	Dear Ms Szacki
M.D. (doctor of medicine)	James Sinclair, M.D.	Dear Dr. Sinclair
Ph.D. (doctor of philosophy)	Mary Barrington, Ph.D.	Dear Dr. Barrington
Esq. (esquire)	Alistair Willins, Esq.	Dear Mr. Willins
Q.C. (Queen's counsel)	Alistair Willins, Q.C.	Dear Mr. Willins
	Alistair Willins, Esq., Q.C.	Dear Mr. Willins

There are also prescribed forms of addressing and saluting government officials and judges. Some of these are shown below.

Title/position	Inside address form	Salutation
Governor general	Her Excellency the Right Honourable Michaëlle Jean	Excellency
Prime minister	The Right Honourable Paul Martin	Dear Mr. Prime Minister *or* Dear Prime Minister
Lieutenant governor	His Honour, the Honourable James Bartleman	Your Honour
Provincial premier	The Honourable Dalton McGuinty	Dear Premier *or* Dear Mr. Premier
Mayor	His Worship Mayor David Miller	Dear Mayor Miller
Supreme Court chief justice	The Right Honourable Beverley McLachlin, P.C., Chief Justice of Canada	Dear Madam Justice McLachlin
Supreme Court justice	The Honourable Mr. Justice John C. Major	Dear Mr. Justice Major
Federal Court chief justice	The Honourable John D. Richard, Chief Justice	Dear Mr. Justice Richard
Federal Court justice	The Honourable Madam Justice Karen Sharlow	Dear Madam Justice Sharlow
Provincial high court justice	The Honourable Mr. Justice Doe	Dear Mr. Justice Doe
Provincial or county court judge	Judge Roe	Dear Judge Roe

Bartholomew is the other firm's client, who is suing your client, Nicodemus. When you write back, you should change the subject line to

RE: Nicodemus ats. Bartholomew

Complimentary Close

Commonly used complimentary closes include "Yours truly" and "Sincerely yours." Note that the first letter of the second word is not capitalized.

For companies, it is generally enough to leave four to six line spaces after the complimentary close, followed by the sender's name and, if you wish, the sender's title. The sender will then sign inside the space.

Law firms almost always sign letters with the firm name before the signature space and the writer's name. The rationale for this is that the letter is written on behalf of the firm itself, not the individual writer. Sometimes, partners sign only their names, without indicating the firm name. And sometimes, in adherence to tradition, firms add a "Barristers & Solicitors" line in the complimentary close. Here are two examples of different complimentary close formats you might see, depending on the preference of the firm:

```
Yours sincerely,

SMITH, BROWN AND MARTINO, LLP
Barristers & Solicitors




Robert Martino
```

In some firms, law clerks who sign letters must identify themselves as law clerks. For example:

```
Yours sincerely,

SMITH, BROWN AND MARTINO, LLP




Marilyn Benson, Law Clerk
```

Copies

When you send copies of your letter to people other than the recipient, you should add a line that begins *cc:*, *CC:*, or *c.c.:*, two lines below the writer's name. The abbreviation stands for "carbon copy" and is a vestige of the days when copies were made by typing on carbon paper. Some firms have replaced the abbreviation with the words *Copy to:*. Again, the actual form of the copy line you use will be governed by the firm's convention.

Regardless of how the copy line begins, leave two spaces after the colon and add the name of the person receiving a copy of the letter. If more than one person is receiving a copy, list them one below the other.

Sometimes you will see *bcc:*, which means "blind carbon copy." This notation appears only on copies of the letter, not on the original. You use *bcc:* when you don't want the primary recipient of the letter to know who received copies.

Enclosures and Attachments

Very often you will send the recipient copies of items to which you refer in the letter. These items can be either enclosures, which are separate from the letter, or attachments, which are stapled. To indicate that you are sending something with the letter, you should add a final line to the letter stating either "Enc." or "Att." This line goes two lines below the copy line or, if there are no copies, two lines below the writer's name.

Enclosures are often named in this line, and it is particularly useful to name them when there are several. List the names of the documents you are enclosing, one beneath the other. This helps you ensure that you have enclosed all the necessary items, and it is also useful to the reader in identifying the documents.

As you have seen from some of our examples, there are some variations in the way that letters and memos are formatted. Many firms provide staff with a detailed manual that outlines the formatting of letters and memos, going so far as to specify the fonts to use and exactly where to place each element of the letter or memo. Other firms may not formalize their policies in a manual, but they still prescribe certain conventions. In all cases, you follow the conventions of the firm for which you work.

CONTENT

In order to respond quickly to your letter, the recipient requires information that is accurate, complete, and free from confusing or irrelevant detail.

People's attention is generally at its highest at the beginning and end of your message. For this reason, get to the point as early as possible, and reiterate important points at the end. For example, beginning your letter with "We have received your letter" is a wasted opportunity. Since you are replying to their letter, obviously you must have received it, so you have really said nothing. The following first sentence would be much more effective: "As requested in your letter of June 4, I attach a copy of your May account."

Similarly, make good use of your ending. For example, "We hope to hear from you at your convenience" conveys nothing, and it may never be convenient for them to contact you! Instead, say exactly what you need from the reader. If you write, for example, "We would appreciate your sending us the agenda by Wednesday morning, so that we can be prepared for the meeting on Thursday," the reader has a reason to act, which will often prompt him or her to do so (see figure 4.5).

Figure 4.5 Sample Letter

SMITH, BROWN AND MARTINO, LLP
4700 Arbuthnot Street, Suite 2700
Naismith, ON N0P 1V0

July 16, 2006

Mr. William Wilton
22 Penny Lane
Naismith, Ontario N0P 1V0

Dear Mr. Wilton:

RE: Wilton v. Wilton—sale of condominium

Our file W/MA231

As you instructed in our telephone conversation of July 11, 2006, I advised your wife's lawyer, Ms Marjorie Higginbothom, of your offer to pay all the expense incurred in the sale of the condominium, in the amount of $5,256.23. This leaves all the proceeds of the sale, $560,000, available to be divided equally between you and your wife, as you both previously agreed.

Ms Higginbothom has now advised me that your wife accepts this proposal. Therefore, please provide me with a cheque for $5,256.23, which will be deposited in your trust account until such time as we receive the real estate agent's invoice. We will then use the funds to settle the agent's account.

Yours sincerely

SMITH, BROWN AND MARTINO, LLP

Robert Martino

In the body of the letter, use subheadings as appropriate. This not only helps the reader follow the message, but also provides ease of reference for future discussions or correspondence. Also, make use of devices such as bullets, numbered lists, and charts, which make information stand out.

Refer to the material in chapter 3 on grammar and effective writing, and to the section below on paragraphs.

Tone

Adopt a courteous, businesslike tone. The overall impression created by your letter is important. A courteous tone will elicit a response much more quickly than a sarcastic or threatening tone will. Remember that you can be businesslike and still remain pleasant!

Readability

The ease and speed with which your reader can grasp the main points and supporting details of your letter will often determine how the letter is handled. Spelling and grammar mistakes are unacceptable.

Paragraphs

A paragraph is made up of several sentences. Each paragraph contains one main idea. There is no prescribed length for a paragraph, but it must be long enough to fully express your main idea or your purpose for writing.

In order to express your main idea in a paragraph, you must write a *topic sentence*. Every other sentence in the paragraph supports, describes, or explains the main point you are expressing in the topic sentence.

Most paragraphs begin with the topic sentence, although this is not strictly necessary. Examine the following paragraph:

> **I am a creature of impulse. Just yesterday I decided to visit Mexico for a week. Within two hours I had booked my flight, arranged a hotel, and bought a new swimsuit. I spent all yesterday evening dreaming of the warm Mexican sun and the sound of mariachi. Still, tomorrow I might just as easily cancel the whole thing and stay at home.**

The topic sentence in this paragraph is the first sentence. The main idea is that the writer is impulsive. Every other sentence supports this main idea: the quick decision to visit Mexico, the arrangements that are made within two hours, the idea that the arrangements could easily be cancelled without notice. Only a person of impulse would act in this way.

The topic sentence, then, should express the paragraph's controlling idea and convey the writer's point of view. Consider the following topic sentence:

> **Working as a theme park guide for the summer was both rewarding and frustrating.**

Here the author is writing about his or her summer job as a theme park guide (the topic). The experience was both rewarding and frustrating (the controlling idea). The remainder of the paragraph should provide details about how the job was both rewarding and frustrating.

A topic sentence can have a wide variety of controlling ideas, depending on who is doing the writing. A summer job at a theme park could have been rewarding yet frustrating for one writer, and exciting or boring or challenging for others.

Once you have chosen your topic, established your controlling idea, and written your topic sentence, you must provide sentences that support the main idea through detail and example. The example above, on the "creature of impulse," illustrates how supporting details may explain the topic. In this case, the writer of the paragraph has used examples.

Examples are specific illustrations to support the controlling idea. They must be clear and specific. The following paragraph illustrates the use of specific examples that support the controlling idea. The topic sentence is set in italics.

> *My father was a small-town lawyer, and I learned my love of the law from him.* He'd go into his office every morning never knowing what the day would bring, but he could count on drawing up wills, finalizing business deals, or merely sitting and talking with people about the finer points of the law. He gained the respect of the community by giving sound advice and by never pressing for payment of his client's accounts when times were tough, when the crops failed, or when the local mill shut down. He didn't make a lot of money, but he dealt fairly with people and represented them to the best of his ability. Those are the principles I adopted when I entered the legal profession.

Writing Strong Paragraphs

There are different strategies for writing paragraphs: narration (telling a story), description (describing something with an appeal to the senses), exposition (explaining how something is done), comparison/contrast (pointing out similarities or differences between two or more subjects), and cause and effect (describing the effect of one thing on another).

EXERCISE 1

USING DIFFERENT KINDS OF PARAGRAPHS

Using the development suggestions provided, build on the following topic sentences according to the paragraph category assigned them.

1. When I transferred into the Law Clerk/Legal Assistant program, I knew I had found my career. [Write a *narrative* paragraph telling the story of how you came to choose the Law Clerk/Legal Assistant program.]

2. The line of clerks waiting to file court documents was long. [Write a *descriptive* paragraph detailing the length of the line and the attitude of the people waiting.]

3. Making a new client feel welcome on her first visit to your firm is easy if you show courtesy and friendliness as you greet her at Reception. [Write a paragraph of *exposition* describing the process in detail, being careful not to leave anything out.]

4. The style of communication in Canadian law firms is more formal than in American firms. [Write a *comparison/contrast* paragraph that points out similarities and differences.]

5. Lack of honesty between divorcing spouses leads to longer, more combative legal proceedings. [Write a *cause-and-effect* paragraph explaining how dishonesty between spouses can produce delays and frustrations in the legal process. Use specific examples.]

One last word on paragraphs: one paragraph should discuss only one idea. Read your paragraphs carefully to be sure they include nothing off-topic. A single sentence that doesn't belong can ruin the flow of a paragraph and even obscure the paragraph's central message.

EXERCISE 2

COMPOSING SAMPLE LETTERS

1. Your client has, at your request, returned executed copies of an agreement of purchase and sale. However, although you tabbed all the places where signatures were required, one copy is missing his signature on page 4. Write to the client and request that he sign the contract at the appropriate place and return it to you again. You should also advise the client that this delay, short though it is, could jeopardize your ability to return the fully executed agreement to the other party by the promised date. The situation is urgent.

2. Your client is a small corporation for whom your lawyer acts as corporate secretary. The corporation's annual meeting is to be held one month from today. Write to the client, setting out the date, time, and place for the meeting. Then list and enclose all the documents required for the meeting.

Memos

Memos can be either formal or informal, depending on their intended use. Whatever the situation, there are certain guidelines that should be followed. The basic memo format is reproduced in figure 4.6.

Figure 4.6   Memo Format

```
MEMORANDUM

To:

From:

Date:

Subject:

[Body]

Copy to:

[Initials or signature]
```

ADDRESSES

Firm or company culture dictates how names of senders and receivers are written. Your firm may use Ms or Mr. or just the names themselves. Titles are often omitted, but you might decide to include them if the memo is to serve as a future record. Include the names of all who are being directly addressed by the contents of the memo, and put those who are simply receiving a copy for their information in the "Copy to" line at the bottom of the memo.

SUBJECT LINE

The subject line does not have to be a complete sentence. Make it as brief and to the point as possible, and provide file references that will help orient the reader immediately.

```
Subject: Toronto Law Firm Softball League Schedule

Subject: Lien against property of Bob Arnsby,
         file RE06/01/RA
```

CLOSING

Initial or sign your memo after you proofread it. You do this in order to

- personalize the memo and indicate to the reader that you care about the topic;
- signify to the reader that there are no errors in the memo and that you are responsible for its contents; and
- verify to the reader that the memo is indeed yours and sent with your authorization.

Note that there is no complimentary close (e.g., "Yours truly," "Sincerely,") in a memo.

CONTENT

Limit your memo to one topic. If you have two topics to discuss, send two memos. The memo should be accurate, complete, and free from confusing or irrelevant detail.

TONE

Be polite, courteous, and businesslike, even if the memo is on an informal topic.

READABILITY

Proofread your memo for spelling and grammar mistakes.

THE "YOU" APPROACH

In your memo, point out the advantages to the reader in doing what is requested, or make it clear why the information conveyed is important to the reader. These practices are also useful in writing letters.

FORMATS AND WRITING STRATEGY

Memos can be divided into several formats according to their purpose. As a legal assistant or law clerk, you will most often write one of the following kinds:

- information or instruction memo

- problem-solving memo

- opinion or proposal memo (note that the opinion memo is not the same as an opinion letter, which is a formal document sent by a firm to a client)

- memorandum of law.

While there are no hard-and-fast rules for the composition of memos, the following guidelines will help you write memos that fall into these categories.

Information or Instruction Memo

You might adopt this memo format if you are, for example, notifying others in the firm of meeting arrangements, requesting information from internal sources, or reporting the results of your research. A sample of this kind of memo is shown in figure 4.7. Here are some things to remember when you use this format:

1. *Main message:* State the main reason for writing. For example, you might need to tell colleagues about an important meeting, or explain a new procedure.

2. *Details:* State the information or instructions in as much detail as necessary. For example, in a memo about a meeting, you would indicate where and when it will be held and how long it will last. With some memos, you may need an additional paragraph or two to convey all of the information or instructions.

3. *Action required or proposed:* If you need instructions on how to proceed, ask for them here. If you are going to take action yourself, inform the reader of that here. If no action is required, simply tell the reader that this memo is for providing information only.

Figure 4.7   Sample Information/Instruction Memo

```
MEMORANDUM

To: Sylvia Macintosh, John Wilson, Maria Hobson, Josh
Weinberg, Lee Chan

From: Roberta Jones

Date: November 18, 2006

Subject: Orientation meeting with Smartwear Manufacturing

As you know, we have recently acquired a prestigious new
client, Smartwear Manufacturing. Our managing partner,
Peter Martino, has invited us to meet with representatives
of Smartwear in order to learn about their needs and to
formulate a plan on how we can best serve them.

The meeting has been scheduled for Monday, October 14, 2006
at 4 p.m. in the 4th floor Conference Room. Refreshments
will be served at 5 p.m., and we expect the meeting to
last until approximately 6 p.m.

Please confirm by e-mail to me no later than the end of the
day tomorrow that you will attend this important meeting.
```

Problem-Solving Memo

A sample problem-solving memo is shown in figure 4.8. Keep the following in mind when you use this kind of memo:

1. *Statement of the problem:* You want the reader to care about the problem before you provide a solution, so state it from his or her perspective or from the perspective of the firm. Say, for example, that you want to hire a temp for the rest of the summer to help in your department. Point out that the vacation backlog has already resulted in missed deadlines, late submission of expense reports, and other consequences of importance to the reader.

2. *Analysis:* Go into some detail about where and why the problems arise. In this case, provide financial numbers to illustrate the cost and anything else the reader should know.

3. *Proposed solution:* Provide your solution and explain how it would work. Again, provide cost figures for comparison, so that the reader can clearly see the financial benefit.

4. *Proposed action:* Request permission to go ahead, stating exactly what you propose to do.

Figure 4.8   Sample Problem-Solving Memo

MEMORANDUM

To: Pamela Gates, Human Resources Manager

From: Janice Warrington, Real Estate Department

Date: May 28, 2006

Subject: Proposed solution to departmental inefficiencies

We have recently experienced inefficiencies in our department, leading to at least one deadline almost missed and several late billings. [*statement of problem*] There are two reasons for this:

- Mary is on maternity leave and we did not hire a replacement for her. We thought that John and I together could absorb her work, but this has proved impossible. [*analysis*]

- The new online billing system is complicated and the learning curve has been steep. [*analysis*]

I recommend we hire a temp until Mary returns, and assign a training person from IS for two days to familiarize us with the new system. These two measures should help us catch up and ensure our usual level of efficiency. [*solution*]

May I have your agreement so that I can take these actions? [*call for action*]

Opinion or Proposal Memo

Figure 4.9 provides a sample of the opinion or proposal memo. When you use this format, try to include the following:

1. *Statement of opinion:* Suppose you want to change the way something is done in your department or in the firm at large. Begin with clear statements such as "I believe," "I recommend," or "In order to … I would suggest." Take a bold stand here so that there is no doubt what you are recommending.

2. *Reason for suggestion:* State the potential positive outcome if your recommendation is accepted.

3. *Examples:* Provide examples to illustrate the reasons underlying your opinion.

4. *Benefits of change:* Don't exaggerate, but use positive language to portray your proposal in a good light.

5. *Possible disadvantages:* Presumably, since you are making this recommendation, you have thought through the pros and cons and still believe in your idea. Now you must mention any possible drawbacks, but do so in such a way that they appear outweighed by the benefits.

6. *Action requested:* Request action, such as a meeting to discuss your ideas further.

Figure 4.9   Sample Opinion or Proposal Memo

MEMORANDUM

To: Arthur Robinson, Facilities Manager

From: Christine Wojohowitz, Insurance Litigation Department

Date: August 17, 2006

Subject: Proposal for congestion relief in the copy centre

In an effort to relieve the ongoing crowding and congestion in the copy centre, I believe we should rearrange the equipment in the room. [*statement of opinion*] This would have the following benefits:

- It would eliminate crowding. [*reason*] The machine most often used by all employees is the big copier to the right of the door. People lining up for the machine often block the doorway and sometimes even the corridor. [*explanation/example*]

- It would increase speed of work. [*reason*] If we move the collating table to the southwest corner of the room, there will be better traffic flow among the copiers and other machines. This will allow us to complete jobs more efficiently. [*explanation/example*]

I would like to discuss my suggested layout with you. Could we meet in your office this Friday at 10 a.m.? Please let me know whether that is convenient for you. [*conclusion/call to action*]

CW

PLANNING YOUR MEMO

Advance planning will make the actual task of writing the memo much easier and faster. Decide which of the three formats you will use, jot down the relevant elements listed above, and make notes of what to include in each. Having the message clear in your own mind will help you make it clear on paper for your reader.

LANGUAGE AND GRAMMAR

Learn and use the material in the spelling and grammar chapters of this book. The best planned and laid-out memo or letter will fail if it is grammatically incorrect or full of spelling mistakes.

EXERCISE 3

WRITING A MEMO

Write a memo addressed to the manager of food services at your school, on the following topic. Use today's date.

You have been eating lunch in the cafeteria every day for the past two months, and have enjoyed the quantity and quality of food served, and its reasonable price. Today, however, you ordered the filet, and found it undercooked and tasteless. As well, the potatoes were lumpy, and the gravy had an unusual taste that you can't quite describe. You are not a complainer, but in this case you feel you should inform someone of the situation. You also feel that you should be refunded part of the $4.95 you spent on the very poor meal.

EXERCISE 4

WRITING A MEMO

Write a memo to your immediate supervisor, Valerie Locke, based on the following situation. Use today's date.

Twenty employees in your office, including yourself, have formed a softball team and have arranged to play in an out of town tournament next weekend. You have two requests: first, the team would like permission to leave the office early on the Friday before the weekend tournament; second, the team asks that the company cover the costs of travel to the tournament and accommodations for the weekend. You estimate expenses will run to $1,000 for the weekend. In return, the team will wear the company's name on the back of its sweaters as a form of advertising promotion. The team also agrees to work extra hours for the time missed on the Friday. Since registrations have to be submitted this week, you would appreciate a timely response.

EXERCISE 5

REVISING A BAD MEMO

The finance committee at your firm wants to institute a new procedure to take control of delinquent accounts. Following is a poorly written memo informing lawyers about the new procedure. Rewrite the information as an information/ instruction memo to all lawyers, with their individual clients or legal matters in the heading. Remove superfluous language and be sure your instructions are clear and easily understood.

> The finance committee requires that, prior to any further substantial work being performed on the above-noted file(s), you provide a formal memorandum to the finance committee together with a copy to your department head outlining the nature of the file, the work to be performed, the anticipated monthly and total billings, and whether or not a financial retainer and written retainer is in place. A copy of the written retainer and information relating to the financial retainer should be provided with your memorandum. In the absence of an adequate financial retainer, reasons should then be provided as to the basis for the Committee to review whether or not an exemption should be granted so that work may be further undertaken on said file and the extent of that exemption. A copy of the memorandum should be provided to your Department Head.

■ Memorandum of Law

The most specialized form of memo you will use is the memorandum of law. This is essentially a memo that reports the results of legal research.

For example, in order to decide on a course of action in a case, a lawyer may need to examine previous case law for similar parameters and circumstances. The results of this research are presented in a memorandum of law. The lawyer may ask you to do the research, or he may ask an articling student to do it. In either case, you must know how to format the memo correctly.

The elements of a memorandum of law are:

1. *Question:* State the question the lawyer has asked you to research.

2. *Facts:* State the facts of the current case on which you have relied in researching the question. If you have made assumptions, say that they are assumptions.

3. *Issue(s):* Clearly state the issue or issues of law that are to be examined. Here you must define the legal issues that emerge from the facts of the current case.

4. *Law:* Set out the law governing the case law you have found. You must state the provisions of the law exactly as they appear in the statutes, with full citation set out in the prescribed manner (see below).

5. *Discussion:* Analyze the statutes or regulations and the available case law in the light of the current case.

6. *Conclusion:* State what you have concluded after applying the law to the facts of the current situation.

LEGAL CITATION

An essential part of the formatting of a memorandum of law is what is known as legal citation. All aspects of the case law are "cited" in a prescribed manner. You must become familiar with the rules of legal citation.

Case Citations

A correct legal citation of a case consists of several parts as illustrated in the following examples, explained below:

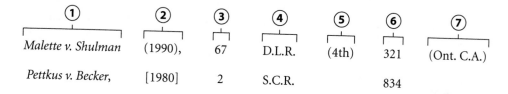

①	②	③	④	⑤	⑥	⑦
Malette v. Shulman	(1990),	67	D.L.R.	(4th)	321	(Ont. C.A.)
Pettkus v. Becker,	[1980]	2	S.C.R.		834	

1. STYLE OF CAUSE OR GENERAL HEADING

The style of cause of the citation sets out the names of the parties (last names only). The names of *all* the parties to the action are not always included in the citation. In a reported case, the editors of the report series will have given the case a short style of cause as well as the complete one if it is long. The names of the parties are separated by a lowercase "v" (which is Latin for "versus," meaning against) and are italicized.

2. YEAR

The year in which the case is decided or reported—that is, published in a report series—follows the style of cause and will be in either round or square brackets.

Some report series number their volumes sequentially no matter what the year, and it is not essential to know the year in which the case was reported in order to find it in the report series. In that case, the year is placed in round brackets—( )—and is followed by a comma.

Other report series start a new set of volume numbers each calendar year, and it is essential to know the year in order to find the case in the report series. In this case, the year appears in square brackets—[ ]—and is preceded by a comma. For example, in each calendar year, the first volume of the *Supreme Court Reports* is volume 1. To find a case that is located in volume 1, you must know the year in which the case was reported to find the appropriate volume 1.

3. LAW REPORT VOLUME NUMBER

This number tells you the volume number of the report series in which your case can be found. Some law report volumes are identified simply by volume number (as in the first example above), while others are identified also by the year in which the volume was published. More than one volume may be published in one year, as illustrated in the second example above. If the report series starts a new sequence of volume numbers each year, then you must make sure you look for the volume number for the correct year. In the example of *Pettkus v. Becker*, you are looking for volume 2 for the year 1980.

4. NAME OF THE LAW REPORT SERIES

This part of the citation tells you the name of the law report series in which the case is reported. Abbreviations are generally used. In the example of *Malette v. Shulman,* "D.L.R." stands for the *Dominion Law Reports.* In the example of *Pettkus v. Becker,* "S.C.R." stands for the *Supreme Court Reports.*

5. LAW REPORT SERIES NUMBER

Many reports do not continue past a certain number of volumes. When the report reaches, for example, volume 75 or volume 100, that series ends and a new one begins. Subsequent editions are identified by "2d," "3d," "4th," and so on (*not* "2nd," "3rd"). If a series or edition number is provided in a citation, be sure that you have the right series as well as the right volume number of the report. In the *Malette v. Shulman* citation, the case can be found in the 67th volume of the 4th series of the D.L.R.

6. PAGE NUMBER

This number tells you the page number on which the case begins in the report volume. In a correct citation, no abbreviation such as "p.," "pp.," or "pg." is used before the page number.

7. JURISDICTION AND COURT

The abbreviation for jurisdiction and the level of court is found in round brackets following the page number of the case. This information is omitted if the jurisdiction and/or court level is obvious from the name of the reporter series.

If the citation refers to a report series that includes cases for one province only, such as the *Ontario Reports* or the *British Columbia Reports,* only the level of court is set out. For example, the citation of a Court of Appeal case published in the *Ontario Reports* will end with "(C.A.)." The citation for the same case in the *Dominion Law Reports* (which publishes cases from across Canada) will end in "(Ont. C.A.)."

If the citation refers to a report series for one court only, the level of court is not included in the citation. For example, the *Supreme Court Reports* reports only Supreme Court of Canada decisions. Therefore, a citation for that report series will omit both the jurisdiction and the level of court, as illustrated in the example of *Pettkus v. Becker.*

Sometimes, the name of the judge who decided the case is included in the citation. If the citation does not include the court, the judge's name appears in round brackets at the end of the citation. If the court is included, the name follows the court, separated by a long (em) dash: for example, "(Ont. C.A.—Robins J.)." The "J." stands for judge or justice; it is not the initial of the judge's first name. "JJ." stands for justices and "JJ.A." stands for justices of appeal. "C.J." stands for chief justice. A judge's own initial is used only if it is necessary to distinguish between two judges with the same last name—for example, "R.E. Holland J." and "J. Holland J."

Parallel Citations

If a case is reported in more than one report series, "parallel" citations are given. A parallel citation tells you about other reports where the same case can be found. The citation for any official report series is given first. For example:

R. v. Carosella, [1997] 1 S.C.R. 80, 142 D.L.R. (4th) 595, 112 C.C.C. (3d) 289.

This citation means that the case can be found in the *Supreme Court Reports*, the *Dominion Law Reports*, and *Canadian Criminal Cases*. Parallel cites are separated by commas.

When parallel citations are given, you need to choose only one of the report series to find the text of the case. However, if the case has been reported in an official report series, you should read and copy the case from that report series, if it is available to you.

WRITING A MEMORANDUM OF LAW

Writing a memorandum of law is a complex process, and it is important that the end result be an accurate description of your research and the conclusions you have reached. You should not rush it. You may write several drafts, or at least do several rounds of heavy editing, before the final version is ready. It is worth the time and effort to produce an effective memorandum of law.

The following steps will guide you through the process.

1. *Analyze the fact situation.*

2. *Research the law.*

3. *Prepare a draft memo of law.* At this point, you should try to see the problem as a whole, and this is necessary in preparing your memo. A draft memo of law gives you a chance to try out different ideas about what you think is going on from a legal point of view, and to settle on the true issues, the important facts, and the relevant law. You may have to rework your draft once or twice before you're satisfied that you've approached the problem from the correct angle.

   In your draft memo, you should *not* start with the facts and work down.

   Start with the question asked by the client or lawyer.

   Then set out the legal issues that arise out of the question, out of the facts, and out of the law you have found in your research.

   Then set out the law.

   When you have done all this, you will be able to look at the facts and decide which ones are relevant to the principles of law involved. Delete irrelevant facts. Emphasize essential facts.

   Discuss the law as it relates to the facts in your particular case.

   Finally, reach a conclusion. Suggest possible action, and potential consequences of such action.

4. *Prepare a final memo of law in the proper format.* Remember that a memo of law is not a 5,000-word term paper; keep it short and to the point. The lawyer reading the memo is also going to read the attached statute, regulatory, and case law and draw his or her own conclusions.

Figure 4.10 shows a sample memorandum of law regarding the execution and registration of security documents by a debtor using his common law name.

Figure 4.10   Sample Memorandum of Law

```
MEMORANDUM

TO:      Lawyer
FROM:    Law Student
DATE:    December 13, 1995
FILE NO: 20056-3
RE:      Security documents executed and registered using
         debtor's common law name
```

FACTS

An individual (the "Debtor") executed security documents on his own behalf using a name which was not his legal name. He signed using the name David Black, which he was using generally as his name at the time he executed the documents. However, his legal name is David Brown, and he has more recently begun using that name instead of David Black.

Our client (the "Bank") is the security holder. The security documents were registered against the Debtor's personal property in British Columbia in favour of the Bank, with the registration listing the Debtor as David Black.

The Bank is now concerned about whether its security is enforceable.

ISSUE

Will personal property security documents granted in favour of the Bank, signed and registered in British Columbia using the Debtor's common law name David Black, be enforceable against the Debtor and the Debtor's creditors now that the Debtor has changed to using his legal name David Brown?

CONCLUSION

The law is clear that the security documents will be enforceable by the Bank as against the Debtor. However, there is a significant risk that the security documents, which have been registered under the name David Black in public registries, will not be enforceable against other creditors of the Debtor. If the Debtor had continued to consistently use David Black as his common law name, the registration would protect the Bank's security. The switch from Black to Brown brings the protection afforded by registration into question.

(Continued on the next page.)

Figure 4.10   Continued

The Bank should take the following steps to protect its
security. The entire transaction does not need to be re-
executed, because the contracts signed by the Debtor are
valid as against the Debtor. However, the security
registration should be updated by a new filing reflecting
the different name. One way would be to file notice of a
change of name. Given the uncertainty as to when the Debtor
goes by Black, and when he goes by Brown, the better route
is to file under both names.

DISCUSSION

General principles concerning names

At common law, a person could adopt any name in the
community, provided that this was not done with any
intention to defraud others. A person's legal name was the
name the person was known by, determined merely as a
question of common usage within the community. Although
occasionally private Acts were used to formally establish
changes of name, the most common pattern was for the name
change to be effected by adoption, use and recognition in
the community. *CED (West. 3rd)*, Vol. 34, "Vital
Statistics", at para. 47.

Legislation now governs legal name changes. However, the
courts have held that the use of a name different from one's
legal name is still not illegal, so long as there is no
intention to defraud or mislead. *CED (West. 3rd)*, Vol. 34,
"Vital Statistics", at para. 50.

The Privy Council considered the effect of signing a deed
using a name different from one's legal name in *Fung Ping
Shan v. Tong Shun*, [1918] A.C. 403 (P.C., on appeal from
the Supreme Court of Hong Kong). At page 407 their
Lordships stated:

> A person who signs, seals, and delivers a deed of
> covenant cannot avoid liability under the deed by
> signing a name which he represents as, but which is
> not in fact, his own, nor can he saddle such liability
> on the person whose name he uses, unless he is the
> duly constituted attorney of such person.

Their Lordships held that although the defendant had
signed his uncle's name to the conveyance document when he
had no authority to do so, the vendor thought it was
dealing with the defendant rather than his uncle, and the
defendant was therefore liable under the deed of conveyance.
This case is cited as authority in both *Halsbury's Laws of
England* (4th ed.), Vol. 12, "Deeds and other Instruments",

(Continued on the next page.)

Figure 4.10   Continued

at para. 1365, note 1, and *CED (West. 3rd)*, Vol. 11A, "Deeds and Documents", at para. 25.

In summary, at common law one was entitled to use a name by which one was commonly known in the community. If one used a different name to sign a legal document, one would still be bound under that document.

Applying this rule to our facts, the Debtor is bound to the Bank under the security documents, even though he did not sign them using his legal name.

Registration regimes

Difficulties with the common law rule have arisen in modern times because of registration regimes that are name-dependent. There are several recent cases debating this issue in the context of PPSA registrations. Most of these cases deal with minor differences between the legal name and the registered name, such as an incorrect or missing middle initial, or a misspelled first name. I have not dealt with these cases. A small body of cases discusses the problems that arise with a significantly different given name. An even smaller body of cases deals with differences in surnames.

The tendency in the more recent cases has been to afford a generous interpretation of the word "name" in the registration requirements, where the legislation does not specify that the name used in the documentation must be the individual's legal name. However, this is balanced against the problems caused to third parties trying to search the registry under the legal name and finding no security documentation registered under that name.

British Columbia

The leading British Columbia case is *Re Lazarchuk* (1994), 7 P.P.S.A.C. (2d) 155 (B.C.S.C.), per Master Powers. The debtor had granted a chattel mortgage on a motor vehicle to the bank in the name of "Lazarchuk". The debtor subsequently filed an assignment into bankruptcy under the name of "Lazarchuk". The debtor's birth certificate read "Lazarczuk" and as a result the assignment was changed to read "Lazarczuk". However, all other identification of the debtor, including his driver's licence and vehicle ownership, contained the spelling "Lazarchuk". The debtor also stated in an affidavit that he always knew himself to be "Lazarchuk" and held himself to be such to the public. He was not aware that his birth certificate contained a different spelling of his surname.

(Continued on the next page.)

Figure 4.10   Continued

The bank had registered its security interest under the name of "Lazarchuk" and under the correct serial number of the vehicle. The trustee in bankruptcy disallowed the bank's claim as a secured creditor on the grounds that a name search would not reveal the bank's interest and hence the error was seriously misleading. The trustee argued that section 9(1) of the *Personal Property Security Act*, S.B.C. 1989, c. 36 ("PPSA") required that the debtor's legal, true or right name, as indicated on some official document, should be recorded on the financing statement, and that strict compliance is necessary to preserve the integrity of the registration system under the Act. Hence, the trustee argued that the bank's security interest was unperfected at the time of bankruptcy and was invalid as against the trustee.

The bank argued that additions should not be read into the PPSA and its regulations. Furthermore, the bank argued that name changes can occur without registration under the *Name Act* and under common law, and there is nothing to invalidate these changes. The bank therefore argued that its registration and security interest should be valid as against the trustee.

Master Powers noted that this was a case of first impression in British Columbia. He made the following general comments about name changes at pages 162 and 163:

> A person may have more than one name, or may be known by more than one name, or may change their name without going through a formal process which results in a record of that change. The person's birth certificate may contain the name under which their birth was registered, or be issued in a different name if that change has been officially recorded with Vital Statistics. A person may use a surname of their spouse, the name they obtained by adoption, or at birth or their surname immediately before marriage, if they are a married person. The *Name Act*, s 2.1, does not appear to place any restriction on when a person begins using a particular surname or any restriction that prevents them from using one particular surname and then another and reverting to the original or, in fact, to what may be a third surname. The *Name Act* does not appear to require any formal registration of such an election or use.

In addition, there does not appear to be anything which invalidates a change of name by common law even though that change might be an offence under the *Name Act*.

(Continued on the next page.)

Figure 4.10   Continued

Master Powers then reviewed the PPSA and its regulations, and concluded that the references to "name" in that legislation were not restricted to the "legal name" of the debtor:

> I conclude that the regulations should not be interpreted to deprive the bank of its security in a case of this nature. The regulations do not say which name the security must be registered in and I would also find from the evidence that the bankrupt's name is Lazarchuk, not Lazarczuk as shown on his birth certificate. The name Lazarchuk is the name which he has acquired at common-law. I am not making any determination as to whether or not his name may not also be Lazarczuk as registered by his birth. This may simply be a case where he had, in fact, two names and the regulations of the PPSA do not specify which name is to be used. Therefore, I conclude the bank has properly registered its security as required by the PPSA and that its security is valid as against the trustee.

This case comes out strongly in favour of the bank and therefore supports the position our client wants to take with respect to the Brown financing. However, there are several problems with relying on this case. It was decided only at the level of a Master. It is the only British Columbia case on this issue. The two surnames in our case are completely different, rather than having a slightly different spelling. Furthermore, the Debtor has now started using Brown, his legal name, as his surname. This confuses the issue and would enable a court to distinguish our case from that of Mr. Lazarchuk.

Alberta

The Alberta Court of Appeal took a similar approach in *Miller, McClelland Ltd. v. Barrhead Savings & Credit Union Ltd.*, [1995] 5 W.W.R. 170 (Alta. C.A.). The bankrupt in that case had three given names, but was commonly known and referred to by only the second of the names. His driver's licence, income tax returns, personal resume and professional certificates, presented when he applied for a loan with the credit union, all identified him by the second name. The credit union registered financing statements under the PPSA (Alta) showing only the second given name. Bankruptcy proceedings were later commenced using the bankrupt's first given name, under which no PPSA registrations were shown. The registrar in bankruptcy disallowed the credit union's claim, and the disallowance was upheld by the bankruptcy judge. These rulings were overturned on appeal.

(Continued on the next page.)

Figure 4.10 Continued

The Alberta Court of Appeal held that neither the *Personal Property Security Act*, S.A. 1988, c. P-4.05 nor the regulations under it prescribed unequivocal identification criteria. They merely provide that the debtor is to be identified by his or her last name, followed by his or her first name and middle name, if any. The term "first name" is not defined in the Alberta PPSA or regulations and should not be presumed to refer to a precise term such as "given name". The Alberta Court of Appeal held that even though registry guidelines published by the Attorney General directed that the birth certificate name be used in registering securities, those guidelines did not have binding legal effect. Accordingly, the registration using only the second given name and the surname was held to be in compliance with PPSA requirements.

The key in both the Alberta and British Columbia cases is that the name used by the debtor on the security documents was the debtor's common law name, in the sense that the debtor consistently used that name and was known by that name in the community. A different result may arise where the debtor does not consistently use the same name, as in our case.

Ontario

In *Re Grisenthwaite* (1987), 43 R.P.R. 304 (Ont. Sup. Ct.) the borrower used different last names. Her maiden name was J.C. Smith. She adopted her first husband's name, Gullins, on marriage. After his death and her remarriage to W. Grisenthwaite, she used various last names, including "Gullins", "Gullins Grisenthwaite", and "Grisenthwaite". A security document and financing statement in favour of the chattel mortgagee with respect to a motor home described the debtor as "J.C. Gullins". The trustee in bankruptcy of the debtor sought directions as to whether this security was valid.

Master Browne noted that the Ontario legislation did not define what is the proper surname for use in a PPSA financing statement. He noted that the *Change of Name Act*, R.S.O. 1980, c. 62 placed some restrictions on common-law rights with respect to name changes, but did not necessarily change those rights. In particular, he held that at common law the debtor was entitled to use the various names she was using. However, he held that her true name and surname for purposes of compliance with the regulations under the *Personal Property Security Act*, R.S.O. 1980, c. 375 was "Grisenthwaite", as she had adopted by usage her new husband's name. That adoption had the effect of an election. Such an adoption was acknowledged to cause a change of name under the *Change of Name Act*.

(Continued on the next page.)

Figure 4.10   Continued

This case implies that the only name that is valid for PPSA registration is the name that is the legal name under the *Change of Name Act*. In this respect, it is narrower than the later case law summarized above. However, this case was decided several years prior to those cases. The recent Alberta and British Columbia case law takes a more liberal approach.

Summary

When considered together and analyzed, the combined effect of this case law appears to be as follows. Where the debtor uses more than one name, then the name to be used for PPSA registration must be the debtor's legal name. On the other hand, if the debtor consistently uses the same name and has therefore adopted it at common law, registration in that name will be valid for PPSA purposes. Thus, in this case, if David Black was continuing to use that name, even though his birth certificate name is David Brown, then registration under David Black should be valid because it would be his common law name. However, if he is using both names, or has abandoned Black in favour of Brown, then the documentation should be registered in his legal name.

Recommendation

As a result of this analysis, the Bank should take the following steps to protect its security. The entire transaction does not need to be re-executed, because the contracts signed by the Debtor will be valid as against him. However, the security registration should be updated by a new filing reflecting the different name. One way would be to file notice of a change of name. Given the uncertainty as to when the Debtor goes by Black, and when he goes by Brown, the better route is to file under both names.

Reprinted with permission from the Best Guide to Canadian Legal Research at legalresearch.org, © 1995-2005. Catherine P. Best.

Reports

Reports can be in either letter or memorandum form. In other words, reports are folded into the letter or memorandum formats.

Reports are made up of two basic parts, the summary and the details. The details can be further subdivided into the following categories:

1. *Background:* The circumstances that led to the report being written.

2. *Facts:* The subject of the report, written chronologically.

3. *Conclusion:* The results; what needs to be done.

The details of a report follow a sequence called Five Ws and an H:

- Who?

- What?

- Where?

- When?

- Why?

- How?

Stylistically, use the Four Cs in your report writing:

- Clear

- Concise

- Complete

- Correct

Remember, then, that the report is made up of the following components:

1. *Summary:* A brief overview of the topic of your report.

2. *Background:* The setting of the scene. Usually written in the past tense, the background section tells what led up to the facts of the report, and answers the questions *Who? Why? Where? When?*

3. *Facts:* The information that needs to be transmitted. The facts section answers the questions *What?* and *How?*

4. *Conclusions:* The consequence of the facts, and what needs to be done.

Figure 4.11 shows a sample memorandum report describing a car accident that befell law clerk J. Roberts as he was driving to court. The report is from him to his supervisor.

ORGANIZING THE REPORT

In a longer report, a useful procedure for organizing information is to

- gather information,

- jot down topic headings,

Figure 4.11   Sample Report

```
MEMORANDUM

TO: Ms J. Kaine, Attorney, Kaine & Yule

FROM: J. Roberts, Law Clerk

DATE: May 31, 2006

SUBJECT: Traffic Accident

While driving from the office this morning to deliver you
the documents you needed for the Smith trial, I was
involved in a traffic accident. As a result, I did not
deliver the documents on time. [summary]

I arrived at the office this morning at 8 a.m. to pick up
the documents you requested for the Smith trial, which was
scheduled to take place at the courthouse at 10 a.m. I left
the office at 8:15 in my car, a 2002 Chevrolet Caprice, and
drove westbound on King Street toward the courthouse. As I
was approaching the intersection of King and Queen streets,
I stopped for a red light. I then proceeded westbound
through the intersection when the light turned green.
It was raining and the roads were slippery. [background]

As I proceeded through the intersection, I was struck on
the passenger side of the car by a 1999 Plymouth Fury,
travelling southbound on Queen Street, that had failed to
stop for the red light. [facts]

No one was injured in the accident. My car sustained $2,000
damage. The other driver and I waited for the police to
arrive after I placed a call to the police station. I also
called Marcia MacMillan of our office, asking her to
contact you and explain the incident and the reason for my
delay. The other driver was charged with failing to stop
for a red light, and since my car was not driveable, it
was towed to Acme Towing and Salvage. I returned to the
office by taxi with the Smith documents. [conclusion]

JR
```

- delete irrelevant information,

- group related topics together,

- arrange topics chronologically, and

- write.

General rules for report writing include the following:

- Start at the beginning.

- Describe events in chronological order.

- Write in the past tense.

- Use specific words—that is, words that have meanings easily understood by the reader.

- Write in the first person when referring to yourself.

- Write in the third person when referring to other people.

- Use complete sentences, unless a list is called for.

- Follow the rules of grammar and spelling.

- Keep sentences to under 20 words.

E-mail

As stated at the beginning of this chapter, e-mail is merely a vehicle for transmitting messages. For that reason, we don't have as many formatting or composition guidelines as for letters and memos. Remember, you can write a letter or a memo and send it via e-mail. You should approach an e-mail letter or memo with the same care and focus as if you were putting it on paper.

There are, however, a few general guidelines that will help you write effective e-mail messages. While these do not necessarily deal specifically with writing, they do deal with communication.

1. Write an effective subject line. People today are overwhelmed with huge volumes of e-mail, and your subject line can influence your reader either to open your e-mail or to delete it without reading it. A good subject line is specific, and as brief as clarity will allow. For example, "Monthly department meeting" is too general. Better would be, "Change of venue for February department meeting."

2. Avoid using in your subject line words that will trigger "spam filters." These currently include words such as *free, dollar, girls, bargain, profit, additional income, billing address, avoid bankruptcy, guarantee, mortgage rates,* and *your income.* This list is growing all the time. So you might use words that are perfectly legitimate and relevant to your message, such as *billing address,* only to have your message caught in spam filters and never delivered. For complete lists, do an online search for "words that trigger spam filters."

3. Given a situation where, in a printed letter, you would normally use a salutation with a courtesy title, such as *Dear Mr.* or *Dear Ms*, use it in your e-mail message.

4. Use upper and lower case as you would on paper. Words that are written all in block capitals create the impression you are shouting, and they are also likely to fall prey to the spam filters. If you omit capitals altogether, your work is not only grammatically incorrect but difficult to read and inappropriately casual.

5. Leave an extra line space between paragraphs, just as you would on paper.

6. Keep paragraphs short. Large blocks of text on a computer screen are hard on the eyes and difficult to read; in other words, they are an automatic barrier to communication.

7. Smiley faces and other "emoticons" have no place in business e-mail. Your words must speak for themselves.

8. Proofread! An e-mail is a business document, and it's just as important that it be correct in all respects as it would if it were on paper. Don't let this method of delivery be an excuse for shoddy work.

9. Include your contact information at the end of the message, together with your name. The easiest way to do this is with e-mail signatures, which are available in all major e-mail programs.

10. Use distribution lists wisely. A list of people in your department, for example, can be useful when the message is for everyone, but sending copies of all your messages to everyone on the list is unnecessary and annoying.

In the legal world, people still print e-mails and put them in their paper files, and they probably will do so for the foreseeable future. So you must write them with as much care and thought as any other piece of written business communication.

As a law clerk or legal assistant, you will perform many and varied tasks. Remember that written memos and letters will be the only lasting, tangible evidence of your work. It is therefore to everyone's benefit, including your own, that your written work be the best product you can make it.

EXERCISE 6

WRITING TO A CLIENT

Write a letter report to a client explaining that your lawyer has been called out of town unexpectedly for a trial that wasn't supposed to start for two weeks. Your client, who was to have a hearing in a child support case, will now have to wait until another court date can be set. You as the law clerk writing the letter report will have to make up appropriate names, addresses, dates, and circumstances, follow the report organization, and draw conclusions. Keep in mind that your client will likely be upset with the delay.

EXERCISE 7

REWRITING A LETTER

Rewrite the following letter, correcting all grammar, form, spelling, and punctuation errors. Remove any unnecessary words and phrases, and correct awkward sentence construction. Arrange the material in appropriate paragraphs.

November 1, 2005

Dr. Norman Wattingford, Doctor of Chiropractic,

2100 Robinson Boulevard,

Suite 207,

Abbotsford, Ontario L6J 4M2

Dear Doctor Wattingford

Big Bad Machinery Company v. Dorothy Langham

We are acting as solicitors for mrs Dorothy Langham who is also a chiropractic patient of yours. It is our understanding from our discussions with dorothy that she suffered a accident on the factory floor of Big Bad Machinery Co where she works on December 14 2004. As a result of said acident (on which a large piece of heavy metal machinery accidently broak of it's hinges and fell at ms Langhams' feet landing on her big toe of her right foot leading to great pain) Ms Langham has been suffering excrutiating pain since the accident. Because of the above reasons she has not worked since the date of the accident. It is my understand that you are the doctor who has treated Mrs Langham for her injuries and you agree she is not in a condition to return to her place of work in case she further injures her toe. Furthermore she is seeing a psychiatrist because of pain and sufering which she has caused her to be afraid of the big machinery so how can she now earn her living with it? Can you please send me all your reports exploring Dorothys' history with this trouble so that as her solicitors I can act on her behalf in dealing with her employer the Big Bad Machinery Company and trying to get her some form of compensation form them. Please kindly contact me with this information at your earliest possible convenience.

Yours very truly,

WILSON Smith & JONES

Billy Smith

EXERCISE 8

WRITING A MEMORANDUM

Your client is the wife in a messy divorce case. The husband has been ordered to pay child support for the two children of the marriage, Rebecca (age 7) and Robert (age 2). He has been paying fairly regularly, if sometimes late, for almost a year.

Today, while your lawyer was in court, you took a telephone call from your client, who was hysterical and barely coherent. Apparently, she received a call that morning from her ex-husband, saying he now knows that Robert is not his child and refuses to pay any more of his "hard-earned cash to support somebody else's kid." Your client repeated over and over to you that there is no truth in this statement and that her ex-husband is indeed Robert's father.

The ex-husband was verbally abusive to your client and threatened her physical safety. He told her that if she did not immediately give up her claim to this money, he would personally "send two big guys to take care of you."

You assured your client that you would convey to your lawyer not only the situation but also her fear of coming to harm at the hands of her ex-husband. Write a memo to your lawyer recounting the details of the telephone conversation.

SPELLING AND DEFINITIONS

Be able to spell and define the following words:

ancillary	foreclosure	order	transcript
bond	hearing	petition	tribunal
calculate	mediator	punitive	trustee
cross-claim	negotiation	redemption	waiver
default	opponent	supplementary	writ

CHAPTER 5
Summary and Paraphrase

Learning Objectives

After completing this chapter, you should be able to

- Write summaries that contain the main ideas of the original works.
- Paraphrase for understanding.
- Detect bias in reporting.

Introduction

There are two different methods of shortening a piece of writing while keeping the main points of the original work: the **summary** and the **paraphrase**. Each is written differently, and with a different emphasis.

Writing a Summary

Law clerks and legal assistants often need to summarize material. A summary allows a reader to understand the contents of an original piece of writing without having to read the entire original. Legal documents must be broken down into their essentials; important information from reports must be analyzed. It is important for law clerks and legal assistants to be able to summarize effectively.

The summary can also be called a *synopsis* or an *abstract*. Its demands are threefold: it requires that you read carefully, select wisely, and write concisely. Summarizing is a valuable skill to develop. In addition to the legal applications mentioned previously, learning to summarize can help you to take notes and to listen more effectively. The ability to summarize will also be useful in legal research.

The purpose of the summary, then, is to condense an original piece of writing and put it into your own words. The summary gives the reader the main ideas of the original passage, thereby allowing him or her to understand the facts contained in the original without having to read the entire passage.

There are a number of rules that apply to summary writing.

1. *Read the document carefully several times.* As you do so, note the thesis and any bias in the original.

2. *Underline the main ideas.* Eliminate anything that is not essential to the meaning of the original.

3. *Count the words in the original.* The summary should be about one-third or one-quarter the length of the original. The summary may consist of one sentence, one paragraph, or several paragraphs, depending on the length of the original. Do not use point form.

4. *Without looking at the original, write a draft summary.* Be sure that the essential points from the original appear in the summary. Although you should use your own words, the summary must reflect the intent of the original passage. It should follow the order of the original and contain a number of supporting examples.

5. *Substitute single words for clauses and phrases.* Whenever possible, details should be summarized with generalizations. Following are some means of doing this:

   a. Change direct speech to indirect speech.

   b. Write in the third person if possible.

   c. Do not make critical comments; report the facts.

   d. Do not lift passages verbatim; you should not use more than three words at a time from the original.

   e. The amount of textual space given to the summarized ideas should be proportional to the amount they receive in the original.

   f. Identify and eliminate minor supporting details.

   g. Eliminate wordy expressions. For example, change *as a result of* to *because* and *in the end* to *finally*.

   h. Identify and eliminate unimportant modifiers such as *extremely, huge,* and *friendly.*

6. *Look again at the original.* Check that you

   a. haven't quoted from the original,

   b. have covered all the main points,

   c. have excluded all non-essential material, and

   d. haven't included your personal point of view.

7. *Edit your summary for spelling and grammar.*

CHANGING DIRECT SPEECH TO INDIRECT SPEECH

The general procedures for changing direct speech to indirect speech are set out below.

1. *Direct words become an indirect statement, question, or command.* Quotation marks are eliminated.

   Direct: "I finished that file yesterday," she said.
   Indirect: She said she finished that file yesterday.

   Direct: "Where are you going?" he asked me.
   Indirect: He asked me where I was going.

   Direct: "Have all of the documents ready for the next hearing," the judge told me.
   Indirect: The judge told me to have all of the documents ready for the next hearing.

2. *Pronouns usually change from first to third person.* For example, *I* changes to *he*, *she*, or *it*.

3. *Verbs in the present tense usually change to some form of the past tense.*

COUNTING WORDS

Your summary should contain one-third or one-quarter the number of words contained in the original, depending on instructions given. Count the words in the original, then count the words in the completed summary. When counting words, observe the following rules:

1. Articles (*a, an, the*) count as one word.

2. Abbreviations count as one word.

3. Numbers count as one word.

4. Dates (23 October 2002) count as three words.

5. Compound words (e.g., *first-rate*) count as one word.

6. Words separated by a slash (e.g., *either/or*) count as one word.

EXERCISE 1

REMOVING WORDY EXPRESSIONS

Find single words to replace the following phrases:

- conduct a discussion of
- perform an analysis of
- create a reduction in
- make a discovery of
- engage in the preparation of
- give consideration to
- make an assumption of
- is of the opinion that
- on account of the fact that
- carry out an investigation of

SAMPLE SUMMARIES

Compare the following passage with the summarized version below it:

> We wish to acknowledge receipt of your letter of 22 September. We regret to inform you that we cannot fulfill your request at this point in time to bring a group of law students to tour our law office because the building is undergoing renovation. Within the next three months, we expect renovations to be complete and we will again allow visitors in the facility.
>
> We do not usually book appointments for tours this far in advance, but under the circumstances, if you are still interested in a tour when renovations are complete, we would be happy to book an appointment with you immediately. I enclose a brochure about our law firm with pertinent telephone numbers.
>
> We hope that this arrangement will meet with your satisfaction. (126 words)

> Concerning your 22 September letter, we cannot meet your request since the building is undergoing renovation and will not be ready for three months. We will, however, book an appointment for a student tour when renovations are complete. A brochure is enclosed for your information. (45 words)

The following passage contains 183 words, the summary version below it 67 words. Main points in the original have been italicized.

> *The great defect in Jack's personality was a strong aversion to work as he defined it.* It wasn't because he lacked ambition or goals in life, for he would sit in a bingo hall, with 10 or 20 bingo cards on the table in front of him, and *play for hours without a murmur,* even though he would *not be encouraged by a single win. He would stop by at the betting shop* during his rounds *every day,* even in the worst weather, *to place a few bets on horses that never seemed to win.* He would *never refuse to assist a drunk* who held his hand out for a few coins and was a *leader in community events,* such as organizing garage sales and fundraisers for the local school. *The local petty criminals,* too, *used to employ him to run their errands and to do odd jobs that their less obliging partners would not do* for them. In a word, Jack was *ready to take care of anybody's business but his own;* but as for *holding a job,* he found it *impossible.* (183 words)

> Jack disliked ordinary work. He would play bingo for hours without a win and bet on horses every day without much luck. However, he would never refuse to help a drunk and was always a leader in community events. He would do odd jobs for criminals that no one else wanted to do and helped everyone but himself, finding it impossible to do an honest day's work. (67 words)

EXERCISE 2

PRACTISING SUMMARY

1. Summarize each of the following paragraphs into no more than two sentences.

   a. Gossip is a message that is not factual. It is not acceptable to consider gossip as fact. There may be several reasons for gossip: mischief, misunderstanding, boredom, or inattention by the person who is passing on the gossip. On the other hand, gossip may be offered as fact because people are in a rush, are busy, or simply don't get the message straight.

   b. It seems as if busy people attract business. There is always more to do for the busy person and more responsibility to accept. It is important that a law clerk keep active and busy when not on the job. The more a person becomes involved with things outside of work, the more that person learns. At the same time, one should not neglect other important things in life such as family and friends.

   c. Every law clerk or legal assistant is faced with problems that need solving. He or she can take the easy way out by reporting each and every problem to the supervisor and then simply following instructions. A better idea, however, is to take some initiative and attempt to solve a problem before it has to be taken to a supervisor.

2. Select two of the readings from appendix B and summarize them.

3. Look in your local newspaper for opinion-based articles on legal issues. It will be especially informative to find articles that consider an issue from different points of view. Articles should be at least 300 words in length. Summarize the articles.

4. Summarize the article "By the Book," which appears on the following page. The original article is 935 words long.

> ### BY THE BOOK

Tara Schauerte

When people think of law, most think only of the work done by lawyers and judges and their related careers. Campus Starter took a closer look at a few of the many other professional careers associated with the administration of justice. While these careers may not be profiled in television courtroom dramas or legal thriller novels, they are just as essential for keeping the justice system running *by the book*.

In the Office

Public agencies, private law firms and corporations all seek the expertise of a variety of professionals in their legal departments. For example, law secretaries handle the firm's correspondence, law librarians provide supporting research for key cases and abstractors summarise pertinent legal or insurance details. Among the many careers at a law office is that of a paralegal (sometimes called a legal assistant) who assists lawyers with a range of administrative legal work.

Lynn Dechaine is a paralegal with the law firm of McLennan Ross, a large firm with over 50 lawyers and numerous support staff. As one of eight paralegals in a Litigation Support department, Lynn is charged with maintaining and organising large files, assembling briefing materials for the lawyers in the firm and preparing undertakings, transcripts, research and appeal books.

To get where she is today, Lynn obtained a Diploma from the Legal Assistant Program at Grant MacEwan College and worked for both a sole practising lawyer and in the legal department of a small software company before joining the firm. "Both positions gave me experience in the various administrative and legal procedures that I now use in my current job," says Lynn. "I also volunteered on various committees that gave me experience in dealing with many different people on one particular matter—a valuable asset now that I work in a larger firm."

"If you have an interest in law and are an organised person (organisation is a key quality in this field), and enjoy working in a very professional environment, then a job as a legal assistant or paralegal may just be the position for you," adds Lynn.

In Court

On the other side of the legal field, the court systems also offer a diverse range of employment opportunities beyond just judges and crown attorneys (the lawyers who prosecute cases). Bailiffs supervise prisoners and keep order in court, court stenographers record the proceedings and court clerks review and file the legal documents that arrive, and then act as an assistant to the judge.

One such court clerk is Rachel Yakimchuk with the Alberta Court of Queen's Bench. Her job as a court clerk is twofold. Part of her time is at a front counter in a team setting, helping the public and judiciary file legal documents correctly. These documents can include payments for fines and Rachel also helps individuals through the steps required to collect on or appeal their judgements. The second part of her job is in the court room—assisting the judge by opening court, swearing in witnesses and interpreters, reading the charge in criminal cases, handling the exhibits assisting the jury, monitoring digital recording equipment and keeping log notes.

Rachel started with a Bachelor of Arts (Criminology) from the University of Alberta and also worked for Campus Security while completing her degree. "Having experience in other areas of the justice system is not required but is a bonus in joining the court clerks—management also looks favourably on any experience in public service or community programs," says Rachel. "The fact that I came from a background in criminology definitely helped me because of its focus on the operation of the justice system. Also, my previous experience in law enforcement and community service with Campus Security was specifically mentioned to me as a reason for a higher pay scale."

"The best advice I could give if you're interested in this career is to speak to someone who works in the field. There are so many areas that use people with legal backgrounds that you never hear about. I would also suggest to think about the importance of a second language as any language abilities outside of English that staff can provide are always an asset."

On Campus

Research is another area within the field of law that is often overlooked but offers a wealth of opportunities individualized to your area of interest. Researchers studying in the fields of criminology, sociology, psychology and anthropology offer insight into criminal behaviour and corrections. They research trends and publish their findings, offer counselling services, make recommendations for changes within the justice system, provide expert testimony in cases before the courts and often also teach at university campuses. Dr. E. Andreas Tomaszewski, an Assistant Professor in the Department of Sociology, Anthropology and Criminology at Eastern Michigan University is an example of one such researcher. He specialises in topics such as Criminology, Deviance, Street Crime and White Collar & Corporate Crime—all with a focus on Canadian Studies.

While completing his Masters in Canadian Studies, Dr. Tomaszewski interned with the International Council for Canadian Studies (funded by the Department of Foreign Affairs) to study Canadian issues and wrote his thesis on "Rethinking Crime and Criminal Justice in Nunavut." This was soon followed by graduate research in Sociology at Carleton University on crime in public housing and led to the publication of refereed articles and a book. Dr. Tomaszewski then took a lecturer position at Ohio University for one year followed by a tenure-track position as an Assistant Professor at EMU. "Due to the university's location [Ypsilanti is near the border with Windsor, Ontario], I can take advantage of my expertise on Canadian issues and incorporate that in all of my classes, which students appear to appreciate," he says.

When asked for his advice for Canadian students interested in research, Dr. Tomaszewski recommended taking courses at your college or university like the ones he teaches—courses where your professor has a background in Canadian issues. "Also," he adds, "schools can help students get excellent internships that are extremely helpful in securing jobs after, and sometimes even before, graduation."

Source: Campus Starter, http://www.campusstarter.com.
Reprinted by permission of the EI Group.

▪ Writing a Paraphrase

The paraphrase and the summary are often thought to be the same. Both are summaries, but with a difference: the main point of the summary is to condense the basic concepts of a longer passage into a specific number of words. The summary is true to the meaning and tone of the original, but significantly reduced.

A paraphrase translates a written passage or discussion into simpler terms; it entails a more radical "rephrasing" or rewording of the original. It does not have to be true to the tone or mood of the original, and *it need not be reduced in length*, but it should offer the reader or listener a clearer understanding of the original. Paraphrasing is one of the methods of effective questioning mentioned in chapter 1 of this book.

When you are attempting to understand what someone is saying, you may use a paraphrase to show the speaker how you are interpreting what has been said. For example, if you ask a person for a telephone number, that person might say, "The number is 905-555-1111." Your response might be, "Did you say 905-555-1111?" The reply might be, "Yes, that's right."

If you state in your own way what another person has said, that person can determine whether or not the message has been getting through. If the speaker thinks that you have misunderstood the message, the parts that seem to be causing difficulty can be reworded or repeated.

Paraphrasing has two additional benefits: it lets the other person know that you are interested in what has been said; and, since you appear to be interested in the other person's views, your own views may also be more readily accepted.

Keep in mind that paraphrasing is not merely a rearranging of words; it is an attempt to reach understanding. The following example shows how a cursory attempt at paraphrasing may produce no further understanding.

JOAN: John should train to become a law clerk.

SANJIT: You mean the legal field is the right career for him?

JOAN: Exactly! The legal field is the right career for him.

There is no understanding achieved in this exchange. Compare it with the following example, where the speakers obtain, through paraphrase, a higher level of understanding.

JOAN: John should have become a law clerk.

SANJIT: Do you mean his skills are suited for the job?

JOAN: I mean that he's interested in the law, he works well in an office environment, and he's very good at detail work.

SANJIT: Oh, I see. He should have gone into a career where he can enjoy what he's doing.

JOAN: Exactly. Being a law clerk is the career for him.

Keep in mind that the paraphrase is not an exercise in mind reading. As the receiver of a message, you're repeating what the message means to *you* in order to establish the speaker's intended meaning.

METHODS OF PARAPHRASING

There are several ways of paraphrasing successfully:

1. Use the speaker's own words in your restatement.

    ORIGINAL: "I hate paperwork!"

    PARAPHRASE: "You say you hate paperwork?"

2. Restate the speaker's words in your own words.

    ORIGINAL: "I hate paperwork!"

    PARAPHRASE: "You have some really negative feelings about paperwork."

3. Talk about an experience of your own that is similar to the speaker's. This self-reference is designed to show the speaker that you understand, not to switch the focus to your own concerns.

    ORIGINAL: "I hate paperwork!"

    RESPONSE: "I know what you mean. When I used to do a lot of paperwork, I had trouble keeping everything straight, and I always seemed to be confused."

4. Identify the underlying implications of the message. This might lead to a deeper understanding of the speaker's message.

    ORIGINAL: "I hate paperwork!"

    RESPONSE: "Are you concerned that you won't be able to do your job properly?"

Since the function of paraphrase is to explain what someone has said and to demonstrate that you understand the speaker's or writer's message, it is important to check that your interpretation is correct.

EXERCISE 3

PARAPHRASING

Working in groups of three, select a legal topic, and ask the members of your group their opinion on that topic. Paraphrase what the other people have said in an attempt to reach understanding.

BIAS IN REPORTING

You're likely aware by now that not everyone agrees with everyone else all the time. In fact, you can have as many different points of view as there are topics to discuss. Most people have a particular point of view because they are biased about certain things or have strong opinions that can't be easily changed.

A bias does not necessarily involve a prejudice. The statement "I don't like people with brown hair" expresses a prejudice, defined as an unfavourable opinion or feeling, formed beforehand without knowledge, thought, or reason. A bias, on the other hand, can be favourable or unfavourable, but it indicates a strong opinion one way or the other, often based on experience.

The following example, taken from a local newspaper, shows two opposite biases on a single subject: dogs running free in local parks.

> Dear Editor:
>
> There are too many dogs running free in local parks while their owners just stand there and watch. This is against the law. Parks are for people. The bylaw states quite clearly that dogs are supposed to be on leashes, and people are supposed to "stoop and scoop" when dogs leave their droppings. Just the other day, I stepped in a pile of droppings that some ignorant owner didn't bother to pick up. Enforce the law! Leash your dogs, or lose them.
>
> —An unhappy taxpayer

———

> Dear Editor:
>
> Why can't parks be leash-free? Most dog owners, like parents of children, are very responsible and take care of their pets, picking up after them and keeping them under control. The animal shelter sells us stray and unwanted pets, but doesn't give us a place to exercise them. Then, Animal Control comes around to the parks and issues tickets to owners of dogs not on leashes. How hypocritical! We're taxpayers too. Give us a place to exercise our pets. Parks are for everyone, including dog owners.
>
> —An unhappy taxpayer

Both letter writers are unhappy taxpayers, but each looks at the issue of dogs in parks from a different point of view. Both are biased: the first writer wants dogs leashed, while the second writer doesn't. Who is right? I guess it depends on whether you own a dog, and whether you decide to obey local bylaws.

EXERCISE 4

UNDERSTANDING BIAS

Other than the leash law mentioned above, there are numerous bylaws that cause controversy. Research some of your local bylaws and try to imagine the biases that might result from their enforcement or their neglect. What might be the reasons for the different points of view?

Bias in the media goes beyond letter writing by readers; it is seen in many newspaper and magazine articles and reports. If you look at the Readings section of this book (appendix B), you'll find articles that contain bias: "Pleading Case for Reform of Legal Aid System" and Susan Clairmont's "Some Day, Victims Won't Fear Us." The first article, from the Canadian Press, contains its thesis in the title; it is a plea to change the legal aid system. The article begins with a vision of the future, where public defenders would be used in place of current legal aid lawyers. There is a bias against the present system because it is difficult to find lawyers who will take legal aid cases; the rates paid to lawyers haven't changed in 15 years, and don't even cover their overheads.

The article seems somewhat biased against lawyers, who can't make ends meet at between $70 and $80 hourly and who went on strike for a pay raise, with judges supporting lawyers' calls for a pay raise of up to $140 hourly. That seems to be a great deal of money, especially to a person who needs legal services but can't pay for them because of their high cost.

The alternative might be a public-defender type of lawyer with his or her own office, staff, and a salary from the government. This would prevent any problem with legal fees and would likely result in higher client satisfaction with the system.

However, there are critics of this vision. These critics say that the public-defender system would not allow representation by independent counsel, and that the attorney general would have direct control of the legal aid system. The system in the United States is cited as a precautionary example. There, public-defender programs are funded unevenly, and lawyers may spend a maximum of three minutes with a client before going to court. By dealing with the American system at some length, the article reveals an understanding of the bias against this model.

Nonetheless, the article's deeper bias is in favour of the public-defender system, and the reader comes away with the impression that, while imperfect, this system will be advantageous for Canadian clients who choose to use it. If nothing else, potential clients can at least count on some form of representation.

Susan Clairmont's article "Some Day, Victims Won't Fear Us" has the unusual twist of being written by a reporter who is reporting on a criticism of the media, and who appears to agree with the accusers. The article begins by referring to a woman who, after being sexually assaulted, told police that she was more afraid of the media than of the man who assaulted her. This statement appears in the second sentence of the article, and immediately turns the reader against the media. The focus of the article is "Jane Doe" of Ontario, victim of a 1986 sexual assault who became famous, subsequently, for successfully suing the police for negligence. Clairmont also describes a New York woman who was assaulted 14 years ago and only now feels that she can use her real name, rather than "the Central Park jogger."

The reader is made to feel sorry for the Canadian Jane Doe, not only because she was sexually assaulted, but also because she has to remain anonymous. Jane Doe is afraid of the media because she thinks that society has not reached a level of understanding that would allow the victim to be both herself and a rape victim. It is not "dignified" for a woman to be a rape victim. People question her character, her morals, and her actions. The victim fears that the newspaper will find out who she is and publish her name. The victim has to remain nameless.

The author concludes by saying that her newspaper does not publish victims' names without their permission. Nonetheless, the story shows a bias against the media and against society in general. The article makes us deplore the plight of rape victims, who, because society stigmatizes them, are afraid to reveal their identities.

Writing a Summary and Bias Essay

The summary and bias essay combines summary writing and essay writing. If you are asked to write an essay that summarizes an article and points out the bias in that article, write your introduction as you would any summary, putting the content of the article in your own words. Be sure to point out the thesis and topic of the article, and be sure that you clearly convey the article's bias. Refer to chapter 4 to remind yourself of the characteristics of a paragraph. Emphasize in your support-ing paragraphs the ways in which the author supports his or her bias and draws conclusions. You can provide your own conclusion, pointing out whether or not the bias was effectively presented, where it fell short, and whether your opinion on the topic was changed by the article.

EXERCISE 5

SUMMARIZING AND COMPARING

1. Look in your library for newspaper or magazine articles that contain opposing points of view on the same topic. For instance, there have been many recent articles supporting the new *Youth Criminal Justice Act* and just as many stating that the new Act lets young offenders off too easily. There are many such articles in the media about a wide range of legal topics.

   Write an essay comparing and contrasting two articles that take opposite points of view on the same issue. In your opening paragraph, state the theses put forward by the opposing authors. Next, either in block form or point-by-point form, summarize the contents of these two articles, pointing out the bias in each and citing the examples each provides. Finally, write a concluding paragraph telling which article was more effective and why.

   The length of your essay will be determined by the length of the articles you use. You must follow the rules of summary writing: each summary should be about one-third of the article's original length. Your articles must be opinion-based, not report-based (there's not much bias in a brief newspaper article reporting the latest fender bender), and should be at least three hundred words.

2. Write an essay on a legal topic about which you feel strongly. Research the topic to gather whatever facts you need. Point out your bias and the reasons for your bias. Remember, it's your opinion that counts, but you must back up your opinion with facts.

■ Summary

The ability to summarize and paraphrase is an effective communication tool for the law clerk or legal assistant. In summaries, you put other people's words, substan-tially reduced, into your own words while retaining the meaning of the original. When paraphrasing, you demonstrate your understanding of a speaker's or writer's meaning. In most newspaper or popular magazine articles, authors reveal a particu-lar point of view, or bias, on a topic. Facts supporting this bias are used to persuade the reader of the author's point of view.

SPELLING AND DEFINITIONS

Be able to spell and define the following words:

barrister	emotional	preamble	statutory
citation	housekeeping	process	subordinate
colleagues	immediately	prosecutor	traumatic
complainant	impediment	proximity	vandalism
compromise	lenient	regulation	vindicate
controversial	minority	reputed	
corporation	nuisance	secretary	
desperate	overrule	solicitor	

CHAPTER 6
Speaking Effectively

Learning Objectives

After reading this chapter, you should be able to

- Speak effectively in front of an audience.
- Select a topic for an oral presentation.
- Organize an oral presentation.
- Understand the mechanics of oral presentations.
- Handle question-and-answer periods.
- Avoid nervousness and distracting gestures.
- Use audiovisual aids to enhance presentations.
- Understand non-verbal communication methods.
- Use influential language.
- Understand the S.I.R. method of impromptu speaking.

▪ Introduction

In order to be effective communicators, law clerks and legal assistants must understand and practise oral communications skills. Whether you are interviewing clients, speaking with colleagues and superiors in your firm, or dealing with difficult clients, effective speaking skills will enhance your effectiveness in the legal field. One way to improve oral communications skills is to prepare and deliver an oral presentation. Many of the skills that you learn and refine by giving oral presentations can be used in all communications situations, personal as well as professional. You should also learn about non-verbal communication skills, so that you can use them yourself and recognize their use by others.

Have you ever noticed that whenever certain people speak, no matter what they say, it hardly seems worth the effort to listen? Other people speak with such authority that whatever they say seems to be worth listening to. Speaking in such a way as to be heard, to be influential, and to be an object of respect depends on three factors:

1. your words

2. your delivery and tone

3. your appearance.

In other words, your message is made up of what you say, how you say it, and how you look when you say it. For a spoken message to be effective, all three must concur. Learning to prepare an oral presentation will help you develop skills that will be of permanent value in your professional and personal life.

Effective Oral Presentations

PURPOSE

An effective oral presentation can enable you to sway a group of people toward your point of view or merely to inform people about something that you think is important. You must ask yourself what you are trying to accomplish through any particular oral presentation. Initially, of course, you are attempting to obtain a good grade from your instructor. However, beyond this, you must decide whether you are trying to inform (through exposition), to persuade, or to tell a story (through narration). Decide on the subject of your presentation, and ask yourself what you expect from your audience after your presentation.

For example, do you want your audience to

- recognize the role of the law clerk,

- realize the complexity of the legal profession,

- understand the nature of real estate transactions, or

- be in favour of hiring additional legal assistants in your firm?

Whatever your purpose, select and develop a topic that suits your interests and those of your audience.

SELECTING A TOPIC

You may be in a position to select a topic that is of particular interest to you, or you may be assigned a topic by your instructor. Selecting your own topic can become one of the most difficult parts of the oral presentation. It is not easy to come up with a topic that is both interesting and manageable in the time allotted for your presentation. If you have the freedom to select your own topic, there are a few guidelines that might be useful:

1. Draw on your own interests, experiences, and opinions.

2. Consider your audience.

3. Select a topic that is timely and of which your audience might already be aware.

A student who is interested in the legal field and is giving a presentation to a class of legal assistants has a wide range of topics to draw from that meet the criteria outlined above. Look in your local newspaper for ideas: stories relating to the field of law are usually well covered. There are a number of readings in the appendix to this book that might help get you started. If a topic is covered in the local newspaper, it is usually timely and of sufficient importance that most of your audience will be aware of it.

EXERCISE 1

ORAL PRESENTATION: STARTING RESEARCH

In your school library, look in local and national newspapers and find between five and ten stories likely to interest people in the legal profession. List the titles of these articles and briefly summarize them. Be sure that each summary contains the article's thesis and main supporting points. For each article, determine the following:

1. Who is the intended audience for the article?

2. What do you yourself know about the topic covered in the article?

3. Do you hold any strong opinions about the topic?

4. What more would you like to know about the topic?

5. How would you obtain additional information about the topic?

NARROWING THE TOPIC

Once you have selected a topic, you don't just start writing out your presentation. Now is the time to give even more thought to your topic and your presentation. Consider the following matters:

1. How much time is available for your presentation?

2. How many ideas can you cover in that time?

3. What are the most important parts of the topic, and how many of them can be covered in the given time?

4. Which ideas will be of most interest to your audience?

EXERCISE 2

ORAL PRESENTATION: GATHERING INFORMATION

Using the articles you have selected for Exercise 1, choose the one that you feel would be most interesting to an audience of legal professionals. Assume that you have been assigned a five-minute oral presentation on the topic covered in this article. Within the time allotted to prepare your presentation, determine the following:

1. What is the purpose of your presentation (e.g., to inform, to teach, to entertain)?

2. What points to support your purpose can you cover within the allotted time? (Assume that the average speaker can deliver between 115 and 120 words per minute.)

3. What are some secondary issues you might want to cover—are there issues related to the main topic that would help your audience understand your main point?

4. How much research on the topic will you need to do in order to make an effective presentation?

5. What is a thesis statement that effectively defines the purpose of your presentation?

6. What is an appropriate title for your presentation?

RESEARCH

Having decided on your topic, you must begin researching it, compiling as much information as you can within the time you have. Summarize any information you find, noting the main points found in your sources. Be sure to keep a full bibliographic record of each source so that you can find the source again if necessary. You may find it useful to record the following information on notecards:

1. a full citation of your source

2. a summary of the article's contents

3. the main ideas in the article

4. any direct quotations you'll be using

5. a paraphrased version of the ideas you'll be using

6. any additional references, indicated in your source, that might provide you with further information about your topic.

This research method will likely require more than one card for each source, but you can organize the cards by putting the name of the source, along with the category of information, at the top of each card, as shown here:

```
Jones, Source                                        Card 1

Summary




Main points
```

```
Jones, Direct Quotations                             Card 2
p. 3
p. 13
p. 16
```

```
Jones, Ideas                                         Card 3
p. 12
p. 34
p. 123
```

Cite evidence accurately; avoid distorting data or taking it out of context. Credit your source for any information and ideas you've used, even when you have paraphrased the material. Edit your cards, eliminating unnecessary material or material that won't fit into your allotted time.

PREPARATION

An oral presentation must be prepared, and prepared well. In this way, it is like any of the written material discussed in this book. Whether speaking to a colleague about a matter relating to your law firm, or making a presentation to a superior, or composing a classroom presentation, you must be prepared. Some things to remember when preparing your oral presentation are set out below.

1. *Prepare an outline.* Include a topic and thesis statement, as you would for an essay or a paragraph. The topic is what you are speaking about, the thesis statement is your point of view, usually expressed at the beginning of your discussion.

2. *List your main points.*

3. *Revise your list.* Review your points, and omit those that are unnecessary.

4. *Arrange your remaining points in logical order.* Use the procedure you would use for writing an essay.

5. *Write your opening sentence.*

6. *Write your introduction and conclusion.*

7. *Prepare your final draft.* Do not write it out or memorize it. Put your main points on cue cards, as well as your topic, thesis, opening sentence, and conclusion. You should know your topic well enough that you need the cue cards only to jog your memory. If you have audiovisual material, you should indicate on the cue cards where the audiovisual material is to be used.

There are various strategies for beginning an oral presentation. Some of the more common ones are as follows:

- Tell a story or an anecdote.

  My only previous contact with the legal system occurred when I was finishing high school. I was arrested on my graduation night. A couple of friends insisted that we go out for a few drinks. No sooner had I sat down in the local pub and had a few sips of beer than an undercover police officer came up and asked me for identification. I was taken to the police station. After what I saw that night, I resolved to do what I could to help those who can't afford legal assistance. I saw a lot of unfortunate people that night.

- Read a quotation.

  As I read in a recent newspaper report, "Judges in this country never cease to amaze me." I have the greatest respect for the Canadian judicial system and for the people who sit behind the bench. However, I want to tell you about some questionable, and humorous, decisions that have recently been reached in our courts.

- Use a gimmick.

  I'm holding in this plastic bag a small amount of marijuana—no, it's not really marijuana, just some common grass clippings from my front lawn. Look at how small the amount of grass is in this bag. If it was marijuana, and I was caught, I'd be risking a jail term. Our marijuana possession laws have to change.

- Reveal an interesting fact.

  The legal aid system is in turmoil. Too few lawyers want to take legal aid cases, because it is too expensive for them within the legal aid guidelines legislated by the province. At the same time, the number of people needing legal aid is exploding, and the system is not able to handle these people.

- Relate a new fact about the subject.

  The federal Cabinet will be looking at new legislation that would give police and security agencies the right to intercept personal e-mails and text messages, and monitor password-secure websites without explicit court approval.

The conclusion of an oral presentation, like the introduction, may be approached in various ways, but try to ensure that you accomplish the following:

- Restate your main topic.

  As I said at the beginning of this discussion, the legal aid system is in turmoil, and I have pointed out only a few examples to prove my point.

- Summarize your main points.

  Law clerk and legal assistant programs are now found in almost every provincial community college, as well as in private training institutions. The need to coordinate these programs becomes essential if students are to graduate with acceptable minimum requirements acknowledged by all law firms. Possibly the provincial government should step in.

- End with whatever method you used to begin.

  So, I guess the only thing I'll be holding in this little plastic bag is my grass clippings—at least until the law changes. I don't want to go to jail.

- Leave the audience with a challenge.

  As citizens of this country, we must stand up and speak out against this contemplated invasion of our privacy.

- Set an example for the audience to follow.

  Talk is cheap. Here's what I intend to do.

EXERCISE 3

ORAL PRESENTATION: MAKING AN OUTLINE

Prepare an outline that is appropriate for the topic you have selected. In point form, list the following:

1. topic,

2. thesis,

3. method of beginning (e.g., anecdote, interesting fact), and

4. the main points you wish to cover.

After creating this broad outline, list any subpoints you wish to cover.

ORGANIZATION

Many experts recommend a three-step method of organizing an oral presentation:

1. Tell the audience what you're going to say.

2. Say what you have to say.

3. Tell the audience what you've said.

These steps can be expanded into the Six Ps of public speaking:

1. *Preface.* What in your background qualifies you to speak on the chosen topic?

2. *Position.* What is your thesis—the position you take on the topic?

3. *Problem.* Define the problem and give some background to the topic, including relevant issues and any terminology that the audience might need to know.

4. *Possibilities.* Be sure to explore all sides of the issue, and be respectful toward points of view different from your own.

5. *Proposal.* Once you've explored an issue, suggest some possible solutions. Are all solutions workable?

6. *Postscript.* Restate the issue you've discussed, pointing out that you have proven something, solved a dilemma, or in some other way accomplished what you set out to do in your introduction.

A presentation that lasts from 5 to 10 minutes can easily be organized along these lines.

EXERCISE 4

ORGANIZING AN ORAL PRESENTATION

Using the principles of organizing an oral presentation, prepare an outline for one of the following topics:

- smokers' (or non-smokers') rights,
- cats make better (or worse) pets than dogs,
- students should have longer (or shorter) weekends, or
- conjugal visits should (or should not) be allowed in prisons.

Write a sentence for each of the Six Ps.

MECHANICS

When the organizational part of your oral presentation is complete, you should begin working on the mechanics of it, including the following:

1. *Volume.* Speak to people at the back of the room. If they can hear you, everyone can hear you.

2. *Rate.* People speak at the rate of 115 to 120 words a minute. Practise this. Nervous speakers speak too quickly.

3. *Pause.* Pause between main ideas, and even slightly after sentences. This will give your audience time to consider what you've said.

4. *Stance.* Don't slouch; project confidence. If you use a lectern, stand behind it with your hands to either side of the lectern; don't lean on it for support. If you don't use a lectern, keep your hands out of your pockets, and do not jiggle your change. Use your hands to express yourself. If you can't think of anything else to do with your hands, leave them at your sides.

5. *Personality.* Be sincere, and smile. Show your audience that you care about the topic you're presenting.

> **DO'S AND DON'TS**

1. Give your audience what it wants to hear: be relevant.

2. Know your audience.

3. Realize that humour can work for or against you.

4. Dress appropriately.

5. Don't read your presentation.

6. Don't exceed your time limit.

7. Use visual aids.

8. Rehearse.

9. Be aware of the level of your vocabulary.

ANSWERING QUESTIONS

You may have a question-and-answer period after your presentation to allow your audience to gain additional information about your topic. Prepare for this beforehand, during the planning phase, by anticipating any questions that might be asked. Know your topic well enough that you can expand on certain points if asked. Prepare potential answers ahead of time.

There are three common categories of questions that might be asked:

1. *Open.* Open questions ask for your opinion about something.

2. *Closed.* Closed questions require a specific "yes" or "no" answer.

3. *Clarification.* Questions seeking clarification invite you to expand on a point.

Here are some general guidelines for responding to all these kinds of questions:

1. *Listen and respond.* Listen to the entire question, and think before you answer. Be objective in your response.

2. *Restate and respond.* Restate the question to the person who asked it, thereby gaining for yourself time to think. Restating the question also ensures that you have understood it.

3. *Categorize and respond.* Be aware of the category of the question, and respond accordingly. Don't give an opinion if a factual answer is requested.

4. *Retain your point of view.* Don't change your point of view from the position you adopted in your presentation.

If you don't know the answer to a question, admit it. You can ask your audience for help, or refer the questioner to a source where the answer may be found, but don't try to fake an answer. This ruins the effectiveness of your presentation.

NERVOUSNESS

Many people are nervous about speaking in front of an audience, but there are ways to overcome this anxiety:

1. *Observe others.* Watch other speakers and pick up on their strengths.

2. *Lower your blood pressure.* Run cold water over your wrists before you begin your presentation; this lowers your blood pressure.

3. *Try to relax.* Loosen tense muscles through stretching and self-massage.

4. *Move your body.* Relax by moving your body unhurriedly and deliberately when you present.

5. *Suck on a candy.* Suck on a small, hard candy before your presentation; this eliminates a dry mouth.

6. *Breathe.* Take deep, regular breaths.

EXERCISE 5

EXPLORING PHOBIA

Fear of speaking in front of an audience is a common phobia. What is a phobia, and why do so many people have this particular phobia? Suggest some ways, apart from the techniques described above, that people might overcome their fear of public speaking.

VISUAL AIDS

Visual aids, when used effectively, can enhance any presentation. There are a few things that must be kept in mind, however, when considering the use of visual aids.

1. *Use visuals to clarify or enhance.* Visual aids should be used judiciously. They should not be used excessively or without a specific reason.

2. *Keep visuals simple.* You don't want to give your audience so much information visually that they're too distracted to listen to your words.

3. *Make visuals large.* Visuals should be large and visible enough that all members of your audience can see them.

4. *Provide time to absorb the visuals.* After displaying a visual, give the audience a moment to absorb the information before you paraphrase it and incorporate it into your presentation.

5. *Practise using visuals.* Don't ignore your visuals when you practise your presentation. Be sure they go where they're supposed to go and work when they're supposed to work.

Visual aids help an audience to understand your presentation and to remember what you have said. It is important that you use appropriate visuals for your presentation. Each kind of visual has particular advantages.

1. *Overhead transparencies.* Overhead transparencies are the most common type of visual. They are easy to prepare and use, and they allow the speaker to maintain contact with the audience during the presentation.

2. *Computerized visuals.* Computerized visuals, such as PowerPoint, have become widely used. They create professional results, can offer sound, movement, and colour, and can be used with a television or computer monitor. Slides and transparencies can be created with the computer. Most computerized visuals are easy to use and inexpensive.

3. *Flip charts.* Flip charts are becoming old-fashioned, but they are easy to prepare and use, are portable, and allow the speaker freedom to create new visuals while the presentation is in progress.

4. *Videos.* Videos can be effective if they are properly prepared in advance. It is very distracting to have to search for the right spot in a video during a presentation, or to find an alternative if the equipment isn't available. Your firm may have in-house training videos that you can use. There are many movies about legal situations.

5. *Slides.* Slides are old standbys, but they need a darkened room, a projector, and a great deal of preparation. There are costs involved if the slides need to be created.

6. *Handouts.* Handouts are still common in presentations, and can be as effective as other visuals. The audience often likes these souvenirs, and they do help retention, but you have to avoid having your audience focus on them rather than on what you are saying. Provide handouts *after* you've made your points.

EXERCISE 6

SPEAKING SKILLS FOR LAW CLERKS AND LEGAL ASSISTANTS

1. As a class, discuss ways in which effective oral presentation skills are valuable to law clerks and legal assistants. Be specific: what situations can law clerks and legal assistants encounter where effective oral communications skills are valuable?

2. Research a software program used in legal offices, and report back to your class on how this software program has increased efficiency in the office, has made the job of the law clerk or legal assistant easier, and, in general, has been a benefit to those people using it.

Non-Verbal Communication

"Actions speak louder than words." This statement is certainly true in oral communication. The use of body language reveals a great deal about both the communicator and the person receiving the communication. Understanding non-verbal communication is essential for effective communication and, in many cases, for discovering the truth.

Approximately 65 percent of our face-to-face communication is non-verbal; many of our messages are transmitted through facial expressions, gestures, eye movements, and tone of voice. Many speakers are unaware of the non-verbal dimensions of their communications, and therefore send unintended messages. Frequently glancing at the clock while a client is speaking, for example, is clearly sending the message that you're impatient or bored or that you consider the speaker's words to be unimportant.

Non-verbal communication can be divided into *visual* elements and *vocal* elements.

VISUAL ELEMENTS

Eye Contact

People who fail to make or fail to maintain effective eye contact are not good communicators. They give the impression of being embarrassed, nervous, at a loss for words. Maintaining eye contact allows a law clerk or legal assistant to send the message that they are honest and concerned about the client. When meeting a client for the first time, for example, maintaining eye contact (without staring) allows the legal professional to send the message that the client is welcome, and that the client's needs are of prime importance. Be aware of cultural differences in non-verbal communication. In most Western cultures, eye contact indicates a desire to communicate and an interest in what is being said. In other cultures, eye contact may be seen as aggressive and disrespectful, and in some cases intimidating.

Facial Expression

Your facial expression, which is the key to non-verbal communication, must match your message in order for you to be taken seriously. Scowling throughout your oral presentation will give the impression that you want to be anywhere else but in front of the class. And a sea of bored faces in a classroom sends an effective message to the teacher regardless of the verbal communication taking place.

Gestures and Posture

Using your hands during an oral presentation can be very effective. On the other hand, your gestures and posture can seriously detract from your message. Fidgeting, nervous hand gestures, shuffling from foot to foot: all of these gestures may be clues that a person is nervous. Exaggerated hand gestures, extreme body movements, or stabbing with the fingers to make a point often indicates a lack of confidence on the part of the speaker.

In one-on-one communications, the use of the hands can send mixed signals. A firm handshake, for instance, can be seen as an appropriate gesture of greeting, but in some cultures—people from the Middle East or parts of Asia, for example—a firm handshake is seen as aggressive. Some Eastern cultures consider bowing, rather than handshaking, an appropriate form of greeting.

Body Orientation

The position in which a person places his or her body during a conversation tells a great deal about that person's approach to the situation. If a person faces you head-on, with squared shoulders and feet, you may gather that the speaker is being aggressive and confrontational.

It's best to position yourself at a slight angle to the client, suggesting both safety and openness. To convey your interest, lean slightly forward when the client is speaking. It is always a good idea to avoid sitting behind a desk when interviewing a client. The desk constitutes a barrier, and inhibits openness by suggesting that the person behind the desk is in a superior position.

Manner of Dress

How we dress sends a message about our professional and social standing. Well-groomed, well-dressed people convey a sense of professionalism and responsibility; they give the impression of taking their positions seriously.

VOCAL ELEMENTS

Loudness

Using a loud voice can indicate that you have control over a situation, but it can also convey the wrong message. A loud voice can indicate aggression toward the other party, and it may elicit a loud voice in response.

"Please speak louder," said in a firm, normal speaking voice asks for cooperation. Shouting "speak louder!" might indicate that you're looking for, and in fact require, an aggressive response. The use of the word *please* is a request for cooperation. The effect of emphasizing certain words in a spoken sentence is discussed below.

Rate

Speaking quickly indicates nervousness. If you speak quickly, the other person may not understand you. Combine speaking quickly with a loud voice and aggressive tone and body language, and you have a potential confrontation.

Emphasis

The emphasis you put on certain words in a sentence can give that sentence completely different meanings.

> "*Are* you sure of your facts?" (You don't sound like you're sure)
> "Are you *sure* of your facts?" (It sounds like hearsay)

EXERCISE 7

PRACTISING VERBAL AND NON-VERBAL COMMUNICATION

Role-play in a number of different situations involving both verbal and non-verbal communication. Assume that you are a law clerk and that you have to deal with each of the following:

- a colleague who wants you to take on an extra file that is not your responsibility,

- a lawyer who wants you to come in on your week off,

- a witness you are interviewing who is not sure of his facts, and

- someone in the office who likes to gossip.

Have someone in your class play the role of the person you have to deal with in each of the above situations. Ask questions of this person, while that person responds using different types of verbal and non-verbal communication. Discuss your responses to the different communication styles.

SPATIAL ELEMENTS

Most people "need their own space"—that area surrounding a person that others aren't allowed to enter or are allowed to enter only under certain circumstances. Someone who "gets in your face" is aggressively asserting himself or herself. There are different types of space or distance.

1. *Personal distance.* Usually between 1½ and 4 feet (roughly ½ to 1¼ metres) from one's body, this "arm's-length" distance is where we allow friends and acquaintances. It is not an intimate distance.

2. *Social distance.* Usually between 4 and 12 feet (roughly 1¼ to 3½ metres) from one's body, this is the distance at which most of our social interactions occur.

3. *Public distance.* Usually 12 feet (roughly 3½ metres) or more, this is the preferred distance for meetings, classroom teaching, and interviews.

Cultural differences are a factor in personal space preferences. Where North Americans usually prefer to communicate at arm's length, people from Asian cultures prefer a greater distance. On the other hand, some cultures from the Middle East or Latin America traditionally communicate at much closer quarters, in some cases toe to toe. When speaking to a client, try to establish a distance that is comfortable for both of you.

Impromptu Speaking: Say What You Mean, S.I.R.

Let's say your lawyer requests a report for an upcoming client meeting, but you don't have it ready yet. Don't succumb to the stress of the moment and offer excuses in a hesitant or garbled manner. Instead, muster your resources, collect your thoughts, and offer an organized, cohesive response. In other words, follow a simple formula whose initials form the acronym *S.I.R.* The letters stand for *statement—information— restatement.*

According to the S.I.R. principle, you would answer the lawyer as follows:

1. *Statement:* "I can't complete the report on the Acme sale transaction, because I'm still waiting for some information."

2. *Information:* (a) "The client has not submitted its royalty figures." (b) "There were errors in the financial statement and I'm waiting for the corrections." (c) "I'm waiting for clarification of the royalty calculation formula."

3. *Restatement:* "Although I still expect to complete the report in time for your meeting with the client, I wanted you to know why it's not ready for your approval yet."

The impression this message creates is of an organized, well-thought-out position. A closer look at the structure of the message reveals the following:

1. Your initial *statement* is your basic position. Take a moment to decide on this main point, then express it simply and clearly.

2. The *information* comes next. One of the key factors in this formula is the provision of three pieces of information. Human beings like things expressed in threes. So, figure out a way to follow your initial statement with three statements of information. You may have more than one sentence for each, but you should clearly enumerate the three points.

3. When you make your *restatement*, take the opportunity to add something. In our example, the lawyer is reassured that the report will be ready. In this way it sounds as if the situation is under control.

The ability to think on your feet and convey a message succinctly with little or no preparation is a highly regarded skill, and one worth cultivating for the sake of your career.

EXERCISE 8

IMPROMPTU SPEAKING

1. Use the S.I.R. method to answer the following questions:

    a. Why were you late for work today?

    b. You didn't return my call. Were you ill?

    c. Where have you been? I've been trying to phone you all morning.

2. Work with a classmate to perfect the S.I.R. technique. Throw questions at each other concerning a variety of topics, and work on coming up with appropriate answers, giving three pieces of information with every answer.

■ A Last Word about Oral Presentations: Don't Read

It is one thing to review a cue card for directions; it is fine to glance down and check a statistic; it is even acceptable to read out a quotation you've copied from your notes. However, it is not acceptable to read a report and pretend that it is an oral presentation. Without eye contact, gesture, and enthusiasm, without visuals and audience involvement, there is no oral presentation—only a reading. Watching someone read is a miserable experience. When someone stands up and reads a presentation, the audience becomes distracted and loses interest. In other words, *the presentation is a failure.* Do not read your report!

Don't read. Don't read.

■ Workplace Communication

Among the challenges you will face as a law clerk or legal assistant is that of having to deal with difficult people and with people severely stressed at finding themselves in a legal situation—facing a lawsuit, for example. Another challenge is that of making an oral presentation to your peers.

DEALING WITH A DIFFICULT CLIENT

In any situation that's confrontational or challenging, the most important thing you can do is be professional. Remember that you are dealing with an emotional person and that your best approach is to try to defuse the emotion and bring the conversation back to a practical level.

There are numerous ways of accomplishing this, many of which have been discussed in chapter 1 under the heading "Nine Rules for Lively Listening." Keep the following in mind:

1. Adjust the behaviour. Clients are emotional or difficult for a reason— they may be angry or fearful; they may feel threatened, or feel that they have been used unjustly. Instead of responding to the emotion, attempt to determine what is making the client difficult or emotional, and then try to remove whatever is triggering that reaction. In other words, try to perceive and acknowledge what is at the root of the client's behaviour, and then use the principles of active listening to adjust the behaviour.

2. Be tolerant. The client's difficult attitude is entirely justified as far as he or she is concerned. Perhaps this attitude has helped the client deal with problems in the past. A client's defensive attitude, for instance, may stem from past experiences of having to ward off outside interference. You are seen as an outsider, even though you are there to help. The client is conscious of the fact that you will get paid or keep your job whether the client goes to prison or goes bankrupt.

3. Reward non-defensive behaviour on your client's part by mirroring it when it occurs; keep the pace of your conversation slow, do not exhibit negative non-verbal communication, listen sympathetically, and bring a calming manner to the situation.

4. Show that you are on the client's side and want to help by using phrases such as "I see what you mean," "I understand what you are saying," or "I think that I can help you." But don't make promises that you can't keep.

5. Give your clients options and let them make decisions that will allow them to feel in control of their own lives. Clients often react negatively to the feeling that their lives are in the hands of a lawyer or legal professional.

6. Reassure the client with empathetic statements like the following: "After all you've been through, I can understand why you're angry."

7. Don't label your client by saying things like the following: "Everyone who is in financial trouble has to fill out these forms." It is embarrassing for the client to be categorized this way.

8. If your client is abusive or non-responsive, respond with verbal and non-verbal attention, and encourage any part of the client's conversation that is appropriate and constructive. Avoid resistance. The following exchange shows a legal assistant responding appropriately to an angry client:

CLIENT: All you ever do is talk! I'm about to lose everything and all you can do is talk!

LEGAL ASSISTANT: I do talk a lot.

CLIENT: If you were paying attention to what I've been saying, you might have some answers for me. That's what I'm paying you for!

LEGAL ASSISTANT: That may be true. I could be paying more attention.

CLIENT: You're just like all of the other people in these lawyer's offices. You take my money and use a lot of language that I don't understand, and I still have to face the consequences!

LEGAL ASSISTANT: So far there are no consequences. I talk a lot and ask questions because I'm trying to find the best way to help you.

In her book *Impact: A Guide to Business Communication*, Margot Northey discusses ways to deal with aggressive behaviour:

Sometimes emotions run high and, if left unchecked, they can create hostility. You can help by encouraging participants to stick to the facts, so that their comments don't become a personal attack … . Try to remain neutral rather than taking sides … . Create a constructive atmosphere where ideas are built up and developed.

In the end, you can maintain your professionalism by simply following good listening habits, responding when appropriate, and offering constructive advice when emotions have subsided.

CONFERENCING WITH PEERS

Small conferences and workshops and discussions with your peers must be structured in much the same way as formal presentations. A presentation to our peers is more than a conversation, and the fact that you might be seated does not allow you to be offhand or casual. Your approach should be based on the following questions:

1. What is the purpose of your presentation?
2. Who is the audience, and how much do they know about your topic?
3. How much time will be allotted to your talk?
4. Will there be a question period?
5. Are other speakers involved?

After answering these questions, begin to prepare by

1. brushing up on your topic,
2. planning a general outline,
3. gathering key facts and statistics, and
4. preparing visual aids, diagrams, or handouts if necessary.

Following these suggestions and practising good speaking skills should allow you to make an effective presentation.

EXERCISE 9

PRESENTING TO SMALL GROUPS OF PEERS

Form the class into small groups and have the instructor assign topics to each member of each group. These topics will either be related to something taught in the course or be something of which the participants have knowledge. Each class member will be responsible for preparing a presentation for his or her small group.

Summary

Effective speaking skills can improve interpersonal communications and are a practical necessity for all law clerks and legal assistants. Whether you are addressing a large group of legal professionals, engaging in a small group discussion, or simply speaking one-on-one with a colleague or a supervisor, you will perform better if you have effective speaking skills.

SPELLING AND DEFINITIONS

Be able to spell and define the following words:

acquaintance	classification	garnishment	trafficking
adamant	convenience	imminent	transfer
alienate	counterclaim	location	transpire
amenable	default	motion	trivial
apt	discontinuance	obstacle	unilateral
authoritative	discovery	perusal	witness
auxiliary	equity	recourse	
circumvent	extrajudicial	sustain	

CHAPTER 7

Legal Forms

There are literally hundreds of forms involved in routine and non-routine legal transactions. In this chapter you will find a selection of those you are most likely to see and use in the course of your work. In each case, there is a brief introductory narrative, followed by the completed forms.

Each of these forms has a specific purpose; they also have a number of general purposes, the most important being to transmit information inside and outside the firm. Completing these forms sometimes involves the use of the summarizing skills you've learned earlier in this book, but also requires the use of the excellent spelling and grammar skills, clarity, and accuracy that are trademarks of the legal profession. These forms are models of the forms that you will encounter on the job, and have been completed in order to suggest the proper formats, contents, and contexts appropriate to each situation.

The details of the information presented in the forms follow the sequence called Five Ws and an H:

- Who?
- What?
- Where?
- When?
- Why?
- How?

Stylistically, the content should accord with the Four Cs:

- Clear
- Concise
- Complete
- Correct

As legal documents, forms must be filled in accurately and completely. Attention to detail is of paramount importance. If a name is misspelled, an address incorrect, a piece of vital information left out, the firm or the firm's client could suffer legal or monetary consequences.

Examine the following forms, noting their purposes, contents, and the specific details that make each unique.

Real Estate

John and Mary Smith have agreed to sell their house for $500,000 to Paul and Isabel Jones. The Joneses have made a down payment of $200,000, leaving a mortgage of $300,000, payable to The Great Canadian Mortgage Company. The payments began on October 1, 2005 and the mortgage will be paid in full on October 1, 2010. When the mortgage is fully paid, The Great Canadian Mortgage Company will provide the Joneses with a discharge of charge/mortgage, which will then be registered at the registry office.

FORMS

The pages that follow show some of the real estate forms relevant to the Smith–Jones transaction:

Figure 7.1: Transfer/Deed of Land

Figure 7.2: Charge/Mortgage of Land

Figure 7.3: Discharge of Charge/Mortgage

Figure 7.4: Land Transfer Tax Affidavit

Figure 7.1 Transfer/Deed of Land

Transfer/Deed of Land
Form 1 - Land Registration Reform Act

Province of Ontario

A

(1) Registry ☐ Land Titles ☒	(2) Page 1 of **1** pages

(3) Property Identifier(s) Block Property
1111-2222 (LT) Additional See Schedule ☐

(4) Consideration **Five Hundred Thousand**
00/00 Dollars $ **500,000.00**

(5) Description This is a Property Division ☐ Property Consolidation ☐
Lot 1, Plan M-123
City of Toronto
Province of Ontario

FOR OFFICE USE ONLY

New Property Identifiers
Additional: See Schedule ☐

Executions
Additional: See Schedule ☐

(6) This Document Contains (a) Redescription New Easement Plan/Sketch ☐ (b) Schedule for: Description ☐ Additional Parties ☐ Other ☐

(7) Interest/Estate Transferred
Fee Simple

(8) Transferor(s) The transferor hereby transfers the land to the transferee and certifies that the transferor is at least eighteen years old and that
We are spouses of one another

Name(s)	Signature(s)	Date of Signature Y M D
SMITH,	John	2005 08 11
SMITH	Mary	2005 08 11
as joint tenants		

(9) Spouse(s) of Transferor(s) I hereby consent to this transaction
Name(s) Signature(s) Date of Signature Y M D

(10) Transferor(s) Address for Service 123 Any Street, Toronto, Ontario M1M 1M1

(11) Transferee(s)

	Date of Birth Y M D
JONES, Paul	1972 01 01
JONES, Isabel	1973 02 02
as joint tenants	

(12) Transferee(s) Address for Service 456 New Street, Toronto, Ontario M1B 1B1

(13) Transferor(s) The transferor verifies that to the best of the transferor's knowledge and belief, this transfer does not contravene section 50 of the Planning Act.

Signature **SMITH, John** Date of Signature Y M D 2005 08 11
Signature **SMITH, Mary** Date of Signature Y M D 2005 08 11

Solicitor for the Transferor(s) I have explained the effect of section 50 of the Planning Act to the transferor and I have made inquiries of the transferor to determine that this transfer does not contravene that section and based on the information supplied by the transferor, to the best of my knowledge and belief, this transfer does not contravene that section. I am an Ontario solicitor in good standing.

Name and Address of Solicitor **Bud Lawyer**
111 Main Street, Toronto, Ontario Signature Date of Signature Y M D 2005 08 11

(14) Solicitor for Transferee(s) I have investigated the title to this land and to abutting land where relevant and I am satisfied that the title records reveal no contravention as set out in subclauses 50 (22) (c) (ii) of the Planning Act and that to the best of my knowledge and belief this transfer does not contravene section 50 of the Planning Act. I act independently of the solicitor for the transferor(s) and I am an Ontario solicitor in good standing.

Name and Address of Solicitor **Purchaser's Lawyer**
999 Downtown Street
Toronto, Ontario M5M 5M5 Signature Date of Signature Y M D 2005 08 10

Planning Act - OPTIONAL
Affix Statement by Solicitor for Transferee(s) here if necessary

(15) Assessment Roll Number of Property Cty. **19** Mun. **04** Map **222** Sub. **222** Par. **12354**

(16) Municipal Address of Property
456 New Street
Toronto, Ontario
M1B 1B1

(17) Document Prepared by:
Bud Lawyer
111 Main Street
Toronto, Ontario

Fees and Tax
Registration Fee
Land Transfer Tax
Total

FOR OFFICE USE ONLY

Figure 7.2   Charge/Mortgage of Land

Figure 7.3   Discharge of Charge/Mortgage

Province of Ontario

Discharge of Charge/Mortgage
Form 3 - Land Registration Reform Act

C

FOR OFFICE USE ONLY

(1) Registry ☐   **Land Titles** ☒   **(2) Page 1 of** 1 **pages**

(3) Property Identifier(s)   Block   Property   1111-2222-(LT)   Additional: See Schedule ☐

(4) Description
Lot 1, Plan M-123
City of Toronto
Province of Ontario

New Property Identifiers

Additional: See Schedule ☐

(5) Charge to be Discharged

Registration Number	Date of Registration Y M D
LT-123456	2005 08 11

(6) This is a

Complete Discharge ☒   Partial Discharge ☐   Final Partial Discharge ☐

(7) Description (cont'd), Recitals, Assignments

Continued on Schedule ☐

(8) Chargee(s) I am the person entitled by law to grant the discharge and this charge is hereby discharged as to the land described herein.

Name(s)	Signature(s)	Date of Signature Y M D
The Great Canadian Mortgage Company	Frank Black, President	2010 10 01
	I have the authority to bind this corporation.	

Additional: See Schedule ☐

(9) Chargee(s) Address for Service
999 King Street West
Toronto, Ontario
M1M 9M9

(10) Document Prepared by:
The Great Canadian Mortgage Company
999 King Street West
Toronto, Ontario
M1M 9M9

FOR OFFICE USE ONLY

Fees	
Registration Fee	
Total	

Figure 7.4   Land Transfer Tax Affidavit

⊘ Ontario

Ministry of Finance
Motor Fuels and
Tobacco Tax Branch
PO Box 625
33 King St. West
Refer to all instructions on reverse side. Oshawa ON L1H 8H9

Property Identifier(s) No.
1111-2222 (LT)

Land Transfer Tax Affidavit
Land Transfer Tax Act

In the Matter of the Conveyance of *(insert brief description of land)*   Lot 1, Plan M-123, City of Toronto, Province of Ontario

BY *(print names of all transferors in full)*   John Smith and Mary Smith

TO *(print names of all transferees in full)*   Paul Jones and Isabel Jones

I   **Paul Jones**

have personal knowledge of the facts herein deposed to and Make Oath and Say that:

1. I am *(place a clear mark within the square opposite the following paragraph(s) that describe(s) the capacity of the deponents):*
   - ☐ (a) the transferee named in the above-described conveyance;
   - ☐ (b) the authorized agent or solicitor acting in this transaction for the transferee(s);
   - ☐ (c) the President, Vice-President, Secretary, Treasurer, Director or Manager authorized to act for _____
     _____ (the transferee(s));
   - ☒ (d) a transferee and am making this affidavit on my own behalf and on behalf of *(insert name of spouse or same-sex partner)*
     Isabel Jones _____ who is my spouse or same-sex partner.
   - ☐ (e) the transferor or an officer authorized to act on behalf of the transferor company and   ☐ I am tendering this document for registration and
     ☐ no tax is payable on registration of this document.

2. **THE TOTAL CONSIDERATION FOR THIS TRANSACTION IS ALLOCATED AS FOLLOWS:**
   - (a) Monies paid or to be paid in cash..$ 500,000.00
   - (b) Mortgages (i) Assumed *(principal and interest)* ....$ _____
   - (ii) Given back to vendor ....$ _____
   - (c) Property transferred in exchange *(detail below in para. 5)* ....$ _____
   - (d) Other consideration subject to tax *(detail below)* ....$ _____
   - (e) Fair-market value of the lands *(see instruction 2)* ....$ _____
   - (f) Value of land, building, fixtures and goodwill subject to
     Land Transfer Tax *(Total of (a) to (e))*...$ 500,000.00 $ 500,000.00
   - (g) Value of all chattels - items of tangible personal property
     which are taxable under the provisions of the
     Retail Sales Tax Act ....$ _____
   - (h) Other consideration for transaction not included in (f) or (g) above. ....$ _____
   - (i) Total Consideration ....$ 500,000.00

   All blanks must be filled in. Insert "Nil" where applicable.

3. To be completed where the value of the consideration for the conveyance exceeds $400,000.00
   I have read and considered the definition of "single family residence" set out in subsection 1(1) of the Act. The land conveyed in the above-described conveyance:
   - ☒ does not contain a single family residence or contains more than two single family residences;
   - ☐ contains at least one and not more than two single family residences; or
   - ☐ contains at least one and not more than two single family residences and the lands are used for other than just residential purposes. The transferee
     has accordingly apportioned the value of consideration on the basis that the consideration for the single family residence is $ _____
     and the remainder of the lands are used for _____ purposes.

   > **Note:** *Subsection 2(1)(b) imposes an additional tax at the rate of one-half of one percent upon the value of the consideration in excess of $400,000.00 where the conveyance contains at least one and not more than two single family residences and 2(2) allows an apportionment of the consideration where the lands are used for other than just residential purposes.*

4. If consideration is nominal, is the land subject to any encumbrance? ☐ Yes ☒ No

5. Other remarks and explanations, if necessary. _____

Sworn before me in the   City of
Toronto
this   11th   day of August   , 20 05

_____
A Commissioner for taking Affidavits, etc.

_____
Signature (s)

Property Information Record

A.   Describe nature of instrument: Transfer/Deed of Land

B.   (i)   Address of property being conveyed *(if available)*   456 New Street Toronto, Ontario M1B 1B1

   (ii)   Assessment Roll No. *(if available)*   19-04-222-222-12354

C.   Mailing address(es) for future Notices of Assessment under the *Assessment Act* for property being conveyed
   as in B (i)

D.   (i)   Registration number for last conveyance of property being conveyed *(if available)*   N/A
   (ii)   Legal description of property conveyed: Same as in D. (i) above. ☐ Yes ☐ No ☒ Not Known

E.   Name(s) and address(es) of each transferee's solicitor:
   Purchaser's Lawyer, 999 Downtown Street, Toronto, Ontario M5M 5M5

For Land Registry Office Use Only
Registration No.

Registration Date (Year/Month/Day)

Land Registry Office No.

School Support (Voluntary Election) *(See reverse for explanation)*

	Yes	No
(a) Are all individual transferees Roman Catholic?	☐	☐
(b) If Yes, do all individual transferees wish to be Roman Catholic Separate School Supporters?	☐	☐
(c) Do all individual transferees have French Language Education Rights?	☐	☐
(d) If Yes, do all individual transferees wish to support the French Language School Board (where established)?	☐	☐

Note: As to (c) and (d) the land being transferred will receive French Public School Board Election unless otherwise directed in (a) and (b)

0449K (2004-04)

Wills and Estates

Mary Smith has died and left a will. Her two sons, Peter Smith and Douglas Smith, are applying to be named trustees in the administration of the will. Peter is also applying to dispense with the need to post a security bond.

FORMS

The pages that follow show a variety of forms relevant to the wills and estates matter described above:

Figure 7.5: Notice of an Application for a Certificate of Appointment of Estate Trustee with a Will

Figure 7.6: Application for Certificate of Appointment of Estate Trustee with a Will (Individual Applicant)

Figure 7.7: Affidavit of Service of Notice

Figure 7.8: Certificate of Appointment of Estate Trustee with a Will

Figure 7.9: Affidavit in Support of Request for an Order that the Requirement of Posting a Bond Be Dispensed With

Figure 7.10: Order to Dispense with Bond

Figure 7.5 **Notice of an Application for a Certificate of Appointment of Estate Trustee with a Will**

ONTARIO
SUPERIOR COURT OF JUSTICE

IN THE ESTATE OF MARY SMITH, deceased.

NOTICE OF AN APPLICATION FOR A CERTIFICATE OF APPOINTMENT OF ESTATE TRUSTEE WITH A WILL

1. The deceased died on July 24, 2001.

2. Attached to this notice are:

    (A) If the notice is sent to or in respect of a person entitled only to a specified item of property or stated amount of money, an extract of the part or parts of the will or codicil relating to the gift, or a copy of the will (and codicil(s), if any).

    (B) If the notice is sent to or in respect of any other beneficiary, a copy of the will (and codicil(s), if any).

    (C) If the notice is sent to the Children's Lawyer or the Public Guardian and Trustee, a copy of the will (and codicil(s), if any), and if it is not included in this notice, a statement of the estimated value of the interest of the person represented.

3. The applicant named in this notice is applying for a certificate of appointment of estate trustee with a will.

APPLICANT

NAME	ADDRESS
Peter Smith	1234 Bell Ave Vancouver, British Columbia L1L 1L1
Douglas Smith	517 Arke Ave Westmount, Quebec H2Y 3E1

(Continued on the next page.)

Figure 7.5 Continued

4. The following persons who are less than 18 years of age are entitled, whether their interest is contingent or vested, to share in the distribution of the estate:

Name	Date of birth (d/m/y)	Name and address of parent or guardian	Estimated Value of Interest in Estate*
Pat Smith	31/06/1987	Peter Smith 1234 Bell Ave Vancouver, British Columbia L1L 1L1	$10,000.00
Alex Smith	01/02/1990	Peter Smith 1234 Bell Ave Vancouver, British Columbia L1L 1L1	$10,000.00
The Children's Lawyer		393 University Ave 14th Floor Toronto, Ontario M5G 1W9	

*Note: The Estimated Value of Interest in Estate may be omitted in the form if it is included in a separate schedule attached to the notice sent to the Children's Lawyer.

5. The following persons who are mentally incapable within the meaning of section 6 of the *Substitute Decisions Act, 1992* in respect of an issue in the proceeding, and who have guardians or attorneys acting under powers of attorney with authority to act in the proceeding, are entitled, whether their interest is contingent or vested, to share in the distribution of the estate:

Name and Address of Person	Estimated Value of Interest in Estate (*Specify guardian or attorney.*)
N/A	N/A

6. The following persons who are mentally incapable within the meaning of section 6 of the *Substitute Decisions Act, 1992* in respect of an issue in the proceeding, and who do not have guardians or attorneys acting under powers of attorney with authority to act in the proceeding, are entitled, whether their interest is contingent or vested, to share in the distribution of the estate:

Name and Address of Person	Estimated Value of Interest in Estate*
N/A	N/A

*Note: The Estimated Value of Interest in Estate may be omitted in the form if it is included in a separate schedule attached to the notice sent to the Public Guardian and Trustee.

(Continued on the next page.)

Figure 7.5   Continued

7.   ~~Unborn or unascertained persons may be entitled to share in the distribution of the estate.~~ *~~(Delete if not applicable)~~*

8.   All other persons and charities entitled, whether their interest is contingent or vested, to share in the distribution of the estate are as follows:

Name	Address
Peter Smith	1234 Bell Ave Vancouver, British Columbia L1L 1L1

9.   This notice is being sent, by regular letter mail, to all adult persons and charities named in this notice (except to an applicant who is entitled to share in the distribution of the estate), to the Public Guardian and Trustee if paragraph 6 applies, to a parent or guardian of the minor and to the Children's Lawyer if paragraph 4 applies, to the guardian or attorney if paragraph 5 applies, and to the Children's Lawyer if paragraph 7 applies.

DATE: September 14, 2001

Peter Smith and Douglas Smith, by their solicitors

Figure 7.6   Application for Certificate of Appointment of Estate Trustee with a Will

Form 74.4

| Ontario
Superior Court of Justice
at Toronto | APPLICATION FOR CERTIFICATE OF
APPOINTMENT OF ESTATE TRUSTEE
WITH A WILL (INDIVIDUAL APPLICANT) |

This application is filed by
NAME AND ADDRESS OF SOLICITOR

DETAILS ABOUT THE DECEASED PERSON

Complete in full as applicable	And if the testator is known by any other name, state below the full names used
First given name Mary	Given name or names
Second given name	
Third given name	Surname
Surname Smith	

Address or fixed place of abode 123 Any Street	Toronto, Ontario

If the deceased person had no fixed place of abode in Ontario, did he or she have property in Ontario? ☐Yes ☐No	Last occupation of the deceased person Housewife

Place of death Toronto, Ontario	Date of death 24 August 2003	Date of last will (marked as Exhibit "A") 29 February 1998

Was the deceased person 18 years of age or older at the date of the will (or 21 years of age or older if the will is dated earlier than September 1, 1971)? ☐No ☒Yes

If not explain why a certificate is being sought. Give details in an attached schedule.

Date of codicil (marked as Exhibit "B") (day, month, year)	Date of codicil (marked as Exhibit "C") (day, month, year)

Marital Status ☐ Unmarried ☒ Widowed ☐ Married ☐ Divorced	Did the deceased person marry after the date of the will? ☒No ☐Yes If yes, explain why a certificate is being sought. Give details in an attached schedule.
Was a marriage of the deceased person terminated by a judgment absolute of divorce or declared a nullity, after the date of the will? ☒No ☐Yes If yes, give details in an attached schedule.	Is any person who signed the will or a codicil as witness or for the testator, or the spouse of such person, a beneficiary under the will? ☒No ☐Yes If yes, give details in an attached schedule.

VALUE OF ASSETS OF ESTATE

Do not include in the total amount: insurance payable to a named beneficiary or assigned for value, property held jointly and passing by survivorship, or real estate outside Ontario.

Personal property	Real estate, net of encumbrances	Total
$316,600.00	$1,185,000.00	$1,501,600.00

Is there any person entitled to an interest in the estate who is not an applicant? ☐No ☒Yes

If a person named in the will or a codicil as estate trustee is not an applicant, explain.

(Continued on the next page.)

Figure 7.6 Continued

Application   Page 2

If a person not named in the will or a codicil as estate trustee is an applicant, explain why that person is entitled to apply.

If the spouse of the deceased is an applicant, has the spouse elected to receive the entitlement under section 5 of the *Family Law Act*?   ☐ No   ☐ Yes

If yes, explain why the spouse is entitled to apply.

(Continued on the next page.)

Figure 7.6   Continued

AFFIDAVIT(S) OF APPLICANT(S)
(Attach a separate sheet for additional affidavits, if necessary.)

I, an applicant named in this application, make oath and say/affirm:

1. I am 18 years of age or older.
2. The exhibit(s) referred to in this application are the last will and each codicil (where applicable) of the deceased person and I do not know of any later will or codicil.
3. I will faithfully administer the deceased person's property according to the law and render a complete and true account of my administration when lawfully required.
4. If I am not named as estate trustee in the will or codicil, consents of persons who together have a majority interest in the value of the assets of the estate at the date of death are attached.
5. The information contained in this application and in any attached schedules is true, to the best of my knowledge and belief.

Name	Occupation
SMITH, Peter	Businessman

Address
1234 Bell Ave, Vancouver, British Columbia, L1L 1L1

Sworn/Affirmed before me at the City
of Toronto
in the Province of Ontario
this   day of September, 2001

A Commissioner for Taking Affidavits
Etc

Signature of Applicant

I, an applicant named in this application, make oath and say/affirm:

1. I am 18 years of age or older.
2. The exhibit(s) referred to in this application are the last will and each codicil (where applicable) of the deceased person and I do not know of any later will or codicil.
3. I will faithfully administer the deceased person's property according to the law and render a complete and true account of my administration when lawfully required.
4. If I am not named as estate trustee in the will or codicil, consents of persons who together have a majority interest in the value of the assets of the estate at the date of death are attached.
5. The information contained in this application and in any attached schedules is true, to the best of my knowledge and belief.

Name	Occupation
SMITH, Douglas	Businessman

Address
517 Arke Ave, Westmount, Quebec, H2Y 3E1

Sworn/Affirmed before me at the City
of Toronto
in the Province of Ontario
this 14th day of September, 2001

A Commissioner for Taking Affidavits
Etc

Signature of Applicant

Figure 7.7   Affidavit of Service of Notice

Form 74.6

ONTARIO
SUPERIOR COURT OF JUSTICE

IN THE ESTATE OF MARY SMITH, deceased.

AFFIDAVIT OF SERVICE OF NOTICE

I, Douglas Smith, of the City of Toronto in the Province of Ontario, make oath and say:

1. I am an applicant for a certificate of appointment of estate trustee with a will in the estate.

2. I have sent or caused to be sent a notice in Form 74.7, a copy of which is marked as Exhibit "A" to this affidavit, to all adult persons and charities named in the notice (except to an applicant who is entitled to share in the distribution of the estate), to the Public Guardian and Trustee if paragraph 6 of the notice applies, to a parent or guardian of the minor and to the Children's Lawyer if paragraph 4 applies, to the guardian or attorney if paragraph 5 applies, and to the Children's Lawyer if paragraph 7 applies, all by regular letter mail sent to the person's last known address.

3. I attached or caused to be attached to each notice the following:

    (A) In the case of a notice sent to or in respect of a person entitled only to a specified item of property or stated amount of money, an extract of the part or parts of the will or codicil relating to the gift, or a copy of the will (and codicil(s), if any).

    (B) In the case of a notice sent to or in respect of any other beneficiary, a copy of the will (and codicil(s), if any).

(Continued on the next page.)

Figure 7.7 Continued

(C) In the case of a notice to the Children's Lawyer or the Public Guardian and Trustee, a copy of the will (and codicil(s), if any) and a statement of the estimated value of the interest of the person represented.

4. To the best of my knowledge and belief, the persons named in the notice are all the persons who are entitled to share in the distribution of the estate.

Sworn before me at the City of
Toronto, in the Province of Ontario
this 14th day of September, 2001

_____
A Commissioner for Taking Affidavits

Douglas Smith
Applicant

Figure 7.8   Certificate of Appointment of Estate Trustee with a Will

Form 74.13   ONTARIO   Court File No. _____
                            # SUPERIOR COURT OF JUSTICE

IN THE ESTATE OF MARY SMITH, deceased

late of City of Toronto

occupation Housewife

who died on July 24, 2001

CERTIFICATE OF APPOINTMENT
OF ESTATE TRUSTEE WITH A WILL

Applicant	Address	Occupation
Peter Smith	1234 Bell Ave Vancouver, British Columbia L1L 1L1	Businessman
Douglas Smith	517 Arke Ave Westmount, Quebec H2Y 3E1	Businessman

This CERTIFICATE OF APPOINTMENT OF ESTATE TRUSTEE WITH A WILL is hereby issued under the seal of the court to the applicant named above. A copy of the deceased's last will (and codicil(s), if any) is attached.

DATE: , 2001

_____
Registrar

393 University Avenue
10th Floor
Toronto, Ontario
M5G 1E6

Figure 7.9   Affidavit in Support of Request for an Order that the Requirement of Posting a Bond Be Dispensed With

SUPERIOR COURT OF JUSTICE
AT TORONTO

AFFIDAVIT IN SUPPORT OF REQUEST FOR AN ORDER THAT THE REQUIREMENT OF POSTING A BOND BE DISPENSED WITH

IN THE ESTATE OF MARY SMITH, late of the City of Toronto, in the Province of Ontario, deceased

I, Peter Smith, of the City of Toronto, in the Province of Ontario, make oath and say that;

1. I am one of the applicants for a Certificate of Appointment of Estate Trustee with a Will in the above named estate.

2. I am the son of the late Mary Smith, who died on the 24th day of July, 2001.

3. I had intimate knowledge of my mother's business affairs prior to her death.

4. At the time of her death, Mary Smith was not and never had been engaged in any form of business.

5. There are no debts outstanding, save for the funeral expenses which have been paid in full and the cost of this Application for Certificate of Appointment of Estate Trustee with Will attached.

6. At the time of her death, the next of kin of the deceased were her sons, Peter Smith and Douglas Smith. The consent of Douglas Smith is attached hereto and marked as Exhibit "A".

7. I make this Affidavit in support of an Order to Dispense with the need to post security and for no improper purpose.

Sworn before me at the City of) Toronto, in the Province of) Ontario, this 21st day of) September, 2001))))	_____ Peter Smith, Applicant

A Commissioner for Taking Affidavits

Figure 7.10   Order to Dispense with Bond

SUPERIOR COURT OF JUSTICE

AT TORONTO

ORDER

IN THE ESTATE OF MARY SMITH, late of the City of Toronto, in the Province of Ontario, deceased

ORDER TO DISPENSE WITH BOND

UPON THE APPLICATION of Peter Smith and Douglas Smith, the Applicants, for a Certificate of Appointment of Estate Trustee with a Will of the Estate of the above named deceased, and upon reading the Affidavit of Peter Smith

IT IS ORDERED that the bond, to be filed by the Trustees herein, BE DISPENSED WITH.

DATED at Toronto this   day of September, 2001

_____
Judge or Registrar

■ Litigation

On August 25, Plaintiff Danny Gill brought suit against Defendants My Gas Bar and Gas Bar Limited. He claims that when he stopped on their property to buy gas, he slipped on black ice and fell, sustaining serious personal injuries. On August 30, Mr. Gill applied to the court to have his action tried by a jury.

On September 2, the Defendants were summoned to attend an Examination for Discovery to be held on September 23. However, on September 20, Mr. Gill served a Notice of Discontinuance of the action, and on September 25 he offered to settle the action out of court. On the same day, he served Notice of Discontinuance of the action.

FORMS

The pages that follow show the forms involved in the litigation described above:

Figure 7.11: Statement of Claim

Figure 7.12: Jury Notice

Figure 7.13: Notice of Examination

Figure 7.14: Affidavit of Service

Figure 7.15: Offer to Settle

Figure 7.16: Notice of Discontinuance

Figure 7.11   Statement of Claim

Court File No.

ONTARIO
SUPERIOR COURT OF JUSTICE

B E T W E E N :

DANNY GILL

Plaintiff

- and -

99999 ONTARIO INC. carrying on business
as MY GAS BAR and GAS BAR LIMITED

Defendants

STATEMENT OF CLAIM

TO THE DEFENDANT

A LEGAL PROCEEDING HAS BEEN COMMENCED AGAINST YOU by the plaintiff. The claim made against you is set out in the following pages.

IF YOU WISH TO DEFEND THIS PROCEEDING, you or an Ontario lawyer acting for you must prepare a statement of defence in Form 18A prescribed by the Rules of Civil Procedure, serve it on the plaintiff's lawyer or, where the plaintiff does not have a lawyer, serve it on the plaintiff, and file it, with proof of service, in this court office, WITHIN TWENTY DAYS after this statement of claim is served on you, if you are served in Ontario.

If you are served in another province or territory of Canada or in the United States of America, the period for serving and filing your statement of defence is forty days. If you are served outside Canada and the United States of America, the period is sixty days.

Instead of serving and filing a statement of defence, you may serve and file a notice of intent to defend in Form 18B prescribed by the Rules of Civil Procedure. This will entitle you to ten more days within which to serve and file your statement of defence.

IF YOU FAIL TO DEFEND THIS PROCEEDING, JUDGMENT MAY BE GIVEN AGAINST YOU IN YOUR ABSENCE AND WITHOUT FURTHER NOTICE TO YOU. IF YOU WISH TO DEFEND THIS PROCEEDING BUT ARE UNABLE TO PAY LEGAL FEES, LEGAL AID MAY BE AVAILABLE TO YOU BY CONTACTING A LOCAL LEGAL AID OFFICE.

IF YOU PAY THE PLAINTIFF'S CLAIM, and $2,500.00 for costs, within the time for serving and filing your statement of defence, you may move to have this proceeding dismissed by the court. If you believe the amount claimed for costs is excessive, you may pay the plaintiff's claim and $400.00 for costs and have the costs assessed by the court.

(Continued on the next page.)

Figure 7.11   Continued

- 2 -

Date _____, 2005   Issued by _____

                                                           Local registrar

                              Address of   Superior Court of Justice
                              court office   Sudbury Regional Municipality,
                                           Northeast Region
                                           155 Elm Street West
                                           Sudbury, Ontario P3C 1T9

TO: 99999 ONTARIO INC.
           carrying on business as MY GAS BAR
           999 Highway North
           Elliot Lake, ON   G5A 2S1

AND TO: GAS BAR LIMITED
           111 Gasoline Alley West
           Toronto, ON M5W 1A3

(Continued on the next page.)

Figure 7.11   Continued

- 3 -

THIS ACTION IS BROUGHT AGAINST YOU UNDER THE SIMPLIFIED PROCEDURE PROVIDED IN RULE 76 OF THE RULES OF CIVIL PROCEDURE.

CLAIM

1.   The plaintiff claims:

    (a)   Special damages in the sum of one hundred thousand ($100,000.00) dollars;

    (b)   General damages in the sum of one hundred and fifty thousand ($150,000.00) dollars;

    (c)   Pre-judgment interest pursuant to Section 128 of the *Courts of Justice Act*, R.S.O. 1990, c.C.43;

    (d)   The costs of this action, and Goods and Services Tax on costs; and

    (e)   Such further and other relief as this Honourable Court deems just.

2.   The Plaintiff resides in the City of Sudbury.

3.   The Defendant, 99999 Ontario Inc., carrying on business as MY GAS BAR, is a corporation incorporated pursuant to the laws of the Province of Ontario with its head office in the City of Elliot Lake, in the Province of Ontario and at all material times was an occupier of a service station at 999 Highway North, in Elliot Lake (the service station).

4.   The Defendant, Gas Bar Limited, is a corporation incorporated pursuant to the laws of the Province of Ontario with its head office at the City of Toronto, in the Province of Ontario, and was at all material times the owner and occupier of the service station.

5.   On Saturday, March 15, 2003, the Plaintiff stopped at the service station to buy gasoline.

6.   The Plaintiff parked his vehicle at the northern-most filling island, and put gasoline into his vehicle.

(Continued on the next page.)

Figure 7.11 Continued

- 4 -

7.   After pumping gasoline, the Plaintiff walked back to his vehicle around the northern side of the filling island, to go into the service station office to pay.

8.   As the Plaintiff walked past the filling island, he suddenly slipped and fell on black ice, sustaining serious personal injuries.

9.   The Plaintiff states that the incident occurred as a result of the negligence, breach of contract and the breach of the *Occupiers' Liability Act* of the Defendants, and the servants, agents and employees of these Defendants, the particulars of which are as follows:

(a)   They failed to see that the service station was reasonably safe for persons entering thereon;

(b)   They failed to keep the service station free of ice and snow;

(c)   They failed to sand or salt the area around the filling island at the service station;

(d)   They failed to regularly inspect the area around the filling island to ensure that it was kept in a safe condition for people using the service station;

(e)   They knew or should have know that ice was likely to form given the weather conditions that prevailed on the day in question;

(f)   They failed to take reasonable care, or any care, to ensure that the Plaintiff, Danny Gill, would be reasonably safe while using the service station;

(g)   They permitted or allowed ice to accumulate on the paved surface surrounding the filling island, thereby creating a danger and a trap to persons using the service station;

(h)   They failed to take reasonable steps, or any steps, to implement a program or a procedure for the routine removal of ice from the service station;

(i)   They employed incompetent servants, agents and employees;

(Continued on the next page.)

Figure 7.11   Continued

- 5 -

(j)   They failed to instruct properly, or at all, their servants, agents, or employees in the proper methods and procedures to be followed to prevent the accumulation of ice;

(k)   They failed to supervise properly, or at all, the removal of ice;

(l)   They caused or prevented the area where the Plaintiff, Danny Gill, was walking to become or to remain a danger and a trap to the Plaintiff, Danny Gill;

(m)   They had at the service station salt and sand available for use, but failed to apply it;

(n)   They failed to take such care as in all the circumstances was reasonable to see that the Plaintiff was safe while on the premises.

10.   As a result of this incident, the Plaintiff sustained serious, lasting and permanent personal injuries including a fracture of the right distal tibia into the ankle joint and tearing of the muscles, tendons, ligaments in the lower right extremity.

11.   The injuries were accompanied by headaches, dizziness, shock, anxiety, depression, emotional trauma, chronic pain, insomnia, weakness, diminished energy and stiffness, which continue to the present, and will continue in the future.

12.   The Plaintiff has sustained and will continue to sustain pain and suffering, loss of enjoyment of life and loss of amenities.

13.   The Plaintiff was unable to participate in recreational, social, household and athletic activities to the extent which he participated in such activities prior to the incident.

14.   The Plaintiff's ability to walk on slopes, uneven ground, and to climb stairs has been impaired.

(Continued on the next page.)

Figure 7.11 Continued

- 6 -

15.   As a further result of this incident, the Plaintiff has undergone and will continue to undergo in the future, hospitalization, therapy, and rehabilitation. In addition, the Plaintiff has received and will continue to receive medication.

16.   The Plaintiff has also incurred and will continue to incur expenses, including expenses for hospitalization, medication, therapy, rehabilitation, home and attendant care, the use of special equipment, medical treatment, and other forms of care, the full particulars of which are not within the Plaintiff's knowledge at this time.

17.   The Plaintiff has sustained a loss of income.

18.   The Plaintiff has sustained a loss of competitive advantage in the employment field, a loss of earning potential, and a diminution of earning capacity.

19.   The Plaintiff is unable to perform handyman chores and housekeeping tasks for himself to the extent he was able to do so before the accident and resultant injuries, and he will require assistance in the future to complete such chores and tasks.

20.   As a result of the negligence, breach of contract, and breach of the *Occupiers' Liability Act* of the Defendants, the Plaintiff has suffered other pecuniary damages up to the present and will continue to suffer pecuniary damages in the future, the full particulars of which are not known at this time.

21.   The Plaintiff pleads and relies upon the *Occupiers' Liability Act*, R.S.O., 1990, c.O.2 as amended, and specifically, Section 3 thereof.

22.   The Plaintiff pleads and relies upon the *Negligence Act*, R.S.O., 1990, c.N.1 as amended, and specifically, Section 1 thereof.

23.   The Plaintiff proposes that this action be tried in the City of Sudbury, in the Province of Ontario.

(Continued on the next page.)

Figure 7.11 Continued

- 7 -

August 25, 2005 (Name of Lawyer) LSUC#: (Insert LSUC No.)
Tel: (416) 350-3500
Fax: (416) 350-3510

Solicitors for the Plaintiff

(Continued on the next page.)

Figure 7.11 Continued

Court File No:

DANNY GILL
Plaintiff

and

99999 ONTARIO INC. carrying on business as MY GAS BAR ET AL
Defendants

ONTARIO
SUPERIOR COURT OF JUSTICE

Proceeding commenced at SUDBURY

STATEMENT OF CLAIM

(Name of Lawyer) LSUC#: (Insert LSUC No.)
Tel: (416) 350-3500
Fax: (416) 350-3510

Solicitors for the Plaintiff

Figure 7.12 Jury Notice

Court File No. 123456/05

ONTARIO
SUPERIOR COURT OF JUSTICE

B E T W E E N :

DANNY GILL

Plaintiff

- and -

99999 ONTARIO INC. carrying on business
as MY GAS BAR and GAS BAR LIMITED

Defendants

JURY NOTICE

THE PLAINTIFF REQUESTS that this action be tried by a jury.

August 30, 2005

(Name of Lawyer) LSUC#: (Insert LSUC No.)
Tel: (416) 350-3500
Fax: (416) 350-3510

Solicitors for the Plaintiff

(Continued on the next page.)

Figure 7.12 Continued

TO: 99999 ONTARIO INC.
carrying on business as MY GAS BAR
999 Highway North
Elliot Lake, ON   G5A 2S1

AND TO: GAS BAR LIMITED
111 Gasoline Alley West
Toronto, ON M5W 1A3

(Continued on the next page.)

Figure 7.12   Continued

Court File No. 123456/05

ONTARIO
SUPERIOR COURT OF JUSTICE

Proceeding commenced at SUDBURY

JURY NOTICE

(Name of Lawyer) LSUC#: (Insert LSUC No.)
Tel: (416) 350-3500
Fax: (416) 350-3510

Solicitors for the Plaintiff

DANNY GILL
Plaintiff

and

99999 ONTARIO INC. carrying on business
as MY GAS BAR ET AL
Defendants

Figure 7.13 Notice of Examination

Court File No. 123456/05

ONTARIO
SUPERIOR COURT OF JUSTICE

B E T W E E N :

DANNY GILL

Plaintiff

- and -

99999 ONTARIO INC. carrying on business
as MY GAS BAR and GAS BAR LIMITED

Defendants

NOTICE OF EXAMINATION

TO: A representative of the 99999 Ontario Inc.

AND TO: A representative of Gas Bar Limited

YOU ARE REQUIRED TO ATTEND FOR AN EXAMINATION FOR DISCOVERY on Friday, September 23, 2005, at 10:00 a.m., at the office of Legal Court Reporters, 730 Wood Ave., Suite 5, Toronto, Ontario, L3R 6X2, telephone no. 416-555-1212.

YOU ARE REQUIRED TO BRING WITH YOU and produce at the examination the documents mentioned in subrule 30.04(4) of the Rules of Civil Procedure, and the following documents and things:

All books, contracts, letters, telegrams, statements, records, bills, notes, securities, vouchers and copies of same in your custody, possession or power in any way relating to the matters which are within the scope of this proceeding or have any reference thereto.

September 2, 2005

(Name of Lawyer) LSUC#: (Insert LSUC No.)
Tel: (416) 350-3500
Fax: (416) 350-3510

Solicitors for the Plaintiff

(Continued on the next page.)

Figure 7.13   Continued

TO: 99999 ONTARIO INC.
            carrying on business as MY GAS BAR
            999 Highway North
            Elliot Lake, ON   G5A 2S1

AND TO: GAS BAR LIMITED
            111 Gasoline Alley West
            Toronto, ON M5W 1A3

(Continued on the next page.)

Figure 7.13 Continued

Court File No. 123456/05

DANNY GILL
Plaintiff

and

99999 ONTARIO INC. carrying on business
as MY GAS BAR ET AL
Defendants

ONTARIO
SUPERIOR COURT OF JUSTICE

Proceeding commenced at SUDBURY

NOTICE OF EXAMINATION

(Name of Lawyer) LSUC#: (Insert LSUC No.)
Tel: (416) 350-3500
Fax: (416) 350-3510

Solicitors for the Plaintiff

Figure 7.14   Affidavit of Service

Court File No.   123456/05

ONTARIO
SUPERIOR COURT OF JUSTICE

B E T W E E N :

DANNY GILL

Plaintiff

- and -

99999 ONTARIO INC. carrying on business
as MY GAS BAR and GAS BAR LIMITED

Defendants

AFFIDAVIT OF SERVICE

I, Mary Law Clerk, of the City of Toronto, in the Province of Ontario, **MAKE OATH
AND SAY:**

1.   I served the defendant, 99999 Ontario Inc., carrying on business as My Gas Bar with the Notice of Discontinuance by sending a copy of same by regular mail to 99999 Ontario Inc., carrying on business as My Gas Bar at 999 Highway North, Elliot Lake, Ontario, G5A 2S1 on September 20, 2005.

2.   I served the defendant, Gas Bar Limited, with the Notice of Discontinuance by sending a copy of same by regular mail to Gas Bar Limited at 111 Gasoline Alley West, Toronto, Ontario, M5W 1A3 on September 20, 2005.

SWORN BEFORE ME at the City of
Toronto, in the Province of Ontario, on
September _____, 2005.

_____
Commissioner for taking affidavits

_____
Mary Law Clerk

(Continued on the next page.)

Figure 7.14 Continued

Court File No. 123456/05

DANNY GILL
Plaintiff

and

99999 ONTARIO INC. carrying on business
as MY GAS BAR ET AL
Defendants

ONTARIO
SUPERIOR COURT OF JUSTICE

Proceeding commenced at SUDBURY

AFFIDAVIT OF SERVICE

(Name of Lawyer) LSUC#: (Insert LSUC No.)
Tel: (416) 350-3500
Fax: (416) 350-3510

Solicitors for the Plaintiff

Figure 7.15   Offer to Settle

Court File No. 123456/05

ONTARIO
SUPERIOR COURT OF JUSTICE

B E T W E E N :

DANNY GILL

Plaintiff

- and -

99999 ONTARIO INC. carrying on business
as MY GAS BAR and GAS BAR LIMITED

Defendants

OFFER TO SETTLE

The Plaintiff offers to settle this action on the following terms:

1.   The defendants will pay to the plaintiff the sum of $30,000.00 for damages;

2.   The defendants will pay to the plaintiff prejudgment interest on the aforesaid amount pursuant to the *Courts of Justice Act*, R.S.O. 1990, c. C.43, as amended.

3.   The defendants will pay special damages in the amount of $1,125.14, representing the amounts paid for treatment to the Ministry of Health under the Ontario Hospital Insurance Plan.

4.   The defendants will pay to the plaintiff partial indemnity costs as agreed or assessed;

5.   This offer to settle will remain open for acceptance until one minute after the commencement of trial.

September 25, 2005

(Name of Lawyer) LSUC#: (Insert LSUC No.)
Tel: (416) 350-3500
Fax: (416) 350-3510

Solicitors for the Plaintiff

(Continued on the next page.)

Figure 7.15   Continued

- 2 -

TO: 99999 ONTARIO INC.
           carrying on business as MY GAS BAR
           999 Highway North
           Elliot Lake, ON   G5A 2S1

AND TO: GAS BAR LIMITED
           111 Gasoline Alley West
           Toronto, ON M5W 1A3

(Continued on the next page.)

Figure 7.15   Continued

Court File No: 123456/05

DANNY GILL   and   99999 ONTARIO INC. carrying on business
     Plaintiff   as MY GAS BAR ET AL
                         Defendants

ONTARIO
SUPERIOR COURT OF JUSTICE

Proceeding commenced at SUDBURY

OFFER TO SETTLE

(Name of Lawyer) LSUC#: (Insert LSUC No.)
Tel: (416) 350-3500
Fax: (416) 350-3510

Solicitors for the Plaintiff

Figure 7.16   Notice of Discontinuance

Court File No.   123456/05

ONTARIO
SUPERIOR COURT OF JUSTICE

B E T W E E N :

DANNY GILL

Plaintiff

- and -

99999 ONTARIO INC. carrying on business
as MY GAS BAR and GAS BAR LIMITED

Defendants

NOTICE OF DISCONTINUANCE

The plaintiff wholly discontinues this action against the defendants.

September 25, 2005

(Name of Lawyer) LSUC#: (Insert LSUC No.)
Tel: (416) 350-3500
Fax: (416) 350-3510

Solicitors for the Plaintiff

(Continued on the next page.)

Figure 7.16   Continued

TO: 99999 ONTARIO INC.
         carrying on business as MY GAS BAR
         999 Highway North
         Elliot Lake, ON   G5A 2S1

AND TO: GAS BAR LIMITED
         111 Gasoline Alley West
         Toronto, ON M5W 1A3

NOTE: If there is a counterclaim, the defendant should consider rule 23.02, under which the counterclaim may be deemed discontinued.

NOTE: If there is a crossclaim or third party claim, the defendant should consider rule 23.03, under which the crossclaim or third party claim may be deemed to be dismissed.

(Continued on the next page.)

Figure 7.16   Continued

Court File No.   123456/05

ONTARIO
SUPERIOR COURT OF JUSTICE

Proceeding commenced at SUDBURY

NOTICE OF DISCONTINUANCE

(Name of Lawyer) LSUC#: (Insert LSUC No.)
Tel: (416) 350-3500
Fax: (416) 350-3510

Solicitors for the Plaintiff

99999 ONTARIO INC. carrying on business
as MY GAS BAR ET AL
Defendants

and

DANNY GILL
Plaintiff

■ Corporate Procedures and Transactions

There are many corporate procedures and transactions whose completion requires the filing of federal and/or provincial government forms. Some of the most common procedures are as follows:

- ABC Corporation is incorporated under the Canada Business Corporations Act.

- ABC Corporation is formed by the amalgamation of Flybynight Inc. and 90210 Productions Inc.

- Apple Corporation is a federal company and wishes to continue as a provincial company.

- EDF Corporation is being dissolved.

- ABC Corporation is changing the number of its directors.

- Star Productions Inc. is filing its annual return, as required by the *Canada Business Corporations Act*.

FORMS

The following pages show the forms needed for the corporate procedures described above:

Figure 7.17: Articles of Incorporation

Figure 7.18: Articles of Amalgamation

Figure 7.19: Articles of Continuance

Figure 7.20: Articles of Dissolution

Figure 7.21: Articles of Amendment

Figure 7.22: Annual Return

Figure 7.17   Articles of Incorporation

[flag] Industry Canada Canada Business Corporations Act	**Industrie Canada** Loi canadienne sur les sociétés par actions	FORM 1 **ARTICLES OF INCORPORATION** (SECTION 6)	FORMULAIRE 1 **STATUTS CONSTITUTIFS** (ARTICLE 6)

1 - Name of the Corporation .... Dénomination sociale de la société

ABC Corporation

2 - The province or territory in Canada where the registered office is situated .... La province ou le territoire au Canada où est situé le siège social

Ontario

3 - The classes and any maximum number of shares that the corporation is authorized to issue .... Catégories et le nombre maximal d'actions que la société est autorisée à émettre

The Corporation is authorized to issue an unlimited number of common shares.

4 - Restrictions, if any, on share transfers .... Restrictions sur le transfert des actions, s'il y a lieu

See attached Schedule "A".

5 - Number (or minimum and maximum number) of directors .... Nombre (ou nombre minimal et maximal) d'administrateurs

Minimum of 3. Maximum of 5

6 - Restrictions, if any, on business the corporation may carry on .... Limites imposées à l'activité commerciale de la société, s'il y a lieu

None.

7 - Other provisions, if any .... Autres dispositions, s'il y a lieu

See attached Schedule "B".

8 - Incorporators - Fondateurs

Name(s) - Nom(s)	Address (include postal code) Adresse (inclure le code postal)	Signature	Tel. No - N° de tél.
Michele Mendes	84 Baidway Court Toronto, ON M1B 2S7		416-555-5555

FOR DEPARTMENT USE ONLY - À L'USAGE DU MINISTÈRE SEULEMENT

IC 3419 (2003/06)

Canadä

(Continued on the next page.)

Figure 7.17   Continued

<u>SCHEDULE "A"</u>

Restrictions on Share Transfers:

The right to transfer shares of the Corporation shall be restricted in that no shareholder shall be entitled to transfer any share or shares of the Corporation without the approval of:

(a)   the directors of the Corporation expressed by resolution passed by the votes cast by a majority of the directors of the Corporation at a meeting of the board of directors or signed by all of the directors of the Corporation; or

(b)   the shareholders of the Corporation expressed by resolution passed by the votes cast by a majority of the shareholders who voted in respect of the resolution or signed by all shareholders entitled to vote on that resolution.

(Continued on the next page.)

Figure 7.17   Continued

SCHEDULE "B"

Other Provisions:

(a) The number of shareholders in the Corporation, exclusive of employees and former employees who, while employed by the Corporation were, and following the termination of that employment, continue to be, shareholders of the Corporation, is limited to not more than fifty, two or more persons who are the joint registered holders of one or more shares being counted as one shareholder.

(b) Any invitation to the public to subscribe for securities of the Corporation is prohibited.

(c) If authorized by by-law which is duly made by the directors and confirmed by ordinary resolution of the shareholders, the directors of the Corporation may from time to time:

    (i) borrow money upon the credit of the Corporation;

    (ii) issue, reissue, sell or pledge debt obligations of the Corporation; and

    (iii) mortgage, hypothecate, pledge or otherwise create a security interest in all or any property of the Corporation, owned or subsequently acquired to secure any debt obligation of the Corporation.

Any such by-law may provide for the delegation of such powers by the directors to such officers or directors of the Corporation to such extent and in such manner as may be set out in the by-law.

Nothing herein limits or restricts the borrowing of money by the Corporation on bills of exchange or promissory notes made, drawn, accepted or endorsed by or on behalf of the Corporation.

(d) The directors may appoint one or more directors, who shall hold office for a term expiring not later than the close of the next annual general meeting of shareholders, but the total number of directors so appointed may not exceed one third of the number of directors elected at the previous annual general meeting of shareholders.

Figure 7.18   Articles of Amalgamation

🇨🇦 **Industry Canada** Canada Business Corporations Act	**Industrie Canada** Loi canadienne sur les sociétés par actions	FORM 9 **ARTICLES OF AMALGAMATION** (SECTION 185)	FORMULAIRE 9 **STATUTS DE FUSION** (ARTICLE 185)

1 - Name of the Amalgamated Corporation	Dénomination sociale de la société issue de la fusion

ABC Corporation

2 - The province or territory in Canada where the registered office is to be situated	La province ou le territoire au Canada où est situé le siège social

Ontario

3 - The classes and any maximum number of shares that the corporation is authorized to issue	Catégories et tout nombre maximal d'actions que la société est autorisée à émettre

The Corporation is authorized to issue an unlimited number of common shares.

4 - Restrictions, if any, on share transfers	Restrictions sur le transfert des actions, s'il y a lieu

See attached Schedule "A".

5 - Number (or minimum and maximum number) of directors	Nombre (ou nombre minimal et maximal) d'administrateurs

Minimum of 3. Maximum of 5.

6 - Restrictions, if any, on business the corporation may carry on	Limites imposées à l'activité commerciale de la société, s'il y a lieu

None.

7 - Other provisions, if any	Autres dispositions, s'il y a lieu

See attached Schedule "B".

8 - The amalgamation has been approved pursuant to that section or subsection of the Act which is indicated as follows:	La fusion a été approuvée en accord avec l'article ou le paragraphe de la Loi indiqué ci-après.
	[ ] 183
	[X] 184(1)
	[ ] 184(2)

9 - Name of the amalgamating corporations Dénomination sociale des sociétés fusionnantes	Corporation No. N° de la société	Signature	Date	Title Titre	Tel. No. N° de tél
Flybynight Inc.	595385-6		03/10/05	President	416-555-5555
90210 Productions Inc.	385985-8		03/10/05	President	416-555-5555

FOR DEPARTMENT USE ONLY - À L'USAGE DU MINISTÈRE SEULEMENT

IC 3190 (2003/06)

Canadä

(Continued on the next page.)

Figure 7.18 Continued

<u>SCHEDULE "A"</u>

Restrictions on Share Transfers:

The right to transfer shares of the Corporation shall be restricted in that no shareholder shall be entitled to transfer any share or shares of the Corporation without the approval of:

(a) the directors of the Corporation expressed by resolution passed by the votes cast by a majority of the directors of the Corporation at a meeting of the board of directors or signed by all of the directors of the Corporation; or

(b) the shareholders of the Corporation expressed by resolution passed by the votes cast by a majority of the shareholders who voted in respect of the resolution or signed by all shareholders entitled to vote on that resolution.

(Continued on the next page.)

Figure 7.18   Continued

SCHEDULE "B"

Other Provisions:

(a)   The number of shareholders in the Corporation, exclusive of employees and former employees who, while employed by the Corporation were, and following the termination of that employment, continue to be, shareholders of the Corporation, is limited to not more than fifty, two or more persons who are the joint registered holders of one or more shares being counted as one shareholder.

(b)   Any invitation to the public to subscribe for securities of the Corporation is prohibited.

(c)   If authorized by by-law which is duly made by the directors and confirmed by ordinary resolution of the shareholders, the directors of the Corporation may from time to time:

(i)   borrow money upon the credit of the Corporation;

(ii)   issue, reissue, sell or pledge debt obligations of the Corporation; and

(iii)   mortgage, hypothecate, pledge or otherwise create a security interest in all or any property of the Corporation, owned or subsequently acquired to secure any debt obligation of the Corporation.

Any such by-law may provide for the delegation of such powers by the directors to such officers or directors of the Corporation to such extent and in such manner as may be set out in the by-law.

Nothing herein limits or restricts the borrowing of money by the Corporation on bills of exchange or promissory notes made, drawn, accepted or endorsed by or on behalf of the Corporation.

(d)   The directors may appoint one or more directors, who shall hold office for a term expiring not later than the close of the next annual general meeting of shareholders, but the total number of directors so appointed may not exceed one third of the number of directors elected at the previous annual general meeting of shareholders.

Figure 7.19   Articles of Continuance

Industry Canada Canada Business Corporations Act	Industrie Canada Loi canadienne sur les sociétés par actions	FORM 11 **ARTICLES OF CONTINUANCE** (SECTION 187)	FORMULAIRE 11 **CLAUSES DE PROROGATION** (ARTICLE 187)

1 - Name of the Corporation	Dénomination sociale de la société	2 - Taxation Year End Fin de l'année d'imposition

Apple Corporation

		M	D-Y
		12	31

3 - The province or territory in Canada where the registered office is to be situated

La province ou le territoire au Canada où se situera le siège social

Ontario.

4 - The classes and any maximum number of shares that the corporation is authorized to issue

Catégories et tout nombre maximal d'actions que la société est autorisée à émettre

The Corporation is authorized to issue an unlimited number of common shares.

5 - Restrictions, if any, on share transfers

Restrictions sur le transfert des actions, s'il y a lieu

See attached Schedule "A".

6 - Number (or minimum and maximum number) of directors

Nombre (ou nombre minimal et maximal) d'administrateurs

Minimum of 3. Maximum of 5.

7 - Restrictions, if any, on business the corporation may carry on

Limites imposées à l'activité commerciale de la société, s'il y a lieu

None.

8 - (1) If change of name effected, previous name

(1) S'il y a changement de dénomination sociale, indiquer la dénomination sociale antérieure

N/A

  (2) Details of incorporation

(2) Détails de la constitution

N/A

9 - Other provisions, if any

Autres dispositions, s'il y a lieu

N/A

Signature	Printed Name - Nom et letters moulées Michele S. Mendes	10 - Capacity of - En qualité de Director	11 – Tel. No. – N° de tél. 416-555-5555

FOR DEPARTMENT USE ONLY - À L'USAGE DU MINISTÈRE SEULEMENT

IC 3247 (2003/06)

Canadä

(Continued on the next page.)

Figure 7.19   Continued

<u>SCHEDULE "A"</u>

Restrictions on Share Transfers:

The right to transfer shares of the Corporation shall be restricted in that no shareholder shall be entitled to transfer any share or shares of the Corporation without the approval of:

(a)   the directors of the Corporation expressed by resolution passed by the votes cast by a majority of the directors of the Corporation at a meeting of the board of directors or signed by all of the directors of the Corporation; or

(b)   the shareholders of the Corporation expressed by resolution passed by the votes cast by a majority of the shareholders who voted in respect of the resolution or signed by all shareholders entitled to vote on that resolution.

(Continued on the next page.)

Figure 7.19   Continued

SCHEDULE "B"

Other Provisions:

(a)   The number of shareholders in the Corporation, exclusive of employees and former employees who, while employed by the Corporation were, and following the termination of that employment, continue to be, shareholders of the Corporation, is limited to not more than fifty, two or more persons who are the joint registered holders of one or more shares being counted as one shareholder.

(b)   Any invitation to the public to subscribe for securities of the Corporation is prohibited.

(c)   If authorized by by-law which is duly made by the directors and confirmed by ordinary resolution of the shareholders, the directors of the Corporation may from time to time:

     (i)   borrow money upon the credit of the Corporation;

     (ii)   issue, reissue, sell or pledge debt obligations of the Corporation; and

     (iii)   mortgage, hypothecate, pledge or otherwise create a security interest in all or any property of the Corporation, owned or subsequently acquired to secure any debt obligation of the Corporation.

Any such by-law may provide for the delegation of such powers by the directors to such officers or directors of the Corporation to such extent and in such manner as may be set out in the by-law.

Nothing herein limits or restricts the borrowing of money by the Corporation on bills of exchange or promissory notes made, drawn, accepted or endorsed by or on behalf of the Corporation.

(d)   The directors may appoint one or more directors, who shall hold office for a term expiring not later than the close of the next annual general meeting of shareholders, but the total number of directors so appointed may not exceed one third of the number of directors elected at the previous annual general meeting of shareholders.

Figure 7.20   Articles of Dissolution

Industry Canada Canada Business Corporations Act	Industrie Canada Loi canadienne sur les sociétés par actions	FORM 17 **ARTICLES OF DISSOLUTION** (SECTION 211)	FORMULAIRE 17 **CLAUSES DE DISSOLUTION** (ARTICLE 211)

Note: All corporations are to complete Items 1, 2, 3 and 6, and either complete Item 4 or 5 .
Nota : Toutes les sociétés doivent remplir les rubriques 1, 2, 3 et 6 , ainsi que la rubrique 4 ou 5 .

1 - Name of the Corporation - Dénomination sociale de la société

EDF Corporation

2 - Corporation No. - N° de la société

960795-7

3 - Is the Corporation bankrupt or insolvent within the meaning of the *Bankruptcy and Insolvency Act* ?
La société é est-elle en faillite ou insolvable au sens de la *Loi sur la faillite et l' insolvabilité?*

☐ Yes - Oui   ☒ No - Non

Complete either Item 4 or 5, but not both - Remplir la rubrique 4 ou 5, mais non les deux

4 - Has the corporation previously filed a statement of intent to dissolve (Form 19) under subsection 211(4) of the Act ?
La société a-t-elle déjà déposé une déclaration d' intention de dissolution (formule 19) en vertu du paragraphe 211 (4) de la Loi?

☐ Yes - Oui   If the answer is negative, please complete only item 5 - Si la résponse est négative, veuillez remplir
                   seulement la rubrique 5

If yes, has the corp. provided for the payment or discharge of its obligations and distributed its remaining property as required by subsection 211(7) of the Act ?
Dans l'affirmative, conformément au paragraphe 211(7) de la Loi, la société a-t-elle constitué une provision pour honorer ses obligations et réparti le reliquat de l'actif ?

☐ Yes - Oui   ☐ No - Non

5 - Is the Corporation applying for dissolution under Section 210 of the Act? (To apply under Section 210, the corporation cannot have previously filed a statement of intent to dissolve (Form 19) under subsection 211 (7) of the Act)   La société dépose-t-elle une demande de dissolution en vertu de l'article 210 de la Loi? (Pour être admissible en vertu de l'article 210, la société ne peut pas avoir déposé une déclaration d' intention de dissolution (formule 19) en vertu du paragraphe 211(7) de la Loi.)

☒ Yes - Oui   If the answer is negative, please complete only item 4 - Si la réponse est négative, veuillez remplir
                   seulement la rubrique 4

If yes, under what subsection of the Act is the corporation applying for dissolution? (CHECK ONLY ONE ITEM)
Dans l' affirmative, en vertu de quel paragraphe de la Loi la société procède-t-elle? (COCHER UNE RUBRIQUE SEULEMENT)

☐   Subsection 210(1) of the Act applying to a corporation that has not issued any shares.
     Paragraphe 210(1) de la Loi applicable à une société qui n' a pas émis d'actions.

     or / ou

☒   Subsection 210(2) of the Act applying to a corporation that has no property and no liabilities.
     Paragraphe 210(2) de la Loi applicable à une société sans biens ni dettes.

     or / ou

☐   Subsection 210(3) of the Act applying to a corporation that has discharged its liabilities and distributed its property.
     Paragraphe 210(3) de la Loi applicable à une société qui a réglées dettes et réparti ses biens.

6 - Name, address and occupation of the person keeping the documents and records of the corporation for six years after the date of dissolution
Nom, adresse et profession de la personne qui garde les document s et livres de la société pour une période de six ans suivant la date de dissolution

Mary Jane Parker
Law Clerk
EDF Corporation
195 Conway Drive
Toronto, ON M5J 4J8

Signature	Printed Name - Nom et letters moulées Michele Mendes	7 - Capacity of - En qualité de Director	8 - Tel. No. - N° de tél. 416-555-5555

FOR DEPARTMENT USE ONLY - À L'USAGE DU MINISTERE SEULEMENT

IC 3317 (2003/06)

Canadä

Figure 7.21   Articles of Amendment

For Ministry Use Only
A l'usage exclusif du ministère

Ontario Corporation Number
Numéro de la société en Ontario

1

7164626

Form 3
Business
Corporations
Act

Formule 3
Loi sur les
sociétés par
actions

ARTICLES OF AMENDMENT
STATUTS DE MODIFICATION

1. The name of the corporation is: (Set out in BLOCK CAPITAL LETTERS)
   Dénomination sociale actuelle de la société: (Écrire en LETTRES MAJUSCULES SEULEMENT)

   A B C   C O R P O R A T I O N

2. The name of the corporation is changed to (if applicable): (Set out in BLOCK CAPITAL LETTERS)
   Nouvelle dénomination sociale de la société (s'il y a lieu): (Écrire en LETTRES MAJUSCULES SEULEMENT)

   V E N U S   R E D   M E D I A   I N C .

3. Date of incorporation/amalgamation:
   Date de la constitution ou de la fusion :

   05/10/03
   (Year/Month/Day)
   (année, mois, jour)

4. **Complete only if there is a change in the number of directors or the minimum / maximum number of directors**
   Il faut remplir cette partie seulement si le nombre d'administrateurs ou si le nombre minimal ou maximal d'administrateurs a changé.

   Number of directors is/are: **or**   minimum and maximum number of directors is/are:
   Nombre d'administrateurs :   **ou**   *nombres minimal et maximum d'administrateurs :*

   Number   **or**   minimum   and   maximum
   Nombre   **ou**   *minimal   et   maximum*

5. The articles of the corporation are amended as follows:
   Les statuts de la société sont modifiés de la façon suivante:

   To change the name of the Corporation to **VENUS RED MEDIA INC.**

07119 (03/2003)

(Continued on the next page.)

Figure 7.21   **Continued**

2

6.   The amendment has been duly authorized as required by sections 168 and 170 (as applicable) of the *Business Corporations Act.*

La modification a été dûment autorisée conformément aux articles 168 et 170 (selon le cas) de la loi sur les sociétés par actions.

7.   The resolution authorizing the amendment was approved by the shareholders/directors (as applicable) of the corporation on

Les actionnaries ou les administrateurs (selon le cas) de la société ont approuvé la résolution autorisant la modification le

2005/10/03
(Year, Month, day)
(*année, mois, jour*)

These articles are signed in duplicate.
Les présents statuts sont signés en double exemplaire.

ABC Corporation
(Name of Corporation) (If the name is to be changed by these articles set out current name)
(Dénomination sociale de la société) (Si l'on demande un changement du nom, indiquer ci-dessus la dénomination sociale actuelle).

By:
Par :

Director

(Signature)   (Description of Office)
(*Signature*)   (*Fonction*)

Figure 7.22   Annual Return

Industry Canada   Industrie Canada
Corporations Canada   Corporations Canada

Form 22
Annual Return
(Section 263 of the CBCA)

Corporations must file with Corporations Canada an Annual Return (Form 22) along with the prescribed fee within six months following the end of the corporation's taxation year (section 263 of the *Canada Business Corporations Act* (CBCA)).

INSTRUCTIONS

3 Indicate for which taxation year you are filing as well as the taxation year-end as defined in the Income Tax Act. For more information, visit the Canada Revenue Agency (CRA) Web site at **www.cra-arc.gc.ca**. Note that a change to the taxation year-end needs the approval of the CRA.

4 Indicate the date of the last annual meeting or the date of the written resolution in lieu of a meeting, signed by all the shareholders entitled to vote. The resolution must deal with at least the following:

- consideration of the financial statements;
- consideration of the auditor's report (if any);
- appointment of the auditor (shareholders of a nondistributing corporation may resolve not to appoint an auditor); and
- election of directors (if applicable).

5 A *non-distributing corporation* is a **private** corporation that is not a reporting issuer under any provincial securities legislation.

A *distributing corporation* is a **public** corporation that is a reporting issuer under provincial securities legislation.

6 Declaration

This form may be signed by any individual who has the relevant knowledge of the corporation

and who is authorized by the directors (subsection 262.1(2) of the CBCA).

For example:
- a **director** of the corporation;
- an authorized officer of the corporation; or
- an authorized agent.

Fees: Online filing, $20; filing by mail or by fax, $40. Fees are payable to the Receiver General for Canada.

File documents online:
Corporations Canada Online Filing Centre:
http://corporationscanada.ic.gc.ca

Or send documents by mail:
Director, Corporations Canada
Jean Edmonds Tower South
9th Floor
365 Laurier Ave. West
Ottawa ON K1A 0C8

By Facsimile:
(613) 941-0999

IC 2580 (2004/11)

---

1   Corporation name

Star Productions Inc.

2   Corporation number (as it appears on the certificate)

285987-8

3   Year of filing

| Year | Y 2005 | Taxation year-end | M 12 | D 31 |

4   Date of last annual meeting of shareholders or date of written resolution in lieu of meeting

| Y 2004 | M 06 | D 27 |

5   Which of the following boxes meets your situation (check only one item)? Please refer to the instructions for definitions

☒ Non-distributing corporation with 50 or fewer shareholders

☐ Non-distributing corporation with more than 50 shareholders

☐ Distributing corporation

IMPORTANT REMINDER

Change of registered office address?
Complete and file a Change of Registered Office Address (Form 3).

Change of directors or change of address of a current director?
Complete and file a Changes Regarding Directors (Form 6).

These changes can be done electronically, free of charge, via Corporations Canada Online Filing Centre at: **http://corporationscanada.ic.gc.ca**

General
If you require more information, please visit the Forms, Policies, Fees and Legislation section of our Web site at **http://corporationscanada.ic.gc.ca** or contact us at (613) 941-9042 or toll-free at 1 866 333-5556.

6   Declaration

I hereby certify that I have the relevant knowledge of the corporation, and that I am authorized to sign and submit this form.

SIGNATURE

Michele Mendes, authorized officer   416-555-5555
PRINT NAME   TELEPHONE NUMBER

Note: Misrepresentation constitutes an offence and, on summary conviction, a person is liable to a fine not exceeding $5000 or to imprisonment for a term not exceeding six months or both (subsection 250(1) of the CBCA).

Canada

Proofreading

Proofreading Techniques

Following are some useful proofreading techniques:

- Read your work aloud, slowly. This will help you see errors you could easily miss if reading silently.

- Read one line at a time, and read each word in the line individually.

- If proofreading on screen, temporarily increase the size of the type or zoom in closer to the material to make it easier to read.

- Personalize your proofreading. What mistakes do you or your lawyer typically make? Keep an eye out for those mistakes in particular.

- Read backwards. Reading in the normal way, we sometimes see what we expect to see, based on the context of the words, instead of what is actually there. If you read the material backwards, you will automatically see any misspelled words.

- Work with a colleague. Once you have typed something several times, it becomes difficult to spot mistakes. Arrange with a colleague to proofread each other's work, either individually or by reading aloud to each other.

Practise the above techniques, and look out for the following:

- transposed letters (e.g., *adn, htat, edlerly*)

- missing or extra letters (e.g., *repot, stilll*)

- missing words (e.g., *Please to page 10*)

- numbers (check against the numbers in the draft, and do the arithmetic to confirm amounts)

- dates on the calendar (e.g., Is the 15th really a Wednesday?)

- typos

- wrong word in context (e.g., did you use *too* when you wanted *two* or *to*?)

When unsure of a word or a spelling, check your dictionary or thesaurus.

EXERCISE 1

PROOFREADING FOR SPELLING

One or more words have been misspelled in each of the following sentences. There are 20 mistakes in total. (*Note:* Canadian spellings are not errors.)

1. Susie, anxious to secure an apartment, actualy included a charecter reference with her letter of application to the building superintendant.

2. She was determined to have a pleasent appearance at college and so naturally wanted to buy some beautifull new clothes.

3. She had transferred money into a convinient chequing account, but every bank statement proved it was impossible for her to maintain even a minimum balance.

4. She usually was without transportation and therefor found it practicle to shop by catalogue.

5. She was obliged to make partial payments on her annual income, regretting the lack of assistence from her parents.

6. Although it was with some endevor that she read the instructions on the examination envalope, she finally understood them.

7. By Febuary her funds were extremaly low, and so, after some concideration, she made the decicion to accept a position as a waitress.

8. An additional inquery was unnecessary as the description of the car left no dobt that it was a foreign model.

9. Evedently it is advisable to remember to ask for a guarentee.

10. She prefered to believe that the difference between succes and failure was all in the mind.

EXERCISE 2

PROOFREADING FOR SPELLING

One or more words have been misspelled in each of the following sentences. There are 25 mistakes in total. (*Note:* Canadian spellings are not errors.)

1. We are planning to deliver the balance of the shippment either on Wednesday or on Saterday.

2. Thousands of Canadian woman are undoutedly begining to realise the value of business experience.

3. Imagine how greatfull I am for an opportunity to get expierience at this temprary job.

4. With only my business training certificait, I should have had difficulty in getting a permanant job.

5. In this office, a general knowlege of business practice is a neccessity.

6. Even though no definate length of time was specefied, in my opinon, the job will last approximetely three months.

7. Prehaps, if my work is satisfactary, the firm will allow me to use its name as a referance.

8. Every customer, without exception, knows that it is our policy to give promt and excellent service under all circumstances.

9. We ashure you that out association will make every effort to furnish various types of merchandize in accordance with your individual requirements.

10. They showed their appreceation of our curtesy and co-operation by replying immediately to our communication.

EXERCISE 3

PROOFREADING FOR SPELLING

One or more words have been misspelled in each of the following sentences. There are 25 mistakes in total. (*Note:* Canadian spellings are not errors.)

1. To acomplish an adeqate amount of work, it is usually advisable to begin before mid-morning.

2. If you were allert, you would be able to follow his valueable argument instead of apologizing.

3. The small capitol investment in our monthly bullettin has benefited the company's competetive position.

4. She continually demonstrates curtesy, wears appropriate cloths, and exhibits a pleasant temperment in the office.

5. Bedouins are dessert Arabs and are strongly dependant on a sense of danger for successfull protection of their herds.

6. Until she trys, I will be disatisfied with the elementery work she has completed in her sophomore year.

7. The element of surprise is continually upsetting the goverment in Parlament these days.

8. Forty inspectors from the ministry were fined on principal for being predjudiced against immegrants.

9. In my opinion, quitting early to devote one's time to a passtime shows lack of intelligence.

10. The humourous sales representative was sincerely seized with passion for my neice; nevertheless, let's keep the preceeding information confidential.

EXERCISE 4

PROOFREADING FOR SPELLING

One or more words have been misspelled in each of the following sentences. There are 25 mistakes in total. (*Note:* Canadian spellings are not errors.)

1. The counsellor was holy accesible to the delinquent adolesent, but the young villian failed to take advantage of his friendship.

2. I became a little ancious when the bride's father began to relate an extrordinary anecdot as he accompanied his daughter up the isle.

3. The suspicions of the beureau were arroused when the man who had sworn vengence was found unconscious in the cemetery; however, it was determined that he had attempted suiside.

4. The army kernel paid a conspicus complement to the lieutenant in a solemm ceremony attended by several eminent generals.

5. The disasterous consequences of circulating the counterfeet currency made the juvenile forger despised by his fellow convicts.

6. The doctor did endevour to cover up his fundamental error, but under cross-examination by his predecessor and a psychology professor, his hypocricy was revealed.

7. The persistent and irresistable nature of the phenomenon paralyzed the department despite our optimistic outlook.

8. His mischievious behaviour exhausted his parents, who felt that the teacher was an obstacle to their son's reform.

9. Poor pronounciation of the word "minature" results from the students' resistance to spelling instruction.

10. On receit of the grievance, he took his scissors and, giving the appearance of a lunatic, he raced through the office in an unforgettable state of hysteria.

EXERCISE 5

PROOFREADING: SUBJECT–VERB AGREEMENT

Correct the mistakes in subject–verb agreement in the following sentences:

1. Across from the hospital are a collection of old homes.

   _____

2. Either Tom or Jerry have agreed to confess to the crime.

   _____

3. The entire briefcase, including my pens, cellphone, and address book, were taken from my locker.

   _____

4. Some consideration for the needs of others are expected from the social worker.

   _____

5. All the members of the lacrosse team and the coach was given a rousing cheer.

   _____

6. Either Tom or his brothers is responsible for the damage.

   _____

7. In front of the house stand two oak trees.

   _____

8. One of the shoes have disappeared.

   _____

9. None of the dishes are of any value.

   _____

10. A package of toys were given to the boy.

    _____

EXERCISE 6

PROOFREADING: COMMA SPLICES

Correct the comma-splice errors in the following sentences. Some of the sentences are correct.

1. The instructor's late, let's go to the pub!

2. Just let me get out of here, I might say something that I'll regret.

3. I keep buying Lotto 6/49 tickets, but I've never won anything.

4. My brother golfs and swims every day, he's quite healthy, he's only in his thirties.

5. As long as you use correct grammar, you can be accepted in any profession.

6. Montreal used to be called Ville Ste. Marie, I think, but before that it had an Indian name.

7. Students today need summer jobs, tuition and living expenses are more than most families can afford.

8. Tam will be going to the University of Toronto if accepted, he'll be trying to get a scholarship.

9. My word processor makes writing much easier, though it doesn't seem to spell any better than I do.

10. I am seeking a hero after whom I can model my life, so far I've rejected all Canadian politicians.

EXERCISE 7

PROOFREADING FOR SENTENCE FRAGMENTS

Identify the sentence-fragment errors in the following passage, then revise to correct them.

Going shopping with my wife is a waste of time. Because she never knows what she is looking for. After I have arrived home from work. My wife comes into the room. Gathers up her purse. And announces that she is going shopping. And would I like to come. It is a difficult situation to avoid. So off we go. When we get to the grocery store. She goes running up and down the aisles. Trying to remember what she needs. Finally, when we get to the check-out counter, she remembers a number of items that she didn't pick up. So back she goes while I hold the place in line. And other shoppers glare at me. Finally, we get to the car. With me carrying all the groceries and her complaining. About the price of food. The next time. I must figure out a way to gracefully decline. A trip to the grocery store.

_____

_____

_____

_____

_____

_____

_____

_____

_____

_____

_____

EXERCISE 8

PROOFREADING: APOSTROPHES

Identify the apostrophe errors in the following sentences, then correct them.

1. Its never too late if an opportunity presents itself.

2. Children find 9s hard to make.

3. Someone elses brothers car was stolen.

4. Bill picked up his friends costs for them.

5. Youre going to be his helper, arent you?

6. Childrens hands have a way of getting dirty.

7. Lightning hit the Joness house last night.

8. The cars horns beeped angrily as traffic backed up.

9. Dangers cousin is carelessness.

10. Performing a citizens arrest was Peters favourite trick.

11. The walkers feet were sore after the days hike.

12. The stones momentum grew as it rolled down the mountain.

13. Smiths car and Greens truck collided at Brantfords main intersection.

14. The mistakes of the young arent their parents fault.

15. As the weeks slip by summers approach is felt.

16. Its not Jamess fault that Mikes away.

17. Usually a buss tires arent very soft.

18. Greetings arent enemies usual remarks.

19. As she heard the stairs creak, she recognized her daughters footsteps.

20. Castles walls were built to withstand the enemies attack.

EXERCISE 9

PROOFREADING: MISPLACED MODIFIERS

Rewrite the following sentences to eliminate misplaced modifiers.

1. We can only supply one of the items that you ordered with the blue trimming.

   _____

2. The little girl was balancing a basket on her head held down by a stone.

   _____

3. George lived with a friend he trusted in a small apartment.

   _____

4. Students who miss classes frequently fall behind in their studies.

   _____

5. Today I saw a woman whose car side-swiped yours in front of the hotel.

   _____

6. You should not keep a dog that is used to a warm apartment in a doghouse.

   _____

7. Most cars have sun visors above the windshield, which can be adjusted to shade
   the eyes.

   _____

8. Buried in an old trunk for half a century, the owner of the painting discovered
   that it was done by a famous artist.

   _____

9. The antique table was purchased by a blonde lady with Queen Ann legs.

   _____

10. The stadium nearly seated 40,000 people.

   _____

EXERCISE 10

PROOFREADING: DANGLING MODIFIERS

Rewrite the following sentences to remove the dangling modifiers.

1. Driving through the mountains, several bears were seen.

   _____

2. Riding my bicycle, a dog chased me.

   _____

3. Working at my computer, the morning seemed endless.

   _____

4. Being made of glass, I did not expect the door to withstand abuse from children.

   _____

5. Spanning the river, I admired the bridge over the St. Lawrence.

   _____

6. Fearing cats, he noticed that the birds only came to the feeder early in the
   morning.

   _____

7. After putting a worm on my hook, the fish began to bite.

   _____

8. Before exploring Algonquin Park, our car was tuned up.

   _____

9. On opening the letter, a loonie fell out.

   _____

10. While rowing on the lake, the boat overturned.

   _____

EXERCISE 11

PROOFREADING: AMBIGUOUS PRONOUN REFERENCES

Rewrite the following sentences to eliminate ambiguous pronoun references.

1. The farmer went to his neighbour and told him his cattle were in his field.

   _____

2. The clerk told his employer that whatever he did he could not please him.

   _____

3. Charles's guilt was revealed to James in a letter to his wife.

   _____

4. He sent the man to his neighbour with the money he wanted.

   _____

5. Tom asked his cousin to bring his wallet as he was going on an errand.

   _____

6. Alice promised Jane that she would pay her debt.

   _____

7. The lawyer had an argument with a client, and he won.

   _____

8. When David met Shawn, he shook his hand.

   _____

9. The girls asked the boys whether the books that they had in their hands were the ones they had seen on their desks.

   _____

10. He blushed while describing his accident, which was very embarrassing.

    _____

EXERCISE 12

PROOFREADING FOR PRONOUN ERRORS

Correct the faulty pronoun references in the following paragraph.

When a person does not know their way around a new town, you should always stop and ask for directions. If they don't do this, the person will waste a lot of their time driving their car around, searching for one's destination. If we would just take a few seconds to ask questions, we would save many minutes of one's valuable time. And no one will think you are stupid; they will think that person is just unfamiliar with their surroundings. One must overcome needless shyness if they want to use their time more efficiently. If a person is overly shy, I would force myself to go out more and talk to more people, if you are really serious about overcoming the problem. We must always think positively if you expect to solve a problem, no matter how difficult one may find it to do. It is just an attitude you must develop if one wants a more profitable future for themselves.

EXERCISE 13

PROOFREADING: PRONOUN CASE

Correct the errors in pronoun case in the following sentences.

1. Wait for Agnes and I.

   _____

2. Everybody was late except we.

   _____

3. Him and Gary played together.

   _____

4. Mother told you and she to stay here.

   _____

5. I never saw Wayne and they together before.

   _____

6. We expect you and they at the meeting.

   _____

7. You and me are both invited.

   _____

8. Father expects you or I to meet him at the airport.

   _____

9. The Smiths are going, and us too.

   _____

10. I initiated the lawsuit, but it was him who raised the money for the court costs.

   _____

EXERCISE 14

PROOFREADING LETTERS

Transform the following text into a business letter that uses modified block style with open punctuation. Correct all errors in grammar, spelling, punctuation, and word usage. Organize the text into paragraphs. The letter is to Kevin Muise, who is the president of Muise Brothers, 700 Bloor Street West, Toronto, Ontario, M3T 4E8. The letter is from you. Provide an appropriate date, salutation, and complimentary close.

On December 17th I wrote the manager of the furniture department Andrew Lerner regarding a wall unit I had purchased during a recent sale celebrating the stores 75th anniversary. The price was 600 dollars. The unit arrived in damaged condition and I am still awaiting advise from Mr. Lerner regarding how he proposes to handle the matter. As I indicated in my letter to Mr. Lerner there are three major defects in the unit. The left cabinet door doesnt close the edge of the bottom shelf is rough and unfinished and the edge of the top shelf has nicks in it. Their are a number of minor defects beside the major ones and the overall effect is a unit that all ready looks like a much used poorly made peace of furniture. This is not the first time I have purchased furniture from Muise Brothers however it is the first time that I have been so displeased. It is difficult to hide the fact that I am mad. If a manufacturer is lax about inspecting furniture before it leaves the factory Muise Brothers should inspect it before delivery is made to the customer. Mr. Lerner is taking all together to much time to reply to my first letter which was sent the same day the unit was received. Therefore I would appreciate your taking care of this matter and advicing me how it is to be settled.

_____

_____

_____

_____

_____

_____

_____

_____

_____

_____

_____

_____

_____

(Continued on the next page.)

_____

_____

_____

_____

EXERCISE 15

PROOFREADING LETTERS

Turn the following text into a letter that uses block style with open punctuation. Correct all errors in grammar, spelling, punctuation, and word usage. Organize the text into paragraphs. Address the letter to Grace Smith, president of Smith Decorators, Inc., 360 Wolfe Street, Hamilton, ON X0X 0X0. It is from you. Provide an appropriate date, salutation, and complimentary close.

Im now able to give you the final results of the legal assistants poll regarding their ideas for redecorating the word processing centre which was set up three years ago. The centre is a large room and its chief asset is a sunny exposure most of the day. In addition to the natural light and existing lighting fixtures a lamp on each assistants desk makes for a bright cheerful work area therefore it isn't necessary to install additional lighting fixtures. The assistants unanimous choice for carpet colour is blue the supervisors choice of carpet colour for her office is green. The colours of the firm's insignia blue and white will be carried out in the centres wall colours. There isn't much time left before we receive delivery of our final equipment order. Therefore we would appreciate your expediting the work. Please advise the supervisor Bess Marks when you plan to begin. Besss work schedule will be arranged to accommodate your activities.

_____

_____

_____

_____

_____

_____

_____

_____

_____

_____

(Continued on the next page.)

_____

_____

_____

_____

EXERCISE 16

PROOFREADING LETTERS

Turn the following text into a letter that uses block style with open punctuation. Correct all errors in grammar, spelling, punctuation, and word usage. Organize the text into paragraphs. The letter is from the registrar, Mohawk College, Fennell Avenue and West 5th, P.O. Box 2034, Hamilton, ON X0X 0X0. It is addressed to you. Provide an appropriate date, salutation, and complimentary close.

Thank you for your resent letter requesting advise regarding procedures that should be followed when enrolling in Mohawk College. Please submit to us copies of your previous school records which should be sent directly by the schools three letters of reference and a letter stating why you wood like to enter Mohawk. Our admissions committee will consider your application at that time. Because of the dofficulty in choosing between the m,any candidates who would like to enrol on the program of your choise an extrance examination is administered to those who are given preliminary approval by the comittee. The next entrance examination is scheduled for November. You expressed interest in our legal program. Our program will enable you to qualify for a entry level position with a law firm indeed many of our graduates have been successful in this field. Besides the legal field we offer excellent programs in many disciplines. The admissions comittee is all ready studying records of potential spring enrollees therefore do not loose any time in sending your documents.

_____

_____

_____

_____

_____

_____

_____

_____

_____

(Continued on the next page.)

_____

_____

_____

_____

_____

EXERCISE 17

PROOFREADING MEMOS

Correct all spelling and grammar errors in the following text, and put it into memorandum form. Divide it into paragraphs. The memo is from you to the employees of the firm. Use today's date.

You are cordially invited to atend the firm's annual retreat, to be held at Riordan's banquent Centre, 7886 Communication Road, on Saturday, Febuary 21. An agenda will be posted to your interoffice e-mail by the end of the week. The annal retreat is a tradition that was started by our founder Mr. Frederick Larson more than 20 years ago. It has proved to be a valuable moral booster and an excellent opportunity to exchange information between the various departments. We usualy begin with a breakfast meeting and carry on until lunch, which will be catered. You can count on being finsihed by 4 p.m. Dress is office casual.

_____

_____

_____

_____

_____

_____

_____

_____

_____

_____

Readings

Clients Without Lawyers Disturb Chief Justice

Tracey Tyler, *Toronto Star*, August 14, 2005, A2

Reprinted with permission—Torstar Syndication Services

"Complex problem" due to lack of money, but money alone won't help

VANCOUVER—The increasing trend of Canadians representing themselves in court, despite their lack of legal knowledge, is causing "serious repercussions" for the justice system, Canada's top judge says.

"While we have a great justice system, increasing numbers of Canadians do not have access to it," Chief Justice Beverley McLachlin of the Supreme Court of Canada told the opening conference of the Canadian Bar Association here yesterday.

"This has serious repercussions for the justice system, which is based on litigants being represented by lawyers. Even more serious are the repercussions for the public." Pre-trial meetings and trials become longer as judges struggle to explain the process to unrepresented parties, all the while having to be careful they don't appear to favour one side, McLachlin said.

Ironically, say legal experts, those who go it alone for financial reasons often end up adding to the cost and complexity of court proceedings.

McLachlin said money is just one of the issues. "It would be facile and simplistic of me to attempt to tell you what I think the problems are," she told reporters at a news conference following her speech. "It's not just a money problem. It's a complex problem that requires more than just a simplistic solution."

The problem is particularly acute in family courts, where "the cost of litigation uses up precious resources that could better be used in providing housing and clothing for children and parents," the country's top judge said.

One possible solution being tried in the family courts of some provinces, McLachlin said, is to make mediation and counselling services available in order to resolve custody and property disputes more quickly, cheaply, and with the least rancour possible.

In her speech, McLachlin said part of the answer may lie with the country's richest law firms, which she suggested might do more to offer free legal services to those who can't afford a lawyer. "I wonder if some of our largest and most profitable law firms might be more active in constructively supporting their lawyers who would like to give more time to pro-bono work."

Government, judges and lawyers all have to do their part, McLachlin said.

That may be difficult for lawyers, who already feel they are on a "treadmill" and often face "serious pressures" to bill for 2,000 or more hours of work each year, which adds up to 65 or 70 hours in the office each week, she added.

Judges are so concerned about the problem that the Canadian Judicial Council has undertaken a study on unrepresented litigants, hoping to understand the dimensions of the problem, she said. But already judges across the country are reporting that the number of self-represented litigants is rising, she added.

McLachlin said she's also concerned about the process for naming federally appointed judges, who sit on the Supreme Court of Canada, provincial superior courts, and courts of appeal. A House of Commons standing committee on human rights and justice will hold hearings this fall on how the process can be improved ... .

In contrast to the process underway for the confirmation of Justice John Roberts to the United States Supreme Court, Canada's newest Supreme Court appointees were not questioned. Instead, [Justice Minister Irwin] Cotler appeared before the justice committee to explain whom he consulted with and the personal and professional qualities that merited the appointments.

While from her vantage point, the Canadian judiciary already meets high standards of competence, impartiality, empathy and wisdom, McLachlin said it's legitimate for the public to seek the best process possible.

But, she stressed, it's "equally legitimate" to insist the process respect the independence of judges and all appointments be made on the basis of merit.

"I think this is a political matter, the appointment of judges. They're studying it and it's their job to find a good system. I'm not interested so much in the mechanics."

Some Day, Victims Won't Fear Us

Susan Clairmont, *The Hamilton Spectator*,
May 12, 2003, A05

Reprinted by permission of The Hamilton Spectator

I was covering a sexual assault case recently when one of the cops told me something about the victim.

He said she was more afraid of the media than the man who assaulted her.

That's a hard thing for a journalist to hear. For a woman journalist to hear. Especially when that journalist tries to write stories that will make readers care about victims of crime. In fact, I had written about this sexual assault victim before. My heart goes out to her.

I was disturbed by what the cop said.

Then I interviewed Jane Doe. THE Jane Doe. The one who turned the Toronto Police and the whole Canadian legal system on its head. The one who was attacked by the infamous balcony rapist in 1986 and then refused to fit into the justice system's stereotype of what a rape victim should be.

Jane Doe was the first raped woman in Ontario to obtain her own legal counsel. Her lawyer won the right to sit in the courtroom during her rapist's trial.

After the serial rapist was convicted of breaking into the upper-floor apartments of five Toronto women and sexually assaulting them, Jane took the Toronto police to civil court. She was the first Canadian to win the right to sue the police for their actions in the investigation of a crime. She claimed Toronto police were grossly negligent by failing to warn women in her neighbourhood that there was a serial rapist at work. Police were afraid if they warned women, the women might become hysterical and scare the rapist away. So instead of taking action to prevent further rapes, they used unsuspecting women as bait in their quest to catch the predator.

In 1998, 12 years after her rape, Jane Doe won her lawsuit against the police.

Jane is very intelligent. Quite funny. A strong feminist.

She has just written a quirky, thought-provoking and strangely entertaining book about her experience with rape and the systems that investigate and prosecute rapists. The book is called *The Story of Jane Doe.*

Jane Doe. That is the name she continues to use. She, a fearless woman who has spent much of her adult life fighting to change the way raped women are thought of and treated. A crusader who has, over and over again in a very public forum, bared her soul.

Why not use her real name? Why not break down that barrier?

The Central Park Jogger did it. For 14 years that's how she was known. She is the New York City woman who was raped and beaten to within an inch of her life while jogging in Central Park. Her brain was so badly injured that she had to learn to walk again. Just recently she published her autobiography.

The author? Trisha Meili. The Central Park Jogger put her real name on the book. She says she did so because it was time to come out of the closet. Time for people to know the whole story. She believes this is another step in her healing process and hopes it will show other rape victims they don't have to live in fear and secrecy.

But Jane Doe says for her, it isn't time yet. She's ready, but society isn't.

"I'd love my name to be on my book," she says. "This is my book. My sorrow. My joy."

But society has not yet reached a level of understanding that would allow her to be both herself and a rape victim, Jane says. If people know she is Jane Doe, "that will become my sole and first identity."

It's simply not "dignified" to be a rape victim. Rape is humiliating and so is being known for being a rape victim. We may think we've come a long way in our understanding of rape, says Jane, but that is really just "the illusion of change. The impression of change." Deep down, society still puts some of the blame at the feet of the woman. Still questions her character. Her morals. Her actions. There is still a stigma about being a rape victim.

Back to the sexual assault case I was covering.

Apparently what the victim really feared was having her name in the paper. She didn't know *The Spectator* does not name sexual assault victims unless the victim requests that her name be used.

We have a policy because we too believe there is a stigma attached to sexual assault victims. Perhaps when that stigma disappears, our policy will change. But for now, the victim remains nameless.

Pleading Case for Reform of Legal Aid System

Toronto Star, October 6, 2002, A01

Reprinted with permission—Torstar Syndication Services

The legal aid lawyer of the future works in a University Ave. office with three law clerks, a receptionist, a support worker, and a box of teddy bears.

She gets a regular paycheque and generous benefits, including a pension. Paying the office rent isn't a problem.

"I get to do the work I like doing, on a salaried basis, and it's not feast or famine," said Sheilagh O'Connell, a staff lawyer with the Family Law Office, a downtown legal aid clinic, funded by the Ontario government.

She's one of the first in what could be a province-wide system of public defenders.

To some, the difference between her job conditions and those of her counterparts in the private bar is the difference between a shiny new Cadillac and a battered 1987 Tempo.

With rates that have barely changed in 15 years, lawyers in private practice say they can't take on legal aid cases without going into the red. Hourly rates of $70.35 to $80.93 won't cover their overhead, they say. Years ago, some sent their secretaries packing and began working from home.

A recent legal aid strike by Ontario lawyers to back their calls for a pay raise became what might be considered a victim of its own success: faced with judges supporting the lawyers and ordering the province to pay them up to $140 an hour in some cases, Attorney General David Young last week introduced legislation that would pave the way for public defender bureaucracy to deliver legal aid services.

What's gone virtually unnoticed in the turmoil is that small public defender programs are already up and running in Toronto, Ottawa, and Thunder Bay.

Three years ago, Legal Aid Ontario, the agency set up to run the system independent of government, established pilot projects in each city to compare family law services performed by government lawyers with the more traditional method of issuing certificates to legal aid clients so they could hire their lawyer of choice. On Sept. 20, the agency's board decided to make the three clinics permanent.

In Toronto, an evaluation found that the average cost per case for the Family Law Office last year was $1,857 compared with $1,700 when handled by the private bar.

The study also considered intangibles, such as client satisfaction.

On Friday, a mother of two, who didn't want her name used, said she feels less self-conscious at the clinic than she did going to a private law office as a legal aid client.

Although lawyers may not treat their legal aid clients differently from the others, "the comfort level for me is knowing we're all equal," she said. "To me, that is very important."

O'Connell is one of four full-time lawyers at the clinic ... . In the waiting room, there's a pint-size table and chairs, and boxes of stuffed animals and toys. About 65 per cent of the clients are women.

"I think the success of the office is we improve justice by taking on ... more complicated cases," O'Connell said.

In addition to the usual mix of custody, support and child protection cases, the clinic handles all uncontested divorces from an area stretching from Toronto to London, Parry Sound and Cobourg.

The 1,253 cases the clinic has handled in the last three years represent 2 per cent of all legal aid family law cases in Ontario.

But should a public defender system be doing even more?

David Young said federal Justice Minister Martin Cauchon has encouraged him to find other methods of providing legal aid and has called Ontario's current delivery system "inefficient."

At a news conference last week, Young says he believes a public defender system would result in greater efficiencies because lawyers could handle more legal aid cases in a day.

For one thing, they wouldn't have to waste time driving from courthouse to courthouse to represent clients, he suggested. "What I envision is (a public defender office) attached to a courthouse."

Public defenders also would not be paid anywhere near the maximum of $196,000 a year that lawyers can earn for legal aid work, Young said.

However, Legal Aid Ontario's own statistics show that only 10 per cent of Ontario's lawyers earn more than $50,000 a year for legal aid work.

In 2000, the latest year statistics are available, more than a third earn between $10,000 and $49,999, and more than half earned less than $9,999.

The government lawyers who staff the three legal aid offices are paid between $56,600 and $82,400 a year, plus benefits.

Meanwhile, evaluators found the average cost of a case in the Family Law Office in Ottawa to be $1,603 versus $1,577 for those handled by private lawyers working on a legal aid certificate. In Thunder Bay, the situation was reversed: last year, a Family Law Office case cost $1,060 compared to an average $1,557 for the private bar.

The total operating cost of all three offices is $1.8 million a year, while the cost to the province for all legal aid certificates, including family, criminal, and immigration cases, is about $111 million a year.

Overall, the evaluators concluded that the public defender offices were "cost-competitive" and provided "at least an equal level of service" to private bar lawyers. At the same time, they recognized a link between cost efficiency and quality of service.

Janet Tilston, director of the Toronto Family Law Office, said there was initially an expectation that staff lawyers would be able to handle about 140 cases a year, but it quickly became apparent that wasn't realistic.

The number has dropped to about 80 cases a year, with lawyers juggling anywhere from 55 to 60 cases at any time. "There is no way we can replace the judicare system; we complement it," she said, adding the cost of expanding the infrastructure and the overhead for offices to accommodate all legal aid cases would be overwhelming.

Critics of the public defender system say there are even more fundamental problems.

"The proposed legislation jeopardizes one of the fundamental principles of our justice system, which is the right to representation by independent counsel, freely chosen by an accused person," Brian Greenspan, a Toronto criminal lawyer and director of The Advocates' Society, said in a statement last week.

The legislation also gives the attorney general direct control of the legal system, which effectively puts prosecution in charge of the defence, critics say.

Public defenders in the United States say they are stunned that an attorney general would be involved in a public defender system at all.

In Washington, D.C., the public defender's office is governed by an independent board. "Certainly our budget is not contingent on the prosecutor, because that just strikes me as a built-in conflict of interest," said director Ronald Sullivan.

Legal aid is delivered through a mix of public defenders and private bar lawyers whose names are on a panel and are assigned to cases by a court. By statute, public defenders can't represent more than 60 per cent of legal aid clients in the district and they tend to focus only on serious felonies, leaving misdemeanours to the court-appointed lawyers, Sullivan said. As a result, the caseloads are "fairly moderate"—about 25 to 30 cases at any given time, he said.

But it's not always so rosy. Across the U.S., public defender programs run the gamut from well-funded, well-organized systems that cover a state evenly, with good quality controls, down to county-level systems that have no standards at all and pay very little money," said Scott Wallace, director of defender legal services for the Washington-based National Legal Aid and Defender Association, which promotes equal access to justice.

About 30 years ago, the group developed caseload standards. While many states have adopted them, "very often people are exceeding those standards," he said.

"In some areas, lawyers will literally spend no more than three minutes on a client," Wallace said. "They don't interview them, they don't do investigations, and, God forbid, they don't go to trial.

"They meet their clients when they come into court in their orange jumpsuits," he said. "Then they go over and speak to the prosecutor and come back and say, 'Here's the deal I got for you.'"

The Formula from Hell

Candis McLean, *Report/Newsmagazine* (Alberta Edition),
May 13, 2002, vol. 29, no. 10, 54

Reprinted by permission of Candis McLean

*A divorced dad uncovers a deliberate policy to
drive separated parents further apart*

Toronto geologist Alar Soever was going through a divorce early in 1996 when he first encountered the Federal Child Support Guidelines which recommend amounts non-custodial parents should pay for child support. "My lawyer couldn't tell me how the figures were arrived at," he recalls, "so I contacted the federal Department of Justice which said that the documents to explain the formula would be published in the fall of 1996. That made sense, since Parliament was going to debate the guidelines that winter." Mr. Soever then telephoned every two months, but the guidelines were never "ready." The controversial guidelines were passed by Parliament in February 1997 and came into effect two months later. The research report (CSR-1997-1E) which explained the formula was not released until 14 months after Parliament's decision.

Mr. Soever is a methodical man, and was intrigued by a number of issues, including how regulations affecting the lives of hundreds of thousands of divorcing parents could have passed without any public documentation as to how the guideline amounts were calculated. To find out, he undertook four years of investigations. On April 5 [2002] he released his findings to an Ottawa forum, Toward Shared Parenting, co-sponsored by the Family Forum of Ottawa and the National Alliance Advocating for the Needs of Children and Parents. His 31-page document was titled "The Federal Child Support Guidelines: A Breakdown of Democratic Process and the Canadian legal system." According to B.C. resident Ross Bailey who attended the meeting, "Alar's paper has the whole non-custodial and grandparenting community across the country buzzing because they knew something was wrong with the guideline formula, but needed someone to tell them how it was wrong."

The community may buzz even louder with the news that last week, among materials obtained by Liberal MP Roger Gallaway through the Freedom of Information Act, Mr. Soever finally found an explanation of the guidelines which had been prepared in the fall of 1996. He believes the explanation was repressed because it gives examples of the financial consequences of the guidelines, "transparently indicating how unfair the formula is … ." One of those to whom he revealed the document compared the situation to the "tainted blood scandal," in which the government's suppression of information caused irreparable damage. "By not telling the judiciary what the formulas really meant, they caused serious harm which has included driving people into bankruptcy and even suicide."

As a geologist, Mr. Soever examines mineral reserves to separate the truth from self-serving hype, checking assumptions, formulas, and calculations. "When I examined the guidelines," he says, "I realized it was like the Bre-X scandal, complete with flawed assumptions and skewed calculations. It was driven by psychology, with everyone thinking it was child support so it must be good, but it's actually promoting custody battles and hurting children. The bottom line? No one appeared to have done the due diligence on the underlying formula." He ended with a stunning question: "How is it that in a democracy we can have guidelines which contravene the Divorce Act, are based on largely unknown, admittedly deficient formulae, and are derived from undisclosed policy decisions that promote the loss of substantial contact with one parent?"

What Mr. Soever learned is that the guidelines as implemented contain not only child support but spousal support (which contravenes the Divorce Act), and overestimate expenditures on children for the custodial parent while underestimating them for non-custodial parents. That conclusion is also reached by University of Calgary Ph.D. student Paul Millar … in research to be published in the June [2002] edition of the peer-reviewed academic journal, *The Canadian Journal of Law and Society.*

The formula used to generate the guidelines, Mr. Soever learned, makes two key assumptions in all cases, whether valid or not: 1. The paying parent is always assumed to have the expenses of a single adult (i.e., no parenting expenses); and 2. The incomes of the paying and receiving parent are assumed to be equivalent.

In those cases where these assumptions match reality, the model does meet its objectives: equal standards of living and a sharing of expenses between the two parents. In practice, however, the amount of time that the non-custodial parent has custody of the child can range up to 40% (when over 40%, the guidelines do not apply). Among parents with average incomes, if the paying parent spends no time with the children and thus has no expenses, his standard of living tends to be 16% higher than the receiver's. If, however, the paying parent is an involved one, he or she has expenses—often almost as high as the other parent's. Yet the guidelines deny recognition of this. In fact, Mr. Soever has determined, if the parents have average incomes, once custody exceeds 5% (roughly one night every two weeks), the non-custodial parent and the children when they are with him are penalized with a lower standard of living. Once custody approaches 40%, the standard of living in that home is almost 30% lower than in the other home, and barely above the poverty line.

In other words, concluded Mr. Soever, the more time children spend with their divorced non-custodial father, the poorer he gets and the more difficult and impoverished their time together. "The guidelines," he says, "offer clear and powerful financial disincentives to joint parenting by penalizing those payor parents with substantial custody. Most perversely, parents who abandon their children are actually rewarded with a higher standard of living than the children they abandoned."

A further by-product of the guidelines, the researcher says, is that they encourage custody battles as parents strive for the magical 40% threshold, and the benefit to the custodial parent is lost. Mr. Soever knows of one case where a wife was prepared to allow her ex-husband joint custody and about 38% residence time with the children, but not the 50% he desired. This led to protracted mediation and negotiations. The father suspected the guidelines' magical 40% threshold was the root of the problem. To test his theory, the father asked if the children might occasionally have lunch at home with him on Fridays. "Obviously, a hot lunch at home with a parent was preferable to brown-bagging it in a crowded cafeteria," he says. "This, however, would have put him over the magical 40%. It was not really a surprise when the mother's lawyer responded, 'My client is absolutely not agreeable to your suggestion with respect to the children having lunches.' The mother was prepared to fight a costly custody battle just to retain the 40% threshold. Could there be any more blatant example of the insidious nature of these guidelines?"

Ottawa economist Ross Finnie … was one of the developers of the guidelines, but has since published critical articles [of the guidelines]. Mr. Finnie believes the underlying guidelines are fair, but objects to the custodial parent receiving all the tax credits. His major criticism, however, is the same as Mr. Soever's. The 40% threshold with no allowance for expenses, he says, "came out of the air with no real explanation. It came from within the Justice Department. Some people were top-notch, working with technically difficult concepts such as 'What does a child cost?' and just wanting to do the right thing, but that was not uniformly the case. I suspect someone said, 'How can we ratchet up these awards a bit?' Let's just say," he smiles, enigmatically, "it ended messily between myself and the Justice Department."

The Secret Document

Report/Newsmagazine (Alberta Edition),
May 13, 2002, vol. 29, no. 10, 54

Reprinted by permission of Candis McLean

"This says it all!" exulted Toronto geologist Alar Soever at last month's discovery of a 31-page document obtained under a Freedom of Information request. "It is a detailed financial analysis of the Federal Child Support Guidelines showing how impoverished the paying parent would be and the inherent inequities in the model."

Titled "Detailing the Components of the Canadian Child Support Formula, 1997 Edition," labelled draft #6 and dated November 15, 1996, what makes it so different from the guidelines which, pared down to nine pages, were eventually made public, is its level of detail, as well as an appendix of case examples. "This is the comprehensive explanation of the guidelines that Parliament and the Canadian public deserved at the time they were debating and passing this legislation in the fall of 1996," declares Mr. Soever (dadalar@aol.com).

Spokesmen for the Justice Department, however, deny that the document was suppressed, saying it was merely delayed while being fine-tuned for the public. "We struggled mightily with the level of technicality and decided to cut it down to make it short and succinct. If we gave examples, it was too long," attests senior researcher Jim Sturrock, one of the developers of the guidelines. Senior council Lise Lafreniere Henrie adds that MPs had briefing notes while making their decision on the guidelines, but they were not public documents. "It was advice to the ministers, so it was confidential … . However, we published a set of tables and in January 1995 we published an overview illustrated in a more simplistic way, so information was out there."

In the newly discovered draft, a theoretical case is given in which both parents live in Newfoundland, the two children live full-time with the custodial parent and each parent earns $25,000. Utilizing the formula, the document then indicates that the "after-tax, after [child-support] award" income for the custodial parent is $27,369, while the non-custodial parent's income is slashed to almost one-half that, at $14,489. Of the total expenditures on children, $4,435 is paid by the non-custodial parent, while only $2,825 is paid by the custodial parent. "This is without even considering any direct expenditures made by the non-custodial parent during his or her time with the children," points out Mr. Soever.

When the non-custodial parent earns $1,000 more (i.e., $26,000), while the income of the custodial parent remains unchanged at $25,000, the child-support award increases by $170 per year. The actual income of both parents rise: the custodial parent's to $27,539, the non-custodial parent's to $14,983, but while the non-custodial parent now pays $170 more of the children's expenses than before (at $4,605), the custodial parent actually pays $100 less than before. Of the $170 increase in child support, only $70 goes to "direct expenditures on the children," while $100 is directed to the "personal (for parent) disposable income."

So why is an apparent "spousal support" built into the child support in the new formula? Justice officials say it is simply mislabelled and should have been called "household income." Mr. Soever says, "The fact that the larger proportion of the child-support award is going to the receiving parent is perhaps inevitable, but very few people grasp the concept, and that's because it was never made clear when it was passed that the formula was a simple household standard-of-living equalization formula. Even two years after the guidelines were passed, the Supreme Court of Canada still didn't seem to grasp it," he says, pointing to the April 27, 1999, judgment in *Francis v. Baker*:

> "However, even though the Guidelines have their own stated objectives, they have not displaced the *Divorce Act*, which clearly dictates that maintenance of the children, rather than household equalization or spousal support, is the objective of child-support payments."

According to Mr. Soever, "Either the justices didn't know the very basis of the guidelines was a household-equalization formula, or they have ruled that the manner in which the guidelines are constructed contravenes the Divorce Act."

Contends Mr. Soever, "In these case examples, the standard of living of the paying parent is already much lower than that of the receiver, despite using the guidelines' assumption that the household of the paying parent has only a single person and no direct expenditures on the children. In reality, one must remember that the children might be living with the paying parent up to 40% of the time and in that case, his or her direct expenditures on the children would only be marginally less than those of the receiving parent. Clearly being left with a disposable income half that of the receiving parent, the paying parent would not be in a position to provide a comparable standard of living for the children while they are with him.

"This November 1996 draft report with its case examples exposes the deficiencies in the child-support formula. Had it been published in the fall of 1996, as promised earlier, I do not believe the guidelines would have made it through Parliament in their present form. This, I believe, explains why the formula was not published in the fall of 1996.

"In all subsequent drafts, the detailed financial analysis and all the examples which exposed the true financial hardship inflicted by the Guidelines were deleted, so unless you do the detailed analysis yourself—which takes some time and knowledge—you cannot appreciate how it affects families and children. It took the Justice Department 18 months to remove the examples and financial analysis and edit this 31-page draft document down to nine pages which say far less about the nature of the Guidelines than the original. The fact that it has now been revealed that there was a comprehensive draft ready in November 1996 raises serious questions as to why the release of this document was delayed in an open and democratic society."

Judgement Day

John Carpay, *Report/Newsmagazine* (Alberta Edition),
March 27, 2000, vol. 26, no. 50

Reprinted by permission of John Carpay

"Good work, even if you can't do it"

Marleen Tozer became an office assistant in B.C.'s Motor Vehicle Branch (MVB) in 1991 through a cozy deal arranged by her husband, the government agent in Kelowna, and his good friend Ray Jago, regional director of the MVB. They agreed to hire each other's wives without the usual competition. Problems developed in 1992 when Ms. Tozer returned to work after a five-month absence due to a brain aneurysm and stroke. Her error rate while processing permits was too high. The MVB told her to take a 15-week medical leave at 60% pay, or face dismissal. She did, but when MVB declined to rehire her she complained of discrimination on the basis of physical disability. A B.C. human rights tribunal ruled … that the MVB, as employer, should have found her a less demanding government job instead of putting her on disability. The tribunal ordered MVB to pay Ms. Tozer seven months' lost wages plus interest, and $3,500 for hurt feelings.

"No way to treat a lady"

Another B.C. human rights tribunal has ordered Gordon Hass to pay Wendy Larson $5,500. She began working as a lounge manager at the Michel Hotel in Cranbrook on January 3, 1996, at $10 per hour, 40 hours per week, plus free room and board. On three occasions, Mr. Hass asked her personal questions about her boyfriend and their sex life, which she ignored. Eleven days after the owner had grabbed her and tried to kiss her, she quit. Ms. Larson also felt unsafe after realizing Mr. Hass had the key to her room. On February 7 the tribunal ordered him and/or the Michel Hotel to pay her $4,000 for 10 weeks of lost work, plus $1,500 for hurt feelings.

"Please officer, come charge me"

On January 17, the Ontario Court of Appeal affirmed the conviction of Donald Mulligan, arrested on his own property for "having care and control of his vehicle" while impaired. Just after midnight on April 16, an Ontario Provincial Police officer noticed a pickup truck, engine running and lights on, in the parking lot of Mulligan Construction near Flesherton. Suspecting a break-in, the officer found Mr. Mulligan himself sitting in his truck; he smelled of alcohol and was slurring his words. Fully six feet tall and 335 pounds, he took the arrest badly. After being pepper sprayed and struck repeatedly with a baton, he was eventually arrested when four more officers arrived. Although the officer came onto Mr. Mulligan's property without a search warrant and without reasonable and probable grounds to suspect an impaired driving offence, Justice Robert Sharpe ruled the officer did not unlawfully trespass. His entry was authorized by implied invitation, on suspicion that a crime was being committed. The court upheld the $650 fine and one-year licence suspension for being in charge of a vehicle while impaired, and the $200 fine for resisting a justifiable arrest.

"Bias perhaps, but not libel"

Former alderman Henry Merling sued the *Hamilton Spectator* for 23 articles he alleged to be defamatory. Only three of the 23 were published before Mr. Merling's defeat in … a municipal election. Mr. Merling failed to give written notice to the *Spectator* within six weeks of the alleged libel being published, as required by the Ontario Libel and Slander Act. This act states that a publisher who promptly retracts a defamatory article can still be sued, but the damages awarded will be less than if no retraction had been published. On January 24, the Ontario Court of Appeal struck several paragraphs from Mr. Merling's Statement of Claim, based on his failure to promptly notify the newspaper. Chief Justice Roy McMurtry also ruled that 23 articles together did not form "one single libel."

Top Court Lets Dads Appeal Payments

Tara Brautigam, *The Hamilton Spectator*,
August 19, 2005, A1

Reprinted by permission of The Hamilton Spectator

Canada's highest court will hear the appeal of four Alberta fathers who were ordered to pay retroactive child support in a case that could dramatically impact the financial obligations of countless divorced or separated Canadian parents.

Should the Supreme Court of Canada uphold the original January [2005] ruling, it could result in hundreds of thousands of parents being hit with lump-sum support payments totalling millions of dollars, said Deidre Smith, a lawyer in the appeal.

Despite existing court orders and separation agreements, the fathers were ordered by an Alberta judge to make immediate lump-sum child support payments, some stretching as far back as 1997, to reflect changes in their incomes, Smith said.

One of the appellants "is about as opposite from a deadbeat dad as you can get," Smith said from her Toronto office. "(He is) being whacked with this significant retroactive award when a trial judge has said, 'Hey, buddy, you did everything you are supposed to do.'"

The fathers are from the Grand Prairie, Calgary, Edmonton, and Red Deer areas and can't be named because of a publication ban.

Neither provincial legislation, the federal Divorce Act nor federal child support guidelines require parents to make annual adjustments to their payments, Smith said.

The sudden court demand for tens of thousands of dollars has caught the appellants off guard, she said. "They really resent being called deadbeats or being told by the community that they haven't taken care of their kids when they've been paying what the court order or agreement told them to pay," Smith said.

When the new federal guidelines were introduced eight years ago, Ottawa included a process by which the government could calculate child support payments based on tax returns and notify parents of required adjustments in pay.

Those guidelines, however, have not been implemented because the provinces have not yet signed on, Smith said.

Virtually anyone who is paying child support under a court order or separation agreement made within the last 15 years may face large amounts of back claims, Smith said.

The "vast Majority" of Canadian dads earn more after they are separated, Smith said. "If they went back and looked at their old orders, there probably would be additional support owing. I've got to think it would be in the millions."

Currently, separated or divorced parents receive a court order telling them how much they owe, or work out an agreement with their lawyers … . But as child access arrangements change, parents remarry, have more children and incomes fluctuate, the original support arrangements often no longer accurately reflect each parent's situation, Smith said.

Stacy Robb, president and founder of Dads Canada, said mothers and fathers alike often under-report changes in income, day care costs and associated expenses of raising children, which are some of the major factors in determining child support.

The court is expected to begin hearing the appeal between February and May next year [2006].

Index

A

abstract, 123
apostrophes, 74-76, 221
attachments, 95

B

body language, 15, 148-51
business letters
    basic style, 86
    full block style, 89
    modified block style, 87
    traditional style, 88

C

capital letters, 78
clause, 63
client communication, 152-54
colons, 78
comma splice, 65, 219
commas, 72-73
communication
    barriers to, 2-3
    client communication, 152-54
    communication theory, 2
    e-mail writing, 119-20
    grammar skills, 51-82
    importance of, 2
    legal forms, use of, 157-211
    letter writing, 84-99
    listening, 7-25
    memo writing, 99-106
    memorandum of law, 106-16
    multicultural society, and, 3-4
    non-verbal, 14-15, 148-51
    oral presentation, 138-52
    paraphrasing, 130-33
    peer conferencing, 154
    people with disabilities, and, 4
    report writing, 117-19
    speaking, 137-55
    spelling, 27-50
    summarizing, 123-29
communication theory, 2
complete subject, 57

D

dangling modifiers, 66, 67, 223
dependent clause, 63
direct order letter, 84
direct speech, 125

E

effective listening
    barriers to, 18-19
    rules, 10-17
e-mail, guidelines for writing, 119-20
enclosures, 95
exclamation points, 77

G

grammar
    capital letters, 78
    importance of, 51
    pre-test, 52-56
    punctuation
        apostrophes, 74-76
        colons, 78
        commas, 72-73
        exclamation points, 77
        periods, 76-77
        question marks, 77
        quotation marks, 77
        semicolons, 77-78
    sentences
        correlatives, 71
        modifiers, 66-68
        parallel structure, 71
        pronouns, 68-70
        run-on sentences, 65-66
        sentence fragments, 63-64
        subject, 56-57
        subject–verb agreement, 60-62
        verb, 57-60
    voice, 80

complimentary close, 94
contractions, 75
copies, 94
correlatives, 71

I

impromptu speaking, 151-52
indefinite pronoun, 61
independent clause, 63
indirect order letter, 85
indirect speech, 125
infinitive, 59
information memo, 101-2
irregular verbs, 58

L

law clerk
    defined, 1
    working environment, 1
legal assistant
    defined, 1
    working environment, 1
legal citation
    case citation, 107-8
    parallel citations, 108-9
legal forms
    corporate procedures and transactions, 198-211
    litigation, 175-97
    real estate, 158-62
    wills and estates, 163-74
letters
    business, *see* business letters
    content, 95-99
    direct order, 84
    formats, 86-89
    indirect order, 85
    proofreading, 227-29
    style, 90-95
    use of, 84
linking verbs, 58
listening
    acknowledgement and feedback, 12
    barriers to effective listening, 18-19
    body language, 15
    emotional response, control of, 16-17
    listening profile, 8-10
    non-verbal clues, 14-15
    notes, use of, 17
    questioning, role of, 14
    reflective listening, 13
    rules for effective listening, 10-17
    selective listening, 11
    tone of voice, 15

M

memorandum of law
    elements of, 106
    legal citation, and, 107-9
    sample, 110-16
    steps in writing, 109

memos
    addresses, 100
    closing, 100
    content, 100
    format
        basic, 99
        formal versus informal, 99
        information memo, 101
        opinion memo, 103-4
        problem-solving memo, 102-3
    language and grammar, 105
    memorandum of law
        legal citation, 107-9
        steps in writing, 109-16
        use of, 106
    proofreading, 230
    readability, 100
    subject line, 100
    tone, 100
    use of, 84
    writing strategy, 101, 105
    "you" approach, 100
misplaced modifiers, 66-67, 222
modifiers, 66-68

N

non-verbal communication
    listening, and, 14-15
    spatial elements, 150-51
    visual elements
        body orientation, 149
        eye contact, 148
        facial expression, 149
        gestures and posture, 149
        manner of dress, 149
    vocal elements
        emphasis, 150
        loudness, 149
        rate of speech, 150

O

opinion, 16
opinion memo, 103-4
oral presentation
    answering questions, 145-46
    impromptu speaking, 151-52
    mechanics, 144-45
    nervousness, 146
    non-verbal communication
        spatial elements, 150-51
        visual elements, 148-49
        vocal elements, 149-50
    organization, 144
    preparation, 142-43
    purpose, determination of, 138
    research, 140

topic narrowing, 139
topic selection, 138-39
visual aids, 147

P

paragraphs, 97-99
parallel structure, 71
paraphrase
    bias in reporting, 131-33
    distinguished from summary, 130
    methods of, 131
periods, 78
possessives, 74
problem-solving memo, 102-3
pronouns
    ambiguous references, 70, 224
    case of, 69
    indefinite, 61
    proofreading, and, 224-26
    relative, 61
    subject–verb agreement, and, 61
    use of, 68
proofreading, 213-30
propaganda, 16
punctuation
    apostrophes, 74-76
    colons, 78
    commas, 72-73
    exclamation points, 77
    periods, 76-77
    question marks, 77
    quotation marks, 77
    semicolons, 77-78

Q

question marks, 77
questioning, 13-14
quotation marks, 77

R

reflective listening, 13
regular verbs, 58
relative pronoun, 61
reports
    format, 117
    organization, 119
research, 140
run-on sentences, 65-66

S

salutation, 91-92
selective listening, 11
semicolons, 77-78

sentence
    correlatives, 71
    modifiers, 66-68
    parallel structure, 71
    pronouns, 68-70
    run-on sentences, 65-66
    sentence fragments, 63-64
    subject, 56-57
    subject–verb agreement, 60-62
    verb, 57-60
sentence fragments, 63-64, 220
simple subject, 57
S.I.R. method of impromptu speaking, 151
spelling
    misspelled words, 31-32
    misused words, 37-41
    plurals, 34-37
    proofreading for, 214-17
    spelling rules, 32-34
    steps to improve, 28
    troublesome words, 29-30, 37
style, letters
    attention line, 91
    complimentary close, 94
    copies, 94
    date, 90
    enclosures and attachments, 95
    inside address, 90
    salutation, 91-92
    subject line, 92, 94
    "without prejudice," 90
subject, 56-57
subject line, 100
subject–verb agreement, 60-62, 218
summary
    counting words, 125
    direct to indirect speech, changing, 125
    rules for writing, 124
    samples, 126
summary and bias essay, 133-34
synopsis, 123

T

tense, 58
tone
    business letters, 97
    memos, 100
tone of voice, 15

V

verbs, 56, 57-60
visual aids, 147
voice, 80

Y

"you" approach, 100